Vulnerable Workers

Vulnerable Workers

Health, Safety and Well-being

Edited by

MALCOLM SARGEANT
Middlesex University, London, UK

MARIA GIOVANNONE
ADAPT – University of Modena and Reggio Emilia, Italy

Routledge
Taylor & Francis Group

LONDON AND NEW YORK

First published 2011 by Gower Publishing

2 Park Square, Milton Park, Abingdon, Oxon OX14 4RN
711 Third Avenue, New York, NY 10017, USA

Routledge is an imprint of the Taylor & Francis Group, an informa business

First issued in paperback 2016

Gower Applied Business Research
Our programme provides leaders, practitioners, scholars and researchers with thought provoking, cutting edge books that combine conceptual insights, interdisciplinary rigour and practical relevance in key areas of business and management.

British Library Cataloguing in Publication Data
Vulnerable workers : health, safety and well-being.
    1. Industrial safety. 2. Employee rights. 3. Job security. 4. Labor policy.
    I. Sargeant, Malcolm. II. Giovannone, Maria.
    331.1'3 – dc23

Library of Congress Cataloging-in-Publication Data
Vulnerable workers : health, safety and well-being / [edited] by Malcolm Sargeant and Maria Giovannone.
        p. cm.
    Includes bibliographical references and index.
    ISBN 978-1-4094-2662-2 (hbk. : alk. paper)
    1. Precarious employment. 2. Job security. 3. Industrial hygiene. 4. Industrial safety.
I. Sargeant, Malcolm. II. Giovannone, Maria.

    HD5854.V85 2011
    363.11 – dc23

                                                                            2011025534
ISBN 978-1-4094-2662-2 (hbk)
ISBN 978-1-138-26134-1 (pbk)

Contents

List of Figures

List of Tables

List of Tables

About the Editors

Professor Malcolm Sargeant BA, LLB, PhD is Professor of Labour Law at Middlesex University Business School. He is also Managing Editor of the *e-journal of International and Comparative Labour Studies*. His specialist research areas include vulnerable workers, particularly in relation to discrimination issues. His writing and publishing has been extensive. Books include *Age Discrimination* (2011), *Employment Law* (co-authored, 2010), *Essentials of Employment Law* (co-authored, 2011). Edited books include *Age Discrimination and Diversity* (2011) and *The Law on Age Discrimination in the EU* (2008). He is also author of a large number of articles in refereed journals.

Dr Maria Giovannone holds a Ph.D. in Industrial Relations Law. She is a lecturer at the Marco Biagi International and Comparative Study Centre, University of Modena and Reggio Emilia, Italy and is the ADAPT (Association for International and Comparative studies in the field of Labour Law and Industrial Relations) Research Fellow responsible for research into health and safety at work. Her research activity mostly concerns work organization and occupational health and safety issues, from a national, international and comparative viewpoint with special concern with the impact of new forms of work organization and atypical contractual relationships on workers' health and safety. She is author of several articles and publications concerning on labour law; occupational health and safety; new forms of work and its implication on work organization and OSH management. She managed several funded research projects on issues related to occupational health and safety.

About the Contributors

Brenda Barrett is an Emeritus Professor of Law at Middlesex University. Her doctoral thesis was on employers' liability and from that time onwards she has researched and published widely on the law relating to occupational health and safety, having regard to both the criminal and civil law.

Dr Andrea Bernardi is Assistant Professor in Organisation Studies at the University of Nottingham, in service at the Chinese campus of Ningbo. He is also currently Finnish Government (CIMO) Visiting Scholar at the University of Helsinki. Andrea was previously Lecturer of Organisation Studies at the University of Rome, Roma Tre, and Lecturer of Applied Economics at the University of Rome, La Sapienza. He holds a Ph.D. in. Organisational Behaviour from the University of Milan, Bicocca.

Dr Mark Boocock is an Associate Professor and Co-Director of the Centre of Occupational Health and Safety Research at Auckland University of Technology. With over 20 years of experience in research and policy development in injury prevention, Dr Boocock has recently been involved in systematic reviews related to overuse injuries in the work place and biomechanical studies examining loads on the human body arising from different workplace stations and their potential to cause injury.

Barbara Boschetto graduated in social sciences and has worked at the Italian National Institute of Statistics since 2002, at Labour Force Survey. She deals with checking and imput of data. Recently she has also dealt with issues such as health and safety at work and the participation of disabled people in the labour market.

Dr Zeenobiyah Hannif is a Lecturer at the University of Technology Sydney and Senior Research Fellow at the Centre of Occupational Health and Safety Research at AUT. Dr Hannif has researched and published extensively on non-standard and precarious working arrangements, the quality of working life, managing diversity and occupational health and safety in the services sector, in particular call centres. She has also undertaken research on the occupational health and safety of young workers.

Philip James is Professor of Employment Relations at Oxford Brookes University and a visiting professor at Middlesex University. He has researched and published widely in the fields of both employment relations and occupational health and safety. His current research interests encompass the employment implications of public sector outsourcing, union organising among migrant workers and the management of health and safety within supply chains.

Dr Suzanne Jamieson is an Associate Professor at the University of Sydney who has also held a number of senior positions, including Operations Review Committee of the Independent Commission Against Corruption and a member of the New South Wales Anti-Discrimination Board. Her principal research interests include occupational health and safety, particularly as it affects women, human rights and equal pay for women. Recently she has been investigating the efficacy of occupational health and safety prosecutions in New South Wales and Victoria.

Chang Kai is Professor at Renmin University, Ph.D. supervisor and Director of the Institute of Industrial Relations. He was a Professor at Kyushu University from 2003–2004 and a Visiting Professor at Tokyo University in 2009. His social posts include Chairperson – Labour Relations Branch of China Human Resource Development Association, Vice Chairperson – Research Council of Social Law of China Law Society. His books include *An overview on trade union law* (1992), *Labour rights theory: an analysis on legal regulation of labour relations in contemporary China* (2004) and *Industrial relations in China* (2004, in English). He has also published a paper entitled 'The legislation of the right to strike in China' (2002).

J. Ryan Lamare is a Lecturer in Human Resource Management at Manchester Business School, University of Manchester, and a Research Fellow at Auckland University of Technology. He received his B.Sc., M.Sc. and Ph.D. from Cornell University's School of Industrial and Labor Relations and worked previously as a Research Scholar at the University of Limerick.

Dr Felicity Lamm is an Associate Professor and Co-Director of the Centre for Occupational Health and Safety Research at the Auckland University of

Technology. She has researched and published extensively on occupational health and safety, employment relations and the small business sector. She is also co-editor of the *NZ Journal of Employment Relations* and has been on the editorial boards of the *Journal of Industrial Relations, the Journal of Safety Science, Small Enterprise Research* and *Journal of Health and Safety Research and Practice*.

Carlo Lucarelli has worked as a statistician and researcher at the Italian National Institute of Statistics since 1997, and is involved in methodological topics regarding the Labour Force Survey. In recent years he has been dealing with themes concerning health and safety at work and the employment of disabled people.

Dr Christophe Martin has a background in law and political science. He is currently a Senior Research Fellow at the Centre for Research on Risk and Crises at the Ecole Nationale Supérieure des Mines de Paris. He has undertaken extensive research in the area of occupational health and safety (OHS) within the small business sector and more recently has been undertaking research on managing OHS in culturally diverse workplaces.

Dr Nadine McDonnell is a Senior Research Fellow for the Centre of Occupational Health and Safety Research at the Auckland University of Technology. She is a lawyer and legal academic with over 25 years of experience in areas that include work in administrative and compensation law areas, torts, jurisprudence and cultural aspects of law, development and teaching of tertiary level law papers.

Michael Quinlan Ph.D. is a professor in the School of Organisation and Management at the University of New South Wales, Sydney, an honorary professor, Work and Health Research team, Faculty of Health Sciences, University of Sydney, Australia; and adjunct professor in the Business School at Middlesex University. He has published widely on OHS, including a number of books and articles dealing specifically with precarious employment and vulnerable workers.

Cathy Robertson is a Senior Research Fellow for the Centre for Occupational Health and Safety Research at the Auckland University of Technology. She has presented several papers examining the links between management practice and employee health and safety. Her current work is inspired by the plight of precariously employed migrant workers in the construction industry.

Dr Peter Schweder has had over 25 years' experience in various health and safety roles including working for the regulator, work for light and heavy industrial companies and work as a health and safety consultant working with clients in primary industry and associated processing plants. He received his BBS and MBS from Massey University and his Ph.D. from the University of New South Wales. Dr Schweder is currently on the Board of the New Zealand Work and Labour Market Institute.

Boaz Shulruf Ph.D., MPH, B.Sc. is Deputy Director of the Centre for Medical and Health Sciences Education at the University of Auckland. His academic interests include methodology of research and evaluation as well as assessment and measurement in social sciences, health and education.

Rupert Tipples was born into a family of fruit and hop growers in Kent in 1949. Harvest labour was always employed and while growing up work was seen from the employer's point of view. After taking a Land Economics' degree, a research job for the Agricultural Training Board (UK) also gave him the view from the employees' side, as a staff union representative. Research interests moved from the land to the people on the land. A move to New Zealand in 1977 reinforced this shift with lecturing in employment relations at what became Lincoln University. Thirty-four years later a rural employment crisis (Who will milk the cows?) has emphasised the significance of the field and its critical importance for New Zealand's exports and economic future.

Professor Michele Tiraboschi of the University of Modena and Reggio Emilia, Italy, is Full Professor of Labour Law and Labour Relations at the University of Modena and Reggio Emilia. Visiting professor at the University of Paris Pantheon-Assas (Paris II). From 2002–2010 he was consultant and legal advisor to the Italian Ministry of Labour and Welfare in issues related to employment policies, European policies and labour market reform. Since November 2008 he has been consultant to the Ministry of Education, University and Research for the development of an analysis and investigation on the revelation of the situation 'precarious' in school and university. Since December 2004 he has been a member of the technical scientific committee of Isfol (Istituto per lo sviluppo della formazione professionale dei lavoratori). He is the commentator on problems of industrial relations for Il Sole 24 Ore, Avvenire, and was appointed by the President of the Italian Republic as a member of the Guarantee Committee for the implementation of the law on the right to strike for several years and delegated as a government representative to the

Administration Council of the European Foundation for the Improvement of Living and Working Conditions, Dublin.

Professor Tiraboschi is Founding Editor of the *e-journal of Comparative and International Labour Studies* and Deputy Director of the *Journal Diritto delle Relazioni Industriali*. He is Scientific Director of the Marco Biagi Centre for International and Comparative Studies and President of ADAPT – Association for International and Comparative studies in the field of Labour Law and Industrial Relations. He has also published widely and is the author of numerous publications in Italian and English in matters of labour law, trade union law and community law, among which are 4 monographs, 26 books and about 300 articles. He is also coordinator and member of the Teaching board of the International Doctoral School in Human capital formation and labour relations of the University of Bergamo. Professor Tiraboschi has also been project manager of research projects at national, international and EU level. He has attended as a speaker numerous conferences both nationally and internationally.

David Walters is Professor of Work Environment and Director of Cardiff Work Environment Research Centre (CWERC), Cardiff University. His research and writing is on various aspects of the work environment including employee representation and consultation on health and safety, the politics of health and safety at work, regulating and inspecting health and safety management, chemical risk management at work and health and safety in small firms. He is editor of the journal *Policy and Practice in Health and Safety*.

Charles Woolfson is professor of labour studies at REMESO, Institute for Research on Migration, Ethnicity and Society, Linköping University in Sweden. Until 2009, he held the chair of labour studies at the Department of Law, University of Glasgow during which time he spent three years living in the Baltic States as a Marie Curie Chair, researching working environment and social dialogue in the new EU member states. His research concerns labour standards and industrial relations, East–West migration and the enlargement of the European Union.

Preface

This book consists of a selection of papers delivered at a conference held at Middlesex University. The conference was sponsored by ADAPT (the Association for International and Comparative Studies on Labour Law and Industrial Relations). It was a truly international conference and the range of papers in this book reflects that. It was also a conference of the highest quality which we hope you will find when you read the papers contained in this book. We also hope very much to contribute to the understanding of the situation of vulnerable workers in precarious work.

Maria Giovannone

Malcolm Sargeant

1

The Health, Safety and Well-being of Vulnerable Workers

Brenda Barrett and Malcolm Sargeant[1]

Introduction

Each of the contributions to this book addresses situations in which workers are exposed in the course of their employment to unnecessary risk as a result either of their personal circumstances or because of the circumstances in which their employer uses their services. This in turn may depend on the contractual agreement under which they are employed. This chapter is concerned with providing some contextual framework[2] for the chapters that follow. It explains what is meant by the term 'vulnerable worker' and the associated term, 'precarious work'. It then, by way of illustration, reviews the literature on one particular area, namely the vulnerability of domestic workers, and uses it as a case study of vulnerable working.

New Forms of Work Organisation

A report by Anneke Goudswaard published in 2002 by the European Agency for Safety and Health at Work suggested that the new forms of work organisation that have emerged in the shift from an industrial mass production to a knowledge-intensive/service-based society are varied. There has been an increase in decentralisation in organisations with a low 'human factor orientation' such as in lean production. There has also been an increase

---

1 Brenda Barrett is Emeritus Professor of Law, Middlesex University and Malcolm Sargeant is Professor of Labour Law at Middlesex University.
2 This chapter is based upon work funded by a European research contract awarded to ADAPT and collaborating institutions.

in network-based organisations. Companies have retreated to their core competencies and outsourced other functions and formed chains of suppliers and subcontractors. These changing contractual relationships have resulted in an increase in subcontracting to individuals on the understanding that they are 'self-employed'. There have also been increases in part-time employment and increases in temporary employment. In addition there has been an increase in the practice of working long hours, either with one employer or by dint of holding down two or more part-time contracts.

The speed of change has resulted in an increase in the feeling of job insecurity and an increase in the number of 'non-standard' contractual relationships. It is possible that individuals do not change employer more frequently than in the past, but nowadays they are more likely to have to seek alternative employment whereas in the past they may have chosen to do so to advance their careers. A number of authors have tried to analyse the relationship between different contractual relationships and occupational safety and health (OSH). Quinlan et al., in researching such studies, concluded in a paper delivered to a European Union Research Workshop in 2000 that:

1.   The vast majority of studies (74) found a relationship between precarious employment and a negative indicator of OSH;

2.   With regard to outsourcing and organisational restructuring/ downsizing, well over 90 per cent of the studies found a negative association with OSH;

3.   With regard to temporary workers, 14 of 24 studies found a negative association with OSH;

4.   The evidence is less strong with regard to small businesses;

5.   Findings of a small number of studies of part-time workers found no clear relationship between part-time work and negative OSH outcomes;

6.   Five out of seven studies that considered gender issues concluded that women were especially vulnerable to adverse health effects.

PRECARIOUS WORK

An OSHA 'expert forecast' (European Agency for Safety and Health at Work 2007) on emerging psychosocial risks related to occupational safety and health stated that there was growing evidence that there are specific risks for health and safety in the workplace connected with the conditions that characterise these forms of work. Their report cited Rodgers and Rodgers (1989) as proposing four dimensions to precarious working:

- the low level of certainty over the continuity of employment;

- low individual and collective control over work (working conditions, income, working hours);

- low level of protection (social protection, protection against unemployment, or against discrimination);

- insufficient income or economic vulnerability.

Precariousness, according to the report, is caused by a combination of these elements rather than by one aspect only. Work bearing such characteristics is generally considered to increase the risk of illness and injury. Precarious work takes different forms on today's job market. In the scientific literature it is often associated with non-standard forms of work such as temporary, part-time, on-call, day-hire or short-term positions and also with the increase in the prevalence of self-employment. Additionally, work at home and multiple jobs also contribute to the increasing significance of 'non-standard' forms when considering precarious work.

The analysis shows that precarious employment is to be found throughout the European Union, though it is more common in some member states than in others. It cites Eurostat data to show that temporary contracts are especially prevalent in Spain (33 per cent of all employees had this kind of contract in 2005), and quite popular in Portugal (19 per cent), Finland (16.5 per cent) and Sweden (16 per cent), whereas they are rather rare in the United Kingdom (6 per cent), Luxembourg (5.3 per cent) and Ireland (4 per cent). Eurostat data showed that in 2005, taking the average in the EU-25 countries, 15 per cent of women and 14 per cent of men had a temporary job.

Additionally, the employees who seem to be at a special risk of precarious employment are migrant workers. The analysis cites the national data presented in the report written by Ambrosini and Barone in 2007 and published by the Dublin Foundation showing that in many countries temporary contracts are more prevalent among migrant workers than among national employees.

Quinlan et al., in their report, identified three sets of factors which appear to explain why precarious employment was linked to inferior OSH outcomes. First, economic and reward systems result in greater economic pressure in terms of competition for jobs as well as pressure to retain a job and earn a liveable income. A significant group is engaged on piecework or task-based payment systems. As a result there may be 'corner cutting' on safety with pressure to take on high-risk activities that have been offloaded by a larger organisation or refused by permanent workers. Secondly, workers are liable to be less experienced and performing unfamiliar tasks. They are likely to be less familiar with OSH rules. As a result it may be more difficult to coordinate decisions and anticipate dangers. These workers are also less likely to belong to unions or to have bargaining power and also there may be multi-employer work-sites with more complicated lines of management control and more fragmented work processed. Thirdly, there is an increased likelihood of regulatory failure. OSH regulatory regimes are designed to address full-time and secure workers in large workplaces. In a large number of industrialised countries most of the self-employed subcontractors and home-based workers fall outside this regulatory protection.

Benach et al. (2002) describe three impacts of new types of employment on health. First, there is strong evidence that unemployment is associated with 'mortality and morbidity, harmful lifestyles and reduced quality of life'. They suggest that new forms of work organisation and flexibility of employment will share some of these characteristics, in relation to insecure jobs. They cite one study Dooley et al. (1996), for example, which showed that perceived job security was the single most important indicator of a number of psychological symptoms such as mild depression. Downsizing also has been shown to be a risk to some employees. Secondly, the working conditions of non-permanent workers are worse than those of permanent workers, so those in flexible employment are exposed to more hazardous and dangerous work. Temporary workers, when compared to permanent ones, are also more likely to have poor working conditions such as vibration, loud noise, hazardous products or repetitive tasks. Thirdly, some studies have suggested that different types of flexible employment have worse health impacts than more standard types of employment.

TUC COMMISSION

The Trades Union Congress in the UK (TUC) set up a Commission on Vulnerable Employment (CoVE), discussed by Barrett and Sargeant (2008), as a result of concern that unsafe, low-paid, insecure work is causing misery for millions of workers in the UK. It took the view that the well-being of any single employee and that employee's family is too important to be left unprotected. The TUC's final report is entitled *Hard work hidden lives* (Trades Union Congress 2008). The TUC devoted the first chapter of the report to providing its own definition of vulnerable working. The report first defines vulnerable employment as 'precarious work that places people at risk of continuous poverty and injustices resulting in an imbalance of power in the employer–worker relationship'. The Report finds (at p.13) that:

> *Vulnerable work is insecure and low paid, placing workers at high risk of employment rights abuse. It offers very little chance of progression and few opportunities of collective action to improve conditions. Those already facing the greatest disadvantage are more likely to be in such jobs and less likely to be able to move out of them. Vulnerable employment also places workers at greater risk of experiencing problems and mistreatment at work, though fear of dismissal by those in low-paid sectors with high levels of temporary work means they are often unable to challenge it.*

The Commission believed that vulnerable employment is the product of existing social and economic inequalities and is the UK's approach to labour market regulation. Citing *Opportunities for All* (Department for Work and Pensions 1999) it noted that in the ten years immediately prior to the report, employment rates had risen so that 75 per cent of those of employable age were in employment, but there was a 14 per cent gap between overall employability and employment of minority ethnic groups and a 27 per cent gap for people with disabilities and employment rates for the low skilled were only a little above 50 per cent.

The Commissioners believe that much exploitation of workers occurs because the law is not strong enough to prevent it. Some employers find gaps in the law but others break the law. It found that in certain low-paid sectors, including care, cleaning, hospitality, security and construction there was evidence that the law was regularly broken. It believed that enforcement agencies did not have enough resources to guarantee employment rights.

Domestic Work

Relying on published research and other literature the following account uses domestic work as an example of vulnerable work, demonstrating that the problem is not isolated to one nation, but is closely, though not exclusively associated with migrant labour. Domestic work is here defined as 'home working'[3] but focusing on those workers employed to undertake 'domestic work' related to the home such as providing care to or performing housework for those living in domestic premises. According to the International Labour Organisation's *Encyclopaedia of Health and Safety* (1998), 'Domestic work is characterized by labour for another family within their home.'

The term domestic workers should not be confused with homemakers and housewives, who work in their own home, or housekeepers, who work in institutions such as a hospital or school. The position of employment within a home is a unique and often isolated work environment. The position of domestic worker is almost always considered menial or inferior to the family for which they are employed. Indeed in the past, domestic work was sometimes done by slaves or indentured or bonded servants. Some of the job titles today for domestic workers include: servant, maid, housekeeper, au pair and nanny. While domestic workers can be either female or male, female workers are both much more commonly employed and most often paid less than males. Domestic workers are customarily immigrants or members of ethnic, national or religious minorities of the country of employment.

One should also, according to the *Encyclopaedia*, which cites Anderson (2001), distinguish between domestic workers who are employed as live-in servants from those who live in their own home and commute to their place of work. Live-in workers are often isolated both from their own family and their own country of nationality. Because of the worker's disenfranchisement, work contracts and health and other benefits are negligible. This situation is particularly critical for the overseas worker. Sometimes, infractions concerning agreed-upon salary, sick leave, working hours, vacation pay and regulation of hours and duties cannot even be addressed because the worker is not fluent in the language, and lacks an advocate, union, work contract or money with which to exit a dangerous situation. Domestic workers usually have no

---

3 The term 'homeworking' covers all forms of paid employment carried out in the worker's home rather than on the employer's premises. Traditionally it has tended to be manufacturing commodities, for example shoes or Christmas crackers: today it is more likely to be working on a computer linked to the employer's server.

workers' compensation, nowhere to report a violation, and are often unable to quit their employment.

Again, according to Anderson, places where major employers of domestic workers are found include the UK, the Persian Gulf and Arab States, Greece, Hong Kong, Italy, Nigeria, Singapore and the United States. These workers are from various countries, including Bangladesh, Brazil, Colombia, Ethiopia, Eritrea, India, Indonesia, Morocco, Nepal, Nigeria, the Philippines, Sierra Leone and Sri Lanka.

According to work done for the ILO by Ramirez-Machado (2003), typical occupations of domestic workers are housekeepers, gardeners, watchpersons or drivers. The particular human characteristics are that:

- most domestic workers are housekeepers and women;

- more and more immigrants, national and international, are looking for employment in the sector; and

- domestic service draws an important number of child workers.

Domestic work is often exploitative. Major problems include long hours of work and heavy workloads; inadequate accommodation and inadequate food; lack of privacy and interference in personal matters; being vulnerable workers subject to abuse; arbitrary changes to work contracts, pay cuts or non-payment; low pay; lack of working benefits; and violence at the workplace.

DOMESTIC WORK AND EXPLOITATION

According to Blackett (1998) the overwhelming majority of domestic workers are women and, uniquely, their employers are also women – they provide a waged substitute for unwaged labour. Secondly, they are migrants from poorer to richer parts of the economy or world, so while often supporting large families in place of origin, they may not fully appreciate their pay is less than the minimum normally earned in the country where they are working. Thirdly, they work in a private home and live with their employer. Ironically, it is precisely because domestic workers are employed within the 'private sphere' that there is resistance to recognising the domestic work relationship, and appropriately regulating it. The cumulative result is that these workers experience a degree of vulnerability that is unparalleled to that of most other workers.

An ILO report to the International Labour Conference (92nd Session, 2004) states that migrant women domestic workers are among the world's most vulnerable workers:

> *Most are women moving from poorer to richer countries for economic reasons, and most leave their children behind, often in the care of relatives or a hired local maid, creating global care chains. The availability of foreign maids, in turn, allows women with children in destination countries to work for wages, so that many of the world's women between the ages of 15 and 64 years are able to pursue paid employment outside the home.*

The ILO report is not just about the EU of course and it does state that the working conditions of domestic workers vary enormously. Some are treated as members of their employer's family, while others are exploited and subjected to conditions 'which in some cases amount to virtual slavery and forced labour'. Thus

> *Domestic workers often have to work long or even excessive hours of work (on average, 15–16 hours per day), with no rest days or compensation for overtime; they generally receive low wages, and have inadequate health insurance coverage. Domestic workers are also exposed to physical and sexual harassment and violence and abuse, and are in some cases trapped in situations in which they are physically or legally restrained from leaving the employer's home by means of threats or actual violence, or by withholding of pay or identity documents.*

In many countries, labour, safety and other laws do not cover domestic workers, so that there are no legal norms for their treatment or officers and inspectors to enforce them. Even if they are protected by legislation, it can be very difficult for domestic workers to learn about or benefit from available protections, the result being widespread violations of protective labour laws (International Labour Conference, 2004).

A study by Anderson (2001) on the subject of why there is an increasing demand for private domestic services throughout the EU and why this demand is being met by migrant women concluded that migrant labour is flexible and women who are removed from their own family demands can devote themselves to the employing family. In addition their race and citizenship status differentiates them from the female employer.

OCCUPATIONAL HEALTH AND SAFETY (OHS) AND EMPLOYMENT PROTECTION

There is first an issue about the recognition that domestic work is 'work' and that the worker should have a contract of employment and the same rights as workers outside the domestic sphere. As it takes place in the domestic sphere there seems to be an assumption that it should be treated differently. Healey (1994) comments on the failure of the employer to appreciate why people do domestic work:

> *For me one of the most startling aspects is the complete non-comprehension by the employer that these women are workers first and foremost needing to earn a living wage. The fact that they live in on the job should not detract from that reality. Many of the employers in this survey are business people and professionals themselves who wouldn't dream of treating their business staff in this way.*

The development of domestic work within the home was initially considered a matter of family law and this classification was crucial for its exclusion from labour law. Fudge (1997) points out 'the ideologies of domesticity and privacy have historically combined to provide a justification for exempting these workers from some of the basic legal entitlements available to other workers'. Fudge studied the laws in 60 different countries and found that 19 had enacted specific laws or regulations dealing with domestic work; a further 19 had devoted specific chapters or sections of labour codes or acts concerning contracts of employment; 17 countries had no specific employment legislation with respect to such workers; and 9 countries excluded domestic work from the labour code. Only a small number of the national laws analysed require the conclusion of a written contract of employment for domestic work, and only rarely do national laws on domestic work refer to standards and specifications to be dealt with in those contracts. In addition, some countries either exclude domestic work from the requirement of establishing a written contract, or allow such contracts to be of an oral nature. As a result, this legal situation tends to generate uncertainty and create problems in determining and enforcing the conditions of work agreed upon by the parties. To avoid such problems and curtail any possible abuses and uncertainty, some national laws provide a standard form contract to be used as a model. Domestic workers tended by law to work longer hours than workers in other categories. In some countries, they are excluded from general norms on the matter. In some others, the law merely fixes standards of minimum rest. Several national laws on domestic work contain specific provisions stipulating the number of working hours per day and additional regulating mechanisms to avoid, as far as possible, situations of being on-call 24 hours per day. However, according to Fudge, 'given the nature of the work and the lack of control by the authorities, employers have a tendency to disregard such standards when they exist'.

DECENT WORK FOR DOMESTIC WORKERS (INTERNATIONAL LABOUR ORGANISATION CONFERENCE 2010)

This is the title of an ILO publication produced in the context of an agenda item for their 2010 conference on setting labour standards for domestic work. It states that domestic work is undervalued and regarded as traditional women's work. When it becomes paid work it is often undervalued and poorly regulated. In Europe and elsewhere the majority of domestic labourers are migrant women. In recent decades demand for domestic work has led to mass migration of women from one hemisphere to another. A crucial element of the ILO focus on decent work is that domestic workers are workers.

The report made a number of specific recommendations to end forced labour in migrant domestic work. These included:

- forbidding possession of the passport by the employer;

- removing binding requirements or, at least, providing renewable bridge extensions to prevent immediate expulsion on termination of the employment contract;

- removing the requirement to reside in the home of the employer;

- banning the payment of agency fees by workers and restricting similar deductions from their pay;

- requiring agencies to be accredited.

In most of the ILO member states surveyed for this report, domestic workers were not covered by occupational safety and health legislation: the work is mistakenly regarded as safe and non-threatening. There are a number of serious potential risks, which increase as a result of fatigue from working long hours. The work tends to involve a great deal of repetition, bending and reaching, lifting heavy objects, extremes of heat (cooking and ironing), sharp objects (knives), handling potentially toxic cleaning products and prolonged exposure to dust.

Migrant domestic workers may also be more vulnerable because of language issues and their lack of local knowledge. Whilst these risks may be similar to those encountered by migrants who work outside the home, domestic workers do not have the benefit of advice from co-workers as others may have. There is also a lack of autonomy in being able to control how to perform tasks, what tools to use etc. Possible improvements that are suggested include the possibility of inspection visits to ensure that the home is safe and to give advice; and also to ensure that domestic workers receive adequate training.

The discussion at the 2010 conference took the view that the ILO position was that domestic workers were covered by any convention or recommendation unless specifically excluded. Nevertheless several conventions allowed the exclusion of domestic workers and many countries had declared such exclusions when ratifying the convention. The discussion also noted that governments had expressed reservations about the implementation of regulation of domestic work because of the difficulty of monitoring households and the need to balance the privacy of the family against the protection of the domestic worker. It was feared that any convention would have to be very general and would lack effectiveness.

Nevertheless it was proposed that domestic workers should have written contracts which would include:

1.   the starting date of the employment

2.   a job description

3.   paid annual leave

4.   daily and weekly rest breaks

5.   sick leave and any other personal leave

6.   the rate of pay for overtime work

7.   any other cash payment to which the worker is entitled

8.   any allowances in kind and their cash value

9.   details of any accommodation provided and

10.   the period of notice required by either the domestic worker or the
      employer for termination.

    The discussion also addressed other matters including control of hazards
and proposed standards for matters such as overtime, rest period and
accommodation.

United Kingdom

The UK has its share of vulnerable domestic workers. This is in part, though by
no means entirely, due to the migration of wealthy nationals from other parts of
the world who purchase expensive properties in fashionable residential areas,
generally in London. When they move their families into residence they bring
their domestic servants with them. The plight of these domestic care workers
has been monitored by Kalayaan (www.kalayaan.org.uk), which is a UK non-
governmental organisation established in 1987 in London to provide advice,
advocacy and support services in the UK for migrant domestic workers. The
migrant domestic workers that they assist are people who have entered the
UK legally with an employer on a domestic worker visa to work in a private
household. It registers approximately 350 new migrant domestic workers each
year. It stated that

> the isolated, dependant and unregulated nature of working in a private
> household, combined with gender-based and racial discrimination
> means that domestic workers are vulnerable to exploitative practices.
> They can face physical, psychological and sexual abuse, discrimination,
> low pay and long hours. Employers often use passport retention as a
> means of control. Migrant domestic workers are often unfamiliar with
> the UK system and unsure of their rights in this country. Often they
> speak little or no English and are made vulnerable by their dependence
> on one employer for information about their status in the UK, their job,
> their housing and their immigration status.

    In 2008 Kalayaan produced a report, with Oxfam, called *The new
bonded labour* (Wittenburg et al. 208). The theme of the report is that the UK

Government's proposed changes to the visa system would have a detrimental effect on migrant domestic workers. The report is outlined here in some detail because of its importance to this subject.

Every year some 17,000 visas are granted in the UK to domestic workers from non-EU countries to accompany their employers to the UK. Prior to 1998 such workers were given leave to enter as a visitor or a family member, or given a stamp in their passport 'to work with …' Thus they were then not formally recognised as workers and consequently were more vulnerable to exploitation. The report stated that

> *the majority of domestic workers are women. Working within the private sphere of the household, they remain a vulnerable migrant group. Instances of psychological and physical abuse are commonplace.*

There were a number of nationalities of migrant domestic workers identified by Kalayaan, but four predominate. In 2006, out of the 312 migrant domestic workers registered by Kalayaan who gave information on their nationality, 38 per cent were Indian; 30 per cent Filipino; 14 per cent Sri Lankan; and a further 7 per cent were Indonesian. The majority of employers came from the Middle East, making up 59 per cent of the total. The next dominant group came from India with 21 per cent.

The report contained a case study which represented some of the problems with which such workers have to deal:

KALAYAAN CASE STUDY 1

Ramani is 40 and comes from India. She has been a domestic worker for almost ten years, and worked in Singapore and India before arriving in the UK in 2005. Ramani was psychologically abused by her first employer in the UK, who told her 'we have the money, we have the power; you have no rights'. This exemplifies the kind of power employers have over domestic workers. Ramani had no idea what her rights were when she first arrived in the UK. So she believed her employer and her threats. She was told, for example, that if she left the house she would be kidnapped and raped. She suffered serious racial abuse. She was frequently threatened with physical violence, and was never paid the £270 a week she was promised. After less than four months with this employer, Ramani ran away, only to find a second employer who also abused her psychologically and shouted at her constantly. The employer's husband sexually molested her at night, coming into her bedroom which did not have a lock. She was promised £300 a week. But she was not paid regularly and is still owed a large sum of money. Ramani tolerated it for five months, so she could obtain a recommendation letter and renew her visa. Her third employer treated her better, but she was still overworked and underpaid as she often had 24-hour shifts being a carer for a woman with Alzheimer's disease. Ramani must continue to work. 'Employers are bad, but too many mouths [are] dependent on me', she says.

There are examples of exploitation given elsewhere in this report, but Kalayaan gives the following disturbing statistics of abuse from the people that it has helped:

Conditions of work 2006	Percentages
Physical abuse	26
Psychological abuse	72
Sexual abuse	10
No own room	61
No own bed	43
No regular meals	41
No meal breaks	70
No time off	70
Not allowed out of the house	62

The report then examines these conditions more closely:

Physical abuse

The level of physical abuse reported by migrant domestic workers coming to Kalayaan is, according to their report, shocking

> Sometimes this would happen regularly. Or else they would be beaten as a punishment for a small mistake such as burning food, or washing clothes in a way their employer would deem inappropriate. Kalayaan also receives reports of physical abuse in response to the worker asking for entitlements such as their salary owed to them. Another commonly reported type of physical abuse is that of employers burning workers' hands on the stove, or with cooking oil, as punishment for mistakes in cooking.

Psychological abuse

Psychological abuse, including shouting, insults, in particular of a racist nature, and threats to the worker or the worker's family are, according to Kalayaan, highly prevalent among migrant domestic workers. A number of workers interviewed stated that they were constantly shouted at for not working properly, even when they were doing so. Racist insults and name-calling are also a widespread problem recalled by the interviewees when workers and the employers are of different nationalities. Such treatment is, of course, illegal under UK labour law, but is unlikely to be reported.

Sexual abuse

Workers living in their employers' homes are often unable to avoid sexual abuse because they do not have their own room, or if they do, they cannot lock the door. Sexual abuse then becomes another tool of control over the domestic worker. Some male employers may indeed expect their domestic worker to be sexually available to them. Migrant domestic workers (MDWs) may not be able to prevent sexual harassment, as they are tied to their employer in every aspect of their lives and would risk losing their job if they reacted.

Living and working conditions

Food is an issue with over 40 per cent of workers interviewed by Kalayaan stating that they were not given enough. Similarly some 40 per cent stated that they had no bed of their own. Working hours are particularly long, with daily breaks, days off and holidays being an unusual occurrence. Workers registered by Kalayaan in 2006 stated that the average duration of their workday was 16.5 hours, with over 41 per cent of MDWs working between 16 and 20 hours a day. Moreover, 70 per cent of workers registered did not have any time off during the week. Paid holidays were also a rarity: a very low number of workers interviewed having had a paid holiday since being in the UK.

Passport retention

In 2006, 34 per cent of workers registering with Kalayaan reported that their employers still had their passports. Without a passport, any migrant worker is vulnerable, as it is their only form of identification and confirmation that they can legally be in the UK.

An area of concern also was the lack of knowledge of many organisations of the plight of domestic workers and their rights. A further case study from the Kalayaan report highlights this issue:

KALAYAAN CASE STUDY 2

Divia is a 26-year-old migrant domestic worker from India. She and her employer arrived in the UK from Kuwait in May 2000. This employer was a relative of her previous employer in Kuwait. She was forced to sleep on a stone floor in the store room. She was given so little food her sight started to fail and she was continually shouted at and insulted. After six months, Divia ran away from her employer, leaving her passport behind, not knowing that her visa was about to expire. In fact, Divia was never informed about her visa, since the employer applied for it for her and she never had an interview at a UK mission abroad. Divia believes her employer purposefully 'forgot' to renew her visa. When she first ran away, Divia went to the police for help. But they could not understand her because her English was not very good and sent her away. Her embassy just told her to get a new passport. But they did not try to find out what her visa situation was. Divia did not learn of her irregular immigration status until 2005. Since she ran away from her employer, she has been working for free in people's houses, sometimes for a week, sometimes for a month, in exchange for accommodation and food. She has worked for so many people she has lost count. She says some were nice and some were not. She has been beaten, exploited and sexually abused in jobs but cannot take any action against these employers due to her undocumented immigration status. When she cannot find anyone to stay with, Divia sleeps on benches or in parks.

The report then outlined the existing protection offered to migrant domestic workers:

Immigration rights

The entitlement that allows such workers to change employers without being in breach of the immigration rules is seen as vital protection. Without being able to leave an abusive employer, migrant workers cannot challenge the ill treatment. It is important, according to Kalayaan, that the act of leaving an employer does not jeopardise a worker's immigration status, because anyone in breach of that status has no access to any protection under employment law.

The right to decent working conditions and fair pay

Being recognised as a worker is important in order to access employment rights. These rights include the national minimum wage, statutory holidays and sick pay, the right to a contract and wage slips and a notice period. It also means that the migrant worker can go to an employment tribunal to claim their entitlement. In order to exercise these rights a worker would probably have needed to leave the home of the current employer; and it would not be possible to enforce these rights if the migrant worker's immigration status was dependent upon staying with the employer.

The right to health care

Migrant workers are entitled to health care as being 'ordinarily' resident in the United Kingdom. Despite this they have, according to the Kalayaan report, difficulties registering with the health service. Matters are made worse when the employer has kept the passport, so they are unable to provide evidence of their identification.

Conclusion

This chapter began by stating its two objectives were to provide an explanation of what was meant by 'vulnerable employment' and to present the plight of domestic workers as a case study. It was intended to show that vulnerability in employment was a global rather than a national problem although the case study was largely concerned with the situation in the UK. A more recent report, *Vulnerability and adverse treatment in the workplace* produced by the Department for Business, Innovation and Skills (2010), a UK Government Department, although concerned only with the UK well summarises the general findings in this chapter. It finds:

> that certain features of the external labour market, the product market, the employing organisation and the job, as well as characteristics of the employee themselves, each serve to increase the likelihood of adverse treatment.

In the executive summary it continues:

Overall, the results of the analysis supported the notion that vulnerability
to adverse treatment is a function of a variety of characteristics. Some
of these concern the specific nature of the job that an employee may be
doing, but others affect the employment relationship from a distance.
There is also considerable support for the notion that it is those
factors which most affect the balance of power within the employment
relationship which most readily indicate the degree of vulnerability to
adverse treatment.

Turning to the case study on domestic workers it is shocking to find from
the personal stories recorded by Kalayaan that such treatment can continue
in the twenty-first century in the UK. The well-reported abuse and murder
of his servant by a member of the Saudi royal family in 2010 (*The Guardian*
2010) is an example of the continuation of this abuse. It can be little cause for
complacency to learn from the work of the ILO and other researchers that the
problem is not confined to the United Kingdom.

References

Ambrosini, M. and Barone, C. (2007) *Employment and Working Conditions of Migrant Workers*. Dublin: European Foundation for the Improvement of Living and Working Conditions, http://www.eurofound.europa.eu/ewco/studies/tn0701038s/tn0701038s.htm.

Anderson, B. (2001) 'Why Madam has so many bathrobes?: demand for migrant workers in the EU', *Tijdschrift voor Economische en Sociale Geografi*, 92(1), 18–26.

Barrett, B. and Sargeant, M. (2008) 'Health and safety issues and new forms of employment and work organisation', *International Journal of Comparative Labour Law and Industrial Relations*, 24(/2), 241–59.

Benach, J., Gimeno, D. and Benavides, F.G. (2002) 'Types of employment and health in the European Union', http://www.eurofound.europa.eu/pubdocs/2002/21/en/1/ef0221en.pdf.

Blackett, A. (1998) *Making Domestic Work Visible: The Case for Specific Regulation. Labour Law and Labour Relations Programme Working Paper No. 2*. Geneva: ILO.

Department for Business, Innovation and Skills (2010) *Vulnerability and Adverse Treatment in the Workplace*. Employment Relations Research Series 112, H. Bewley and J. Forth. http://www.bis.gov.uk/assets/biscore/employment-matters/docs/e/10-1127-employment-relations-research-series-workplace-treatment.pdf.

Department for Work and Pensions (1999) *Opportunities for All*. Data taken from http://www.dwp.gov.uk/ofa/indicators/indicator-19.asp, accessed April 2008.

Dooley, D., Fielding, J. and Levi, L. (1996) 'Health and unemployment', *Annual Review of Public Health*, 17, 449–65.

European Agency for Safety and Health at Work. *Encyclopaedia of Health and Safety*. International Labour Organisation http://www.ilo.org/safework_bookshelf/english.

European Agency for Safety and Health at Work (2007) *Expert Forecast on Emerging Psychosocial Risks Related to Occupational Safety and Health*, http://osha.europa.eu/en/publications/reports/7807118.

Fudge, J. (1997) 'Little victories and big defeats: The rise and fall of collective bargaining rights for domestic workers in Ontario'. In Bakan, A.B. and Stasiulus, D. (eds) *Not One of the Family: Foreign Domestic Workers in Canada*. Toronto: University of Toronto Press, pp. 119–45.

Goudswaard, A. (2002) *New Forms of Contractual Relationships and the Implications for Occupational Health and Safety*. Luxembourg: Office for Official Publications of the European Communities.

Guardian, The (2010) 20 October 2010, 'Justice even for princes'. http://www.guardian.co.uk/commentisfree/2010/oct/20/saudi-prince-murder-justice.

Healey, M. (1994) 'Exploring the slavery of domestic work in private households' unpublished MA thesis University of Westminster cited in Anderson, B. (2000) *Doing the Dirty Work? The Global politics of Domestic Labour*. Zed Books London and New York: Zed Books.

International Labour Organisation (1998) *Encyclopaedia of Health and Safety*, 4th edn, http://www.ilocis.org.org/en/contilo.html.

International Labour Organisation (2004) *Towards a Fair Deal for Migrant Workers in the Global Economy*, 92nd Session, http://www.ilo.org/public/english/standards/relm/ilc/ilc92/pdf/rep-vi.pdf.

International Labour Organisation (2010) *Decent Work for Domestic Workers*, report for Conference, 99th session, http://www.ilo.org/ilc/ILCSessions/99thSession/lang--en/index.htm.

Quinlan, M., Mayhew, C. and Bohle, P. (2000) 'Contingent work: health and safety perspectives or the global expansion of precarious employment, work disorganisation and occupational health: a review of recent research'. Paper presented to the European Union Research Workshop, Dublin 22–23 May 2000.

Ramirez-Machado, J.M. (2003) *Domestic Work, Conditions of Work and Employment: A Legal Perspective*. Geneva: ILO, Conditions of Work and Employment Series No. 7.

Rodgers, G. and Rodgers, J. (1989) *Precarious Jobs in Labour Market Regulation: The Growth of Atypical Employment in Western Europe.* Brussels: International Institute for Labour Studies, Free University of Brussels.

Trade Union Congress (2008) *Hard Work Hidden Lives,* 4 June. http://www. vulnerableworkers.org.uk/files/CoVE_full_report.pdf.

Wittenburg, V. with contributions from Niyogi, N. and Roberts, K. (2008) *The New Bonded Labour? The Impact of Proposed Changes to the UK Immigration System on Migrant Domestic Workers.* Oxford: Oxfam and Kalayaan.

2

We've Been Down this Road Before: Vulnerable Work and Occupational Health in Historical Perspective

Michael Quinlan[1]

Introduction

Since the mid-1980s, a growing body of scientific research has linked job insecurity and the growth of more precarious or contingent work arrangements – themselves the product of the rise of neoliberal policies and an employer offensive against collectivism – to significant adverse effects on workers (and community) safety, health and well-being in both old industrialized and 'developing' countries (Quinlan et al., 2001; Benach et al., 2010). Paralleling this has been a growing body of research on the occupational health and safety experiences of vulnerable workers in poor and rich countries, notably immigrants/guestworkers and undocumented workers in agriculture, manufacturing/food processing and construction, women employed in domestic service and the like (Debrah and Ofori, 2001; Dong and Platner, 2004; Cho et al., 2007; Premji et al. 2008). Again these studies tend to paint a picture of exploitation, what should be deemed as unacceptable exposure to serious hazards and the inability of these workers either to protect themselves or access protective legislation in any meaningful way compared to other groups of workers. Clearly, the two bodies of research overlap given that vulnerable

1   Professor, School of Organisation and Management, University of New South Wales; Honorary Professor, Faculty of Health Sciences, University of Sydney; and adjunct Professor Business School Middlesex University, London.

workers are typically concentrated in contingent work arrangements – a fact that is sometimes acknowledged and sometimes not (Lipscomb et al., 2008; Toh and Quinlan, 2009). Sargeant and Tucker (2009) argue that the combination of ethnicity/immigrant status and precarious employment can be conceived of as successive or even cascading layers of vulnerability. Such an approach could also include gender and other sources/dimensions of vulnerability (Siefert and Messing, 2006).

Viewed from a historical perspective these findings should not come as a surprise. As this chapter will try to demonstrate, research/investigation and more especially government inquiries into work during the nineteenth and early twentieth centuries clearly pointed to a relationship between precarious employment and vulnerable groups such as casual dock workers and outworkers in the clothing trade with adverse health and safety effects on working and living conditions. Indeed, this evidence had a critical influence on social protection by providing evidence for reform movements and community mobilizations in the late nineteenth and early twentieth century.

There is now a rich research literature on the history of occupational health, much of which adopts a critical perspective that demonstrates how recognition and action on disease and other forms of ill-health was mediated by interest groups and politics (Dembe, 1996). However, little of this research has specifically considered the precariously employed, including the groups and practices (like subcontracting) while historical research into sweating, the early closing movement and de-casualisation has – with some conspicuous exceptions – seldom considered the health and safety consequences of these work arrangements in any detail.

This chapter seeks to redress this gap by presenting evidence covering a range of occupations marked by contingent work arrangements and where the workers involved were clearly viewed as vulnerable by contemporary observers. Drawing on evidence from government inquiries and elsewhere the paper describes the health and safety effects of precarious employment with regard to casual workers, sweating, child labour, shop workers and seamen. As the case of casual workers and sweating are dealt with in detail by two other papers of mine (Quinlan, 2010a, b) this chapter will only briefly summarize the evidence before turning to a more detailed examination of child workers, shop workers and seamen.

The Not so Casual Risks of Casual Work

The widespread use of casual and transient forms of labour in the eighteenth and nineteenth centuries, together with the absence of state social protection – apart from poor laws and later workhouses for the poor (both designed to remove the threat of vagrants and social unrest) – created a welter of social casualties. People who couldn't find work, the injured and the disabled and their children had to beg on the streets. The more accurate urban European streetscape paintings of the eighteenth and nineteenth centuries (as well as early photography) capture this. Less visible from these records – because it is harder to capture visually – is the starvation, long hours/fatigue, poor nutrition and disease associated with precariousness.

Early writers on occupational medicine like Charles Thackrah (1832: 206–209) pointed to the adverse health effects of long hours, intense work and low earnings. Writing 60 years later Thomas Arlidge (1892: 14–20) saw the amount of work, as measured both by its duration and intensity, as one of the key general conditions labour affecting work-related disease. Directly relevant to the health of casual workers – although he does not specifically refer to them – Arlidge also stated that constancy of employment or its absence could affect health. He argued that in industries where demand for work was constant labour was more likely to be treated conservatively (that is sustainably) but this was not the case where demand was declining, or where seasonal work or jobs dictated by fashion resulted in fluctuations between deficient work and overwork. He asserted that 'the health of workers must suffer from fluctuations in one or the other direction, directly and indirectly, needs no demonstration' (Arlidge, 1892: 31). Fast forward a century and we find a growing body of international research documenting the adverse health effects of downsizing/restructuring and job security (for a review see Quinlan and Bohle, 2009) as well as the atypical or irregular working hours (Hughes and Parkes, 2007; Boivin et al., 2007) consequent of the new era of labour 'flexibility'. Researchers have also discovered 'presenteeism' where workers undertake unpaid overtime/extended shifts (to the cost of work–family balance) or attend work even when ill for fear of losing their job or having to make up unperformed tasks (Aronsson et al., 2000; Dew et al., 2005).

For temporary workers the pressures are stark – non-attendance means no pay as well as the risk of being down-shifted in ranking for future work/preferred shifts or losing their job altogether. Again, why should we be surprised at these discoveries? In his book *Health in Relation to Occupation* Vernon (1939: 60–61) quoted US data from the 1920s to demonstrate that workers who received their full wages when off work due to sickness were far more likely to take sickness absence than those denied this benefit. We now rediscover just one good reason why organized labour in the West spent a century pursuing permanency in engagement, trying to standardize working hours, putting financial penalties on overtime and securing sickness absence pay.

Information of the health risks encountered by categories of day labour and other types of temporary work (like seasonal agricultural labour) is more fragmented than is the case with sweating and child labour. The latter were the subject of numerous government inquiries, media exposés, learned commentary and research by a range of persons, including government inspectors, doctors and activists like Engels (1976 reprint: 216). With the partial exception of dockwork, the health of day labour seldom attracted government attention and the very transient nature of the work and workforce meant many of the hazards and its victims remained socially invisible – a notable exception being the Gauley Bridge disaster (Corn, 1992). With regard to dockwork the combination of low pay, irregular but intensive and arduous work posed both health and safety risks. One UK dock company manager was prepared to concede that hunger-induced exhaustion often forced workers to leave a job prior to its completion:

> The poor fellows are miserably clad, scarcely with a boot on their foot ... and they cannot run, their boots would not permit them ... These poor men come to work without a farthing in their pockets ... and by four o'clock their strength is utterly gone; they pay themselves off: it is absolute necessity which compels them (cited in Webb and Webb, 1914: 588).

The combination of lowly paid, irregular but intense work (exacerbated by the bull system of casual employment) was also a recipe for a high incidence of injury, premature disablement and early death. Ogle's analysis of deaths amongst males aged 45 to 55 years reported to the UK Registrar General's Office in 1890–92 found dock/wharf labourers had the third highest death rate (at 40.71 per thousand) of the 40 occupations measured, just behind pottery workers and well ahead of chimney sweeps and miners (Wohl, 1983: 279–281). The costs of a career of insecure work exacerbated by the Great Depression were no better for Sydney dockworkers examined by a government appointed physician in 1942 who observed:

Their endless search for the infrequent job which would keep them and their families from the precarious borderline of malnutrition had taken its devastating toll. The feverish high-tension work performed when the job is secured in order to ensure its repetition had been paid for at the shocking high price of premature old age and physical calamity (cited in Nelson, 1957: 119).

Prior to workers' compensation, some dock unions kept accident books that recorded injuries and illnesses, including diseases aggravated by working in cold wet conditions such as tuberculosis (Oliver, 1997). Handling hazardous cargoes (dust-laden wheat and coal, hides/skins, soda ash and guano) without any form of protective clothing (even gloves) or working on frozen cargoes in light clothing was a serious problem for dockworkers in the nineteenth century and long arduous shifts almost certainly exacerbated exposures (Tull, 1987). These exposures were largely ignored. In the last third of the twentieth century a series of studies examined hazard exposures (see for example, Dimich-Ward et al., 1995 and Bianchi et al., 2001). In another ironic twist of history the re-casualisation of dockwork over the past 20 years will make it harder to identify and address exposures to hazardous substances – a problem that extends to all industries where contingent work has become pervasive and to the community more generally (as more frequent job changes make it more difficult to develop work and exposure histories).

Evidence in relation to other groups of day labourers is equally fragmentary, although a number of studies by historians indicate that there is evidence to be found. For example, a study of 'rockchopper' labourers engaged in building the sewerage system in Sydney after 1880 found they faced a range of serious hazards (injury from rockfalls and explosions, dust, fumes and bad air) but most notably silicosis magnified by the contracting out of work, disorganization and being treated as entirely dispensable by their employers. In 1901 one contractor lamented losing 60–70 per cent of his best men (mostly aged between 30 and 40 years) to silicosis, another spoke of his men pining away to almost nothing within two years, while a third absolved himself of blame by stating that: '*If the men do not complain I shut my eyes to the facts, because in competition you cannot afford to incur greater expense than is necessary*' (Sheldon, 1988).

Overworked and Out of Control: The Health Effects of Sweating and Subcontracting

Sweating – the combination of low pay and long hours – and subcontracting were long linked to poor health outcomes. In the last decades of the nineteenth century broadly based community mobilizations – often in the form of anti-sweating leagues that included unions, religious groups, feminists and others – campaigned for action on sweating. The adverse health and social dislocation effects were central to these campaigns. Doctors working the industrial locations where sweating was concentrated were also aware of its effects as were others. Indeed, in 1888 *The Lancet* commissioned its own special sanitary commission into sweating. In a series of reports on its findings *The Lancet* observed that it had found the problem to be both more pervasive and diverse in its character between different industrial centres (such as Glasgow) than expected. At the same time, *The Lancet* pointed to the exploitive role of middlemen and the recurring connection between low and irregular earnings; poor-quality food; cramped working conditions; crowded, drafty, poorly ventilated and dirty accommodation; filth and poor sanitation; fatigue, chronic injuries and poor health; and susceptibility to all too common infectious diseases (such as scarlet fever) that led to a higher mortality rate amongst children, both those working and those not (*The Lancet*, 7 July 1888: 37–39). Later the same year *The Lancet* (15 September 1888: 540–541) sympathetically reported the resolution of Trades Union Congress calling for the abolition of sweating, noting the representativeness of the attendance and the legislative measures (amendments to factories laws) proposed. The House of Lords had commenced its own inquiry (chaired by Lord Dunraven) into sweating (to which one of *The Lancet's* sanitary commissioners, Adolphe Smith, testified). This inquiry was again duly reported in *The Lancet* (29 September 1888), noting that the House of Lords quickly discovered the immensity and complexity of the problem that extended from London in the south to Glasgow and other centres in the north. Despite the mountain of evidence the final report 'squibbed', with *The Lancet* endorsing Arnold White's criticism of its anodyne results. *The Lancet* not only endorsed White's argument that all homes or workshops where two or three persons were employed should be registered and the subject of factory and shops legislation, it went one step further and urged:

> From a public health point of view we go further, and would substitute the word 'work' for the words 'are employed.' What does is matter whether the people working together are members of the same family who are acting in a sort of partnership with each other, or whether

they call in outsiders to help them? These workers may be members of the same family or strangers, still they consume an equal amount of oxygen and require the same proportion of space. The real basis – the only sound basis to work upon – is the principle that what is made for the public and sold to the public, the public has a right to watch and control through every phase of its manufacture and distribution, whether it be made in a magnificent factory, where hundreds of workers are employed, or in wretched garret where but one or two sweater's victims work together (The Lancet, 2 August 1890: 246).

This prescient statement remains valid today. As rich countries are rediscovering, you cannot isolate the conditions of work and production (including inadequate or unenforced legislation) from broader issues of public health whether that is child labour in poor countries, lead-tainted toys produced in the sweatshop factories of China, unwanted 'additives' used by subcontractors to save costs, or the difficulty of managing food contamination when dealing with elaborate supply chains.

As in poor countries today, the low earnings/poverty associated with sweating and the threat of starvation drove child labour, bringing with it a 'rich' and enduring harvest of health problems due to overwork, constrained posture and affected physical development, and cramped living conditions that was documented in the UK by Edith Hogg (1897), Olive Malvery (1907) and others. While conditions varied between different industries, towns and countries, the key threats to health posed by sweating were essentially the same as those identified by *The Lancet* and the House of Lords. Thus for example, in May 1891 Catherine Powell, a Sydney tailoress, in giving evidence to a Royal Commission (Parliament of New South Wales, 1891: 278) referred to the low wages (with lengthy unpaid trial periods), piecework, dilapidated and cramped workplaces where 'girls [are] so heaped together that they cannot turn around'. The combination of inadequate nutrition, cramped working and living conditions also increased the risk of communicable diseases (Flinn, 1977; Floud et al., 1990). In 1899 a Victorian female factory inspector (Cuthbertson) expressed concern both at the risk of typhoid due to the impure water used in factories and some employers fitting out gas-lit and poorly ventilated basements for 'girls' to work in (Parliament of Victoria, 1900: 19). Articles in *The Lancet* and other medical/health journals, government inquiries and the like repeatedly drew a connection between irregular work (intermixed with bouts of overwork), exploitative subcontracting arrangements and low pay with unhygienic working and living conditions, poor nutrition, injury and disease (Quinlan, 2010b). Recent research is beginning to rediscover the complex interconnections between irregular and low-paid work and poor health outcomes, including the effects of this type of work on living conditions (Lewchuk et al. 2008).

A key aspect of many precarious work arrangements in the nineteenth century was directly linking remuneration to output/service provision. While the archetypal case may be seen as the use of piecework in clothing and other sweated trades, the practice (in various forms) was spread far more widely including whalers (the lays system), shearers, printers, construction workers and miners (hewing rates and contract systems). The reinvention of precarious employment in the late twentieth century was associated with a similar expansion of incentive and output-based payment, including re-emergence of contract schemes, mileage-based pay for truck drivers, garment-based pay for clothing outworkers and 'performance'-based pay for service workers. There is now a body of scientific research linking piecework or incentive-based payment systems to poorer health outcomes including fatigue, distress and higher injury rates (see for example, Lacey et al., 2007; Williamson, 2007). These findings would come as no surprise to unions and social reformers at the end of the nineteenth century – indeed the argument that piecework damaged the health of workers was made repeatedly based direct observations and experience. The connection was repeatedly raised during government inquiries covering a wide range of industries. For example at the 1914 Royal Commission into the mining industry at Broken Hill (Legislative Assembly of New South Wales, 1914: xxxii–xxxv) mineworkers gave extensive evidence as to how piecework induced corner cutting on safety (resulting in increased 'accidents') and exacerbated health problems due to poor dust control, ventilation, drainage and hygiene. Supporting evidence was given by medical witnesses – including the Commonwealth Military Medical Officer for the region. Under the influence of mining interests the Commission refused to prohibit piecework.

The establishment of widespread collective bargaining and regulatory regimes governing hours and wages, and restricting the subcontracting and home-based work associated with sweating in the late nineteenth/early twentieth century did not, as Ethel Osborne's (1919) report into the clothing trade demonstrated, eliminate the intensely arduous and hazardous work experienced by female factory operatives. However, it did remove the worst abuses of the sweating system and the more diabolical threats to health this posed.

While the 'sweating' debate now seems a distant historical event it is more than coincidental that as neoliberal policies and a new wave of corporate business practices (such as outsourcing) took hold from the 1970s evidence of and concerns about the same exploitative practices in rich countries began to re-emerge. In Europe, North America and Australasia campaigns to combat 'sweatshops' and exploitative outwork in clothing trades re-emerged (using symbols such as 'fairwear' or 'clean clothes'). In 1990 the New Zealand government undertook a formal inquiry into 'sweating'. In Australia a concerted campaign based on the adverse OHS effects of exploitative employment of clothing outworkers by 2004 resulted in supply chain legislation that integrated labour standards (industrial relations, OHS and workers' compensation) and included a contractual tracking mechanism (Nossar et al., 2004).

Child Labour and Working Children on the Streets – Visible and Invisible

The appalling conditions and health risks encountered by children in mills, mines, workshops, agriculture and cleaning chimneys was extensively documented in government inquiries such as the Royal Commission on the Employment of Women and Children in Agriculture (1843) and Sir Robert Peel's Committee on Child Labour (1860) in Britain, Canadian parliamentary inquiries into working conditions in 1882 and 1885, and a study of by the US Bureau of Labor published in 1913 (United States Bureau of Labor, 1913).

One important area of child labour in Britain was in agricultural gangs. The gang system that appears to have grown within British agriculture in the 1830s was a system of subcontracting farm work essentially similar to subcontracting in the urban trades (such as clothing described elsewhere). White's investigation of the eastern counties in 1867 found 61 per cent were female (32 per cent of whom were aged between seven and thirteen years) and 87 per cent of males were aged between 7 and 18 years (Verdon, 2001: 50). The gangmaster contracted work for a price, retaining up to a third as their own share while paying workers on piece-rates that might amount to 3d or 4d a day for children (Verdon, 2001: 45). Some also enhanced their profits by selling provisions to gang members (a form of truck-system). Like precarious employment today the gang system enabled farmers to purchase and dispense with labour on a contingent basis.

The 1867 report of the Second Children's Employment Commission drew attention to the both the low wages paid and the serious health consequences of these practices. One obvious health hazard was fatigue. In addition to working long hours the children often had to walk miles to and from the farm to their homes and experienced a range of climate extremes out of doors (Wesley Bready, 1927: 319). The Report is replete with testimony and descriptions of young children worked to a state of complete exhaustion, being forced to work when sick and suffering harsh physical abuse from gangmasters that sometimes led to permanent injuries (and even amputations) as well as 'moral' degradation (Wesley Bready, 1927: 320–321). As with urban-based child workers long hours also affected education. The Gangs Act (1867) – introduced in response to the Commission's report – prohibited the employment of children under eight years, regulated the distances travelled by children, instigated a gangmaster licensing system and required female gangs to be overseen by a female gangmaster. However, other Commission recommendations relating to hours of work, women working in wet corn, establishing a register of those employed and providing for schooling were not acted on. Shaftesbury's efforts to introduce legislation restricting the employment of children in agricultural gangs had limited success but set a precedent (Verdon, 2001: 49).

Another at least equally vulnerable but far less 'investigated' category of child labour were the numerous children, either orphaned or abandoned and living off their wits, or undertaking work to supplement meagre family incomes. As with sweating the harsh realities found its way into popular literature and well-publicized causes. One well-known example is Hans Christian Andersen's story of the *Little Match Girl* published in 1845 (and itself based on a woodcut by Danish artist Johan Lundbye of a child selling matches). Andersen tells the story a child trying to sell matches in the street on New Year's Eve, and afraid to go home without selling any, dies of exposure – being discovered in a nook the next day surrounded by a ring of burnt matches with which she tried to warm herself. In 1867 Irish doctor Thomas Barnardo discovered hundreds of boys living on a rooftop, many orphaned by a cholera outbreak, and resolved to devote his life to destitute children. One evening an 11-year-old named John Somers (nicknamed 'carrots') was turned away because the shelter was full and was found two days later dead from malnutrition and exposure – from then on the shelter bore the sign 'No destitute child ever refused admission'. Again, it is worth noting some contemporary parallels. In its report on employment conditions and health inequalities (Benach et al., 2007) the World Health Organisation's Commission on the Social Determinants of Health devoted considerable attention to child labour, including large numbers engaged in the informal sector undertaking tasks like street hawking in Africa and Brazil that bear striking similarities – including the hazards they face – to many children in similar occupations in developed countries 120 years ago (Baron, 2005).

In comparison to the engagement of children in factories and in mines, which was documented in government reports, the press and elsewhere (including photographs that provide the model for those used in child-labour reports up to the present day), the comparatively greater number of children employed in small-scale hawking and related activities received limited recognition. Nonetheless evidence does exist. In February 1899 a report prepared by the London School Board on children labouring out of school hours found 1143 were working 19–24 hours per week, 729 worked 30–39 hours per week and 285 worked 40 or more hours a week. The occupations they were engaged included newspaper and milk delivery, errands, greengrocery, domestic tasks and shop and factory work, and even undertaker's helper (measuring corpses 23–24 hours a week for 1s.). Not surprisingly, the report found that this extent of work activity induced fatigue and concentration problems that affected school performance. At the same time, the report observed that probably

> some die as a direct result of the severity of the toil inflicted upon them during their early years, and certainly many more of them must become a heavy and permanent charge upon the public purse because of the physical incapacity resulting from the rigour of their early experiences (The Lancet 11 March 1899: 707).

Two months later in April 1899 Sir John Gorst, the Vice President of the Council of Education, provided more comprehensive national data that essentially confirmed the London School's Report about the extent of the problem (*The Lancet* 13 May 1899: 1309). It found 110,000 boys and 34,000 girls were working, with about half (76,173) working in shops, 19,263 in general assistance/delivering, 15,182 selling newspapers, and 6115 in agriculture. Payment was generally minimal with 104,600 receiving 2s. or less (in 47,273 cases it was between 6d. and 1s while in 17,984 cases it was under 6d.). Of these children, many boys and girls 'of tender years' were engaged in excessive jobs 'beyond their powers' in terms of effort and hours (both duration and timing). Of the younger group about 46,000 worked 10 or more hours work out of school hours, with the vast majority (about 40,000) working 20 or more hours – and of these 2390 worked 40–50 hours and 730 worked more than 50 hours a week. In addition to the statistics the report cited numerous illustrative cases of these 'overworked and underfed children' such as a 12-year-old greengrocer's assistant commencing work at 2.30 a.m. and another who rose between 3–4 a.m. for a round to awaken 25 workmen before proceeding a round of selling newspapers between 6–9 a.m. For its part, *The Lancet* (13 May 1899: 1309) noted that, in contrast to children engaged as actors or circus performers, these children lacked any form of legislative protection.

In the United States, Roger S. Tracy undertook a study of the health of workers in cigar-making factories in 1872 and two years later with Nathaniel Emerson did a comparable study of tenement-based cigar production. In the first study Tracy found that the growth of young girls appeared to have been stunted while he found evidence of adverse fertility effects in both locations (Rosen, 1988: 398–399). In a chapter on hygiene of occupations in A. Buck's *Treatise on Hygiene and Public Health* in 1879 Tracy observed:

> *It has appeared to me, from observation made in cigar factories and in dispensary practice ... that sexual development is decidedly retarded in young girls who enter the factories before sexual evolution has begun, and in an investigation made by Dr NB Emerson and myself on the condition of the cigar makers who worked at their trade at home in crowded tenements, were very much surprised at the smallness of the families. In the 124 families of which one of us took notes, there were only 136 children, or an average of 1.09 to each married couple, and in the 201 families visited by the other only 329 children, making an average of 1.63 to each married couple. When we consider the swarms of children that usually grow up in tenement houses, and in the families of the laboring and artisan classes, the paucity of offspring in a particular class becomes significant (cited in Rosen, 1988: 399–400).*

Tracy did not investigate the matter further except to suggest that, based on European research, nicotine in the amniotic fluid led to the death of the fetus and abortions – and to recommend a prohibition on child labour.

Writing in 1910 Owen Lovejoy, General Secretary of the National Child Labor Committee in New York, pointed to the difficulty of children balancing work with learning, the long-term even intergenerational costs of child labour as well as the claims of interference with physical development. Others argued premature employment led to chronic fatigue and other health effects including early onset of chronic injuries. As noted by Derickson (1992: 1282), Albert Frieberg, professor of orthopaedic surgery at the University of Cincinnati observed: '*the prevalence of work-induced deformities as flat feet and curvature of the spine. Dr John Kober attributed to child labor not only musculoskeletal malformations but also predisposition to tuberculosis, rickets, and other diseases.*' For his part Lovejoy (1910: 233–238) argued the most 'dramatic' effect was with regard to injuries at work with statistics in various states indicating *'children 16 years of age and under show almost uniformly a higher percentage than adults in the same industries'*. Lovejoy (1910: 234–235) admitted the statistics were meagre and, it should be added, this data applied to traditional industrial settings that overlooked many areas of work where child labour was conspicuous.

Repeated claims that the combination of poor nutrition and strenuous work affected the physical development of children have subsequently formed the subject of some debate amongst historians. For example, a study of short stature amongst coal-mining children in Britain 1823–850 concluded short stature was not due to poor nutrition as food intake/diet in mining communities was often superior to other working class communities. Rather, Kirby (1995) argued the causal factors lay in a selection process to work in narrow seams and 'long periods of exclusion from ultra-violet radiation that retarded the skeletal development of children working underground and caused them to be shorter than their working class contemporaries'. However, this may represent an exceptional result with the bulk of historical studies finding that stature remains a good indicator of relative deprivation in working communities. A study of fatherless children in early industrial Britain by Horrell et al. (1998) found that a combination of factors contributed to the poorer health and stunted growth of such children. Low income and time constraints on single working mothers contributed to poor nutrition and living conditions (and even the use of restraining opiates) as well as children being put to work at a younger age and 'into more physically demanding and dangerous work' (Horrell et al., 1998: 107). With regard to precarious employment two observations may be added, namely that single mothers were more likely to be found in irregular and low-paid employment and – given the higher mortality rate amongst males in precarious jobs such as casual labour – those rendered single by the death of their spouse were more likely to be members of a precariously employed household prior to being widowed.

From the mid-nineteenth century onwards a stream of government inquiries in Britain, North America and Australia examined the working conditions and OHS of children and juveniles in traditional industrial settings. Like women, children and juveniles were often engaged in tasks requiring considerable dexterity and some of these the combination of unguarded machinery and the rapid pace of work exacerbated by piecework payment systems made such tasks especially hazardous. In 1912 New South Wales Royal Commission into the employment of female and juvenile labour in factories and shops by Commissioner A.B. Piddington described the employment practices and hazards confronting male and female juvenile workers in a wide array of industries (from bakeries and potteries to can-making and food processing). Drawing on Piddington's own observations and the latest publications and expert opinion on work-related hazards (such as Thomas Oliver) the report contains detailed descriptions of serious hazards and the need to both improve legislative provisions with regard to OHS as well as prohibiting the employment of young workers in certain processes. For example, Piddington (1912: xxx) made reference to the already extensive evidence on hazards in UK potteries and the shift to leadless glazes before observing that young girls assisting the glaze dipping process were being exposed to the same hazard, resulting in illness and absence from work. Referring specifically to danger posed by the introduction of piecework and more 'productive' machinery in wire works Piddington (1912: xxx) stated:

> *The boy's duty during the operation of feeding is to control the speed at which the two wires are fed into the coiling-machine from the bobbin; and now that he has two coils to look after, one on each side of him, and that his payment by piece-work gives him an interest in keeping the speed of the feeding machine as high as possible, accidents quite frequently occur, in which a boy loses a finger by the wire jerking up over the top of the bobbin just as he is in the act of putting his hand down to regulate the speed of the reel – an act that must in most cases be done without looking. Whateever may be thought of the system of piece work, it ought certainly to be interdicted in all cases where it is found that speeding up is attended, as it is here, with especial danger.*

In concluding his report, Piddington (1912: xxxiii) argued that had 'medical men' highly critical of the employment of children in factories (a number of whom he had interviewed in the course of his investigation) observed the conditions he had observed it would have not have altered their disapproval. As in the USA, a number of medical practitioners giving evidence to Piddington referred to the adverse effects of extensive labour on the physical development of young workers. The Royal Commission also secured reports from a number of government inspectors, notably Annie Duncan and J.G. Harriott, on outwork. As in earlier inquiries into sweating Duncan and Harriott referred to the very low payments of outworkers, how this encouraged the employment of children to assist adults, and the more casual nature of work in some areas (like box making and artifical flowers).

While the campaign against child labour had been a key part of anti-sweating struggles since the 1880s and an issue in its own right, as US campaigners like Elizabeth Morgan and Florence Kelley were aware, laws restricting child labour were often evaded (or children driven in to more informal occupations), as were laws designed to encourage and lengthen school attendance, in a context where the underlying poverty that drove child labour was not addressed (Scharnau, 1973). At the same time Kelley (1902: 157) criticized the judiciary and inspectors examining the poverty of individual families in granting exemptions to child labour prohibitions, arguing this further depressed wages and that setting effective minimum wages for adult workers was essential in this regard. Just over a decade later Paul Collier's report on wage regulation in Australasia prepared for the Senate of New York State Factory Investigating Commission, provided evidence to support her argument. Collier found that in Victoria (where Wage Boards had set wages since 1896) both the absolute number and proportion of children employed in factories (the only area where data was available) had significantly declined (from 7.3 per cent of the workforce to 4.4 per cent) in the seven years to 1912 even though overall factory employment had grown by 36 per cent. While stricter factory laws (in 1909) played some part in this Collier (1915: 1910–1911) found that *'prosperity and a reduction in the cost of education has induced many parents to keep their children in school longer'.*

Florence Kelley (1902: 162) was also well aware that many working children were denied any form of regulatory protection, not simply those in the cotton factories of the Southern states but in the North

> *newsboys, bootblacks, peddlers, vendors and the thousands of children employed in the tenement houses of New York and Chicago, and in the sweatshops of Philadelphia, remain wholly outside of the law's protection, so far as statutory regulation of the conditions of their work is concerned.*

Reflecting back on the US experience, historian Alan Derickson (1992: 1287) has argued that the child labour movement of the early twentieth century demonstrates the influential role that public health professionals could play in 'building a case for additional reforms' – a message with even more resonance today in the context of widespread precarious employment.

Are You Being Served? From Excessive Hours to Contingent Jobs and Multiple Job-holding

By the 1890s there was a well-recognized connection between long working hours and poor health affected a range of occupations and as the twenty-first century unfolds researchers are again documenting this connection (Dembe et al., 2005). In the retail trade several informed observers had pointed to serious health consequences of long hours well before this. Edward Flower (1843) argued the high mortality rate amongst shop assistants was not apparent to customers because assistants were dismissed and sent home when they grew pale and sickly (Whitaker, 1973: 9). In 1884 Thomas Sutherst (a barrister) published a book entitled *Death and disease behind the counter* and in 1893 Dr Bowrie told a committee of the House of Lords that 38 per cent of shop assistants suffered from consumption (Whitaker, 1973: 30, 55, 99). The Australian colony of Victoria became the first jurisdiction to mandate shop trading hours following a Royal Commission into shops (1882–1883). Like British inquiries, the Royal Commission took considerable evidence from medical practitioners (12 were interviewed) on the effects of long hours on the health of shop assistants. Almost without exception these medical witnesses pointed to serious consequences, including exhaustion/fatigue, digestive disorders, neuraligia, minor glandular enlargements and the use of stimulants. Particular concern was expressed for the health of saleswomen and young workers, as well as the excessive use of gas lighting in shops (Royal Commission, 1883: viii–x). The Commission (1883: ix) found the medical evidence alone provided a compelling case for restrictive legislation. Taking the evidence as a whole, it argued only legislation could achieve a universal and enduring reduction in working hours for shop assistants and recommended an early closing Act be introduced. An Act was introduced in 1885 which was then followed in other jurisdictions/countries over the next 30 years – a trend to intervention reinforced by public health concern-inspired laws addressing shop hygiene.

It is no small irony that the tyranny of working hours dictated by employers which retail workers struggled so long to end in the nineteenth and early twentieth century was reintroduced with the deregulation of trading hours legislation at the end of the twentieth century (Quinlan and Goodwin, 2005).

From 'Coffin Ships' to Contingently-crewed 'Ships of Shame'

While action to improve passenger ship safety had occurred in the mid-nineteenth century following a series of disasters (still inadequate as the *Titanic* was to demonstrate) improvements to merchant ships or mixed merchant/passenger ships (then more common) lagged in the face of fierce resistance from ship owners. As summarized by Jones (2006), the combination of cost-cutting in construction and maintenance, using aged ships with serious structural flaws, overloading, poor rations/accommodation, and undermanning were common practices that resulted in mortality amongst seamen that exceeded all other occupations (including miners) for much of the nineteenth century. The term 'coffin ships' was popularized in the media of the times, including a series of grim cartoons, with good reason. In 1873–4 the British Board of Trade reported the loss of 1,411 vessels, 150 of which simply vanished (another 4,637 ships experienced serious incidents such as collisions) and 6,817 lives. In the same year there were 22,098 wrecks, collisions and other incidents around the coast of the British Isles resulting in the loss of over 8,200 lives (Woodworth, 1876: 79).

High rates of maritime loss were by no means confined to the UK. In 1875, for example, 1,502 US vessels and 85 foreign vessels suffered serious incidents (with 312 being total losses) resulting in 888 deaths with another 73 seamen and others being drowned when washed or falling overboard (Woodworth, 1876: 79). John Woodworth (1876: 80), the Supervising Surgeon-General for the US Marine Hospital Service, endorsed the struggle of Samuel Plimsoll:

> *No thoughtful person will doubt that a large proportion of these casualties are preventable. The loss of these vessels result chiefly from the use of unseaworthy vessels; from the lack of the necessary amount of physical force, resulting from short crews and unseaworthy sailors; from overloading, or from ignorance, inattention or recklessness of officers ... Overloading is given as the cause of only eleven casualties in an aggregate of 7,671, but most of the vessels that go down from this cause are part of the long list of those never more heard from after leaving port.*

Woodworth was in a good position to make statements about the health and safety of merchant seamen. The US Marine Hospital Service instituted in 1798 by an Act of Congress imposed a monthly tax on every person engaged in foreign and coasting trades in order to provide 'for the relief and maintenance of sick and disabled seamen in hospitals or elsewhere' (Smart, 1873).

As with sweating, Plimsoll and others' struggle against 'coffin ships' was closely followed in the Australian colonies (see for example *Perth Gazette* 22 May 1874: 2). This reflected not only the colonies' dependence on maritime transport but also the relevance of such issues to local and overseas shipping visiting the colonies. Losses of ships were all too common, the higher wages of colonial seamen provided an incentive to reduce manning levels, and colonial seamen were essentially employed under the same fixed contract system (though often of shorter duration) as their British counterparts. Further, seamen in the Australian colonies (both those on visiting British or foreign ships as well as colonial vessels) found that protesting or refusing to serve on ships they regarded as undermanned or unseaworthy seldom received a sympathetic hearing before local courts (Quinlan, 1996).

Mortality rates amongst seamen were stark enough and nor was there clear evidence of improvement. Indeed, British data actually suggested deterioration had occurred in the 1880s. In 1862 J.O. McWilliam, Medical Inspector for Her Majesty's Customs, published an extensive study entitled *On the health of merchant seamen*. Using data on home and foreign voyage seamen from the Registrar General of Seaman for 1852–1860 he found an annual average mortality rate of 18.62 per 1,000 (of which 4.3 per 1,000 was due to fever, 1.62 to dysentery, 0.22 to scurvy, 7.72 to drowning and other 'accidents', and 4.83 to causes not ascertained). Twenty years later the situation appeared to have deteriorated. *The Lancet* (12 April 1884: 676–677) noted that the mortality incidence rate for British merchant seamen which was 19 per 1,000 in 1879 had increased to 21.2 in 1880, 23.1 in 1881 and 23.8 in 1882 – with 75 per cent of the deaths in the latter year being due to 'violent causes'. Indeed, the loss of seamen in wrecks steadily increased from 1 in 156 in 1878 to 1 in 62 in 1882. Further, *The Lancet* noted that the mortality figure excluded seamen whose health prevented them engaging on a voyage – an early reference to what is now known as the 'healthy worker' effect. Moreover, the fixed term nature of their employment was also factored into the equation, with *The Lancet* (12 April 1884: 677) arguing that from

> *the nature of the service, which necessitates a certain selection of men at the commencement of each voyage, and which loses sight of those whose health will not allow for re-engagement, it is patent that no materials exist for the calculation of a death rate that can be compared to the death-rate of landsmen.*

Overall mortality rates declined substantially by the 1920s, with a study by Home (1926) finding that by 1901–2 annual mortality rates had fallen to 12.5 per 1,000 for British seamen, 17.7 for foreign seamen and 14.2 by Lascars – and that these figures had halved by 1924 (to 5.47, 9.3 and 6.9 respectively). Nonetheless, this study also found that mortality rate for merchant seamen was still significantly higher than for seamen in the Royal Navy. A number of nineteenth-century studies also suggested the improvement for merchant seamen did not match that found with regard to their counterparts in the British navy. In his 1862 study McWilliam had also compared mortality rates amongst merchant seamen and Royal Navy seamen for the three years 1856–1858. He found that the annual average mortality rate from all causes was 19.85 for merchant seamen for these years (10.98 of which was due to disease and 8.87 to drowning/accidents) while the comparable figure for Royal Navy seamen was slightly higher at 20.25 (18.70 [sic] due to disease and 4.53 to drowning/accidents). What is also notable is that merchant seamen were almost twice as likely to die as a result of drowning or accidents as their Royal Navy counterparts. Twenty years later Sir William Smart (1884), ex-president of the Epidemiological Society, compared mortality ratios for merchant seamen treated by the US Marine Hospital Service in 1882–3 with that of the Royal Navy. He found a higher ratio of disease-related death amongst US merchant seamen, which he attributed to more stringent recruitment standards in the Royal Navy, the extended age of merchant seamen and the naval pension scheme which enabled sailors to escape the 'ultimate risks' of their calling.

From the late 1920s more sustained research confirmed the gap. Comparing mortality data on merchant seamen collected by the Board of Trade to that of the royal navy in 1932 *The Lancet* found the former was significantly higher in all categories (death by disease, injury, drowning and suicide). *The Lancet* (5 November 1932: 1010) reiterated the point it had made 50 years earlier: how official data understated the difference because the precarious employment of seamen contributed to a health worker effect:

> But merchant seamen have not continuous service, and any dying when unemployed are, technically, 'retired' and are not shown in the above figures, a point made by the Fleet-Surgeon Home in an article on the Report which appears in this issue.

Retired Naval Fleet Surgeon W.E. Home, who took a strong interest in the health of merchant seamen over many years, had made the same points a decade earlier. Comparing the death rates amongst merchant seamen to both army and navy personnel for the year 1921 he found that the death rate for British seamen was 4.98 per 1,000, for 'lascars' (Indian seamen) 6.72 per 1,000 and for foreign seamen 8.41 per 1,000 compared to 3.45 per 1,000 for the navy and 4.30 for the army. Home noted that death rates for merchant seamen exceeded the navy and army both for those arising from 'accidents' (including suicide) and disease. Home also noted that these figures understated the actual death rate amongst merchant seamen because the Board of Trade estimates for crew numbers were based on 'first crews of vessel' figures supplied to the Board, not those actually employed on a day-to-day basis. Home (1924: 982) went on to note that unlike the army and navy seamen on merchant ships did not enjoy steady employment throughout the year and that every interruption in service had the effect of overstating the level of employment and understating the frequency rate of death. In other words, as has been noted by more recent research into precarious employment, the irregularity of employment of seamen both obscured and understated their likelihood of suffering injury or disease as a result of their employment.

Home also identified another aspect of irregular employment that helped to mask the incidence of work-related death amongst seamen, namely death while on shore and premature retirement due to illness. In a letter to the *British Medical Journal* Home (1932: 945) argued it was important to include Department of Health data on recently 'retired' seamen in any consideration of mortality rates. In a letter to *The Lancet* Home (1933: 440) compared deaths at sea to those amongst seamen unemployed or retired in the year to 30 September 1930, arguing that medical officers of health in ports should be made aware that more seamen died of pneumonia or tuberculosis within three months of leaving the sea than the vastly larger number on board ships in that year. Nine months later Home (1934) published a more extensive paper exploring this connection further (drawing on Board of Trade and Blue Book data) arguing the evidence strongly suggested that a large number of seamen left the industry and became unemployed/retired because they were ill or dying. He noted that the number of deaths was highest in the first year after leaving the industry (625 deaths – or well over half – out of 1043 for first 5 years, and 2022 for the decade) and steadily declined thereafter. Indeed, almost half those dying in the first year (298 of 625) died within three months of leaving the industry. Home (1934: 1083) noted the absence of any invalidity or compensation scheme – something that again obscured the toll – before caustically asking;

> *is it right for ship owners to unload yearly 100 cases of tubercle on to the general public to be cared for till they die, when many of them,*

without any reasonable shadow of doubt, have become infected at sea?
Should they not be a charge on industry, as are miners suffering from
silicosis, under the Act of 1918?

Also conspicuous in Home's view was the absence of a concerted government response to the toll of death at sea when compared to other areas of employment. Six years earlier Home (1928) had written a letter to the *British Medical Journal* urging that responsibility for the health of seamen be transferred to the Department of Health from the Board of Trade because the latter contained no officials dedicated to this task even though it recorded deaths and via its surveys *'exercised control over the building of ships, and so over the accommodation and sanitary conditions under which seamen live'*. In a paper reviewing deaths in the year 1929 Home (1931) observed that the death rate from violence amongst seamen far exceeded that of coal miners but that the Board of Trade had nothing to say on how to prevent these deaths (431 in 1929) while by way of contrast the Home Office had produced a 178-page report on 982 fatal accidents in British factories that year.

To this death toll could be added a high incidence of injury and illness, as even a cursory examination of ship's logbooks and other documents required by British government from the mid-nineteenth century and now stored at the Maritime History Research Centre at Memorial University, Newfoundland, would readily attest.[2] Prefiguring recent interest in the health effects of downsizing, in addition the hazards of overloaded and poorly maintained ships and the fatigue associated with long hours, both knowledgeable medical authorities and seamen complained of how undermanning made the work more arduous, dangerous and unhealthy. John Woodworth (1876: 82) captured all these points when he observed:

> *It is of common occurrence for a vessel starting on a long voyage to find on the first day out, that one, two, or three of the crew are unfit for service. They become a tax upon the vessel, without rendering adequate return. The ship's crew, probably short at the start, or at least limited to the smallest number considered absolutely necessary to man the vessel, become, by the unexpected reduction, overtaxed and overworked, and consequently more or less inattentive to duty. On arriving in a foreign port, if the vessel is so fortunate, the unseaworthy sailors can claim full pay for the time spent, and the master of the vessel must deposit three*

---

2   I am indebted to Valerie Burton for alerting me to these records and enabling me to briefly examine them during a short visit to Newfoundland in 2006.

month's extra wages with the United States consul for each seaman he discharges. Hundreds of such seamen are returned to the United States from foreign ports every year at the expense of the government. Thus the government and commerce are both unnecessarily taxed, many lives are sacrificed, and property goes to the bottom of the sea from a cause preventable by machinery already existing. The application of the remedy rests with Congress.

In a similar vein Samuel Smith, a fireman, told the NSW Royal Commission on Strikes (Parliament of New South Wales, 1891: 205) that

there have several reductions made in the number of hands employed in the stoke-holds; (8314) they have been reduced to extent of 20 per cent; (8315) such a reduction does not add to the men's contentment, and it does not increase the safety of the ship; (8316) I have very often known firemen to be disabled; (8317) laid up by sickness or injury. I have sometimes seen three or four men incapacitated (8317).

Another witness (Thomas Davis, secretary of the Seamen's Union) told the Commission (1891: 201) that there were not enough seamen to fully man the lifeboats in case of emergency.

While the role of Samuel Plimsoll in fighting the callous disregard for seamen's lives is well recalled in the load line that bears his name, the importance of seamen, their unions and some community groups played in bringing about this and other changes is now largely unrecalled. Seamen had long resisted serving on ships they regarded as unsafe. Between 1870 and 1872 alone 1638 seamen were gaoled in Britain for refusing to serve on ships they regarded as unseaworthy (Jones, 2006: 13). Desertion and refusal to work on grounds of unseaworthiness were also common complaints amongst seamen in the Australian colonies throughout the nineteenth century, as were strikes over other health and safety issues such as poor or rotten rations (Quinlan, 1996). The outcome was much the same as in Britain, with protesting seamen being gaoled for not lodging their complaint in line with law (difficult when leaving the ship to do so would itself constitute an offence). In May 1873, for example, a petition with 400 signatures sought the release five seamen from the *Sea Nymph* in Melbourne who had been gaoled for refusing to unload the ship, having worked 18 hours in the last 24 at the pumps dealing with leaks until it reached port (*Age* 15 and 20 May 1873).

Also largely lost to history is the dogged resistance of shipping interests and their political allies which delayed reforms by more than 30 years (Jones, 2006) and arguments that the load line was not practically feasible and would undermine the global competitiveness of British shipping – arguments used to delay/defeat improvements in OHS to the present day – despite contrary evidence. Arguments about impracticality were also deployed to oppose compensation for those seamen who lost their lives. Debating an (ultimately unsuccessful) effort to include seamen under the Employer Liability Bill then being debated in Queensland parliament in 1886, one member (Black) essentially asserted that seamen were well aware of the hazardous nature of their work and having volunteered to undertake such tasks, like those of the fire brigade, 'employers should not be bound to compensate in such cases' (*Brisbane Courier* 11 August 1886: 2–3).

Despite the introduction of the Plimsoll line and other improvements conditions on ships remained dangerous and primitive. Crowded and unhygienic conditions on ships facilitated the spread of infectious disease. Like 'coffin ships' these concerns were long-standing, especially in the USA where arrival of large numbers of immigrant and merchant ships aroused fears amongst public health authorities about outbreak of disease in major cities like New York. For example, Herber Smith (1875), surgeon in charge of the US Marine Hospital Service for the port of New York, argued the high sickness rate amongst seamen was 'probably greatly augmented by the want of light and air; and the presence of dampness and filth so often observed in the forecastles of even the largest and best equipped sailing and steam vessels'. Smith then went on to illustrate sanitary defects in vessels he had inspected.

A year later Albert Gihon (1876), Medical Inspector for the US Navy gave a public health address in Boston on the urgent need for sanitary reform in both the merchant marine and navy because the combination of poor diet, impure food and water; inadequate/laundering changes of clothing and overcrowded, unhygienic, vermin-infested and damp/poorly ventilated working and living conditions were a breeding ground for infectious disease, phthisis and rheumatism. Gihon (1876: 89) was especially scathing of the conditions on merchant ships, although the crew size on naval vessels resulted in more living in confined circumstances: 'The forecastle of the merchant ship is unclean, its decks slippery with filth, its paint-work black; but eight or ten, or twenty at most live there.' Gihon (1876: 89) claimed that records of the Marine Hospital indicated that the average seaman had a seagoing life of 12 years and that annually 17,000 American seamen died or suffered a disabling injury sufficient to force them from their vocation. Like others already mentioned he point to the flow on effects of poor health to safety, rhetorically asking: 'Is it any wonder, then, that there is a scarcity of efficient seamen, that vessels every day leave port short-handed, and that shipwreck and loss of life grow ever more frequent year by year.' Similar observations are not difficult to find. Twenty years later the Report of the Committee on Steamship and Steamboat Sanitation (Montizambert, 1898) emphasized the need for 'permanent sleeping bunks of the crew, and their daily airing, and necessary cleaning, etc.'.

This information did not bring about a concerted or adequate response from regulatory authorities. Frederick Hoffman (1916), statistician with the Prudential Insurance Company of America, decried both the serious hazards confronting merchant seamen and the absence of any effective regulatory controls, even to collect accurate data on the level of mortality and serious injury comparable to that done in Britain. The American Association for Labour Legislation campaigned for improved laws and to fend off efforts to compromise existing protective standards during World War One (Andrews, 1918).

A point of contrast is the respective treatment of immigrants and merchant seamen during the mass migration wave to the North America between 1880 and 1920. At the European end, regulators showed more interest in the space allocated to passengers than seamen. In an article on the ventilation of ships, Royal Navy Fleet Surgeon W.E. Home (1910) compared the more expansive space and ventilation requirements accorded by some European laws to passengers while the British Merchant Shipping Act of 1906 enlarged the minimum cubic space of seamen from 72 cubic feet to 120 cubic feet – still well below that accorded to navy sailors. At the North American end, the major government concern was ensuring arriving immigrants were healthy, with the imposition of mass medical inspections of immigrants in the USA between the 1890s and 1920s. Ensuring the health of immigrant labour was viewed as a critical priority. Not so the health of seamen who transported goods and immigrants to the USA.

In a short discussion of health in the marine industry, Dr W. Collingridge (1902) emphasized the health risks posed by the combination of overcrowded, damp and unsanitary conditions on merchant ships, poor diet, heat (especially in the case of stokers), exposure to infectious diseases (including tropical diseases like beriberi) and poor or hazardous living conditions when in port. Five years earlier, Collingridge – who was formerly Medical Officer of Health, Port of London – complained that the Board of Trade was not a sanitary authority and – unlike public health authorities – had no sanitary officers to implement even its small sanitary powers under the Merchant Shipping Acts (cited in Home, 1926: 99).

The Board of Trade's limited role was further highlighted by W. Spooner (1906), ex-Medical Inspector with the Board of Trade at Liverpool wrote a detailed paper on the food of seamen. Spooner emphasized that, contrary to common impressions, food scales were decided by employment contracts at the commencement of the voyage rather than being fixed by the Board. Spooner examined a typical example to argue it was based on custom, not designed with the physiological well-being of seamen in mind, lacking variety, relying excessively on salt meat, being deficient in vegetables and also imbalanced in terms of the proportion of ingredients. Spooner (1906: 863) acknowledged an earlier effort in 1883 to promulgate an improved scale of rations had some effect in reducing outbreaks of scurvy. However, Spooner noted the initiative was entirely voluntary (relying on persuasion) – being inserted in the Ship Captain's Medical Guide (a small book edited by himself and authorized by the Board of Trade) – and urged the mandating of an improved scale according to enhanced criteria he had developed. Twenty years later Andrew Balfour (1926: 783) in a speech at the opening of School of Hygiene at Johns Hopkins University lamented that American merchant seamen were generally better housed and fed than their British counterparts – urging (like W.E. Home) that control of seamen's health be passed from the Board of Trade to the Department of Health.

On 25 May 1912 *The Medical Officer* (cited in *American Journal of Public Health* June 1912: 494) noted that the annual report of Dr Herbert Williams, the medical officer for the Port of London, indicated that dark, dirty and damp conditions on ships were conducive to the spread of pulmonary tuberculosis and that legislative action was required to secure the welfare of seamen. Williams repeated his warning, citing a number of cases, a year later (*American Journal of Public Health* November 1913: 1241). Following its earlier forays into the issues of sweating and dock workers *The Lancet* too turned its attention to the merchant marine, writing a series of articles on conditions onboard ships. In May 1913, for example, an article detailed unsanitary conditions on ships, including overcrowded and unhygienic crew quarters, inadequate lavatories, poor ventilation, inadequate food and filth in chain lockers. It noted that sanitary standards were 30 years out of date and that of 2213 coastal and overseas ships inspected in 1912 over 15 per cent were found to have serious sanitary defects. *The Lancet* (17 May 1913: 1396–1397) argued that that while it was customary to

complain of over-inspection (how little things change) there was an urgent need
from more stringent and rigorously enforced legislation on sanitary conditions
on ships. Almost 20 years later virtually identical criticism was made in the
journal *Public Health* (April 1931: 195–196) with the author stating

> *If the Board of Trade devoted to the hygiene of crew quarters a fraction*
> *of the attention they have devoted to the sea-worthiness of ships and*
> *the safety of life at sea, and if ship designers devoted to this question*
> *a fraction of the attention they have given to cargo carrying capacity,*
> *speed and passenger accommodation, condition of life for seamen might*
> *be vastly improved without handicapping our ships in competition with*
> *other nations.*

Injuries and disease remained common and, as *The Lancet* observed, while
little comparative data was prepared that which existed indicated merchant
seaman was one of the unhealthiest of occupations. In the years 1900–1902 'for
every 100 deaths among "occupied" males in England and Wales, there were
167 amongst merchant seamen, the figure for phthisis being 100 to 142, for
pneumonia 100 to 153, and for accidents 100 to 458' (*The Lancet* 14 March 1925:
555). In 1928 – by which time sail represented only a small remnant of total
shipping – of 164,300 British seamen a total of 861 died (an incidence rate of
6.45 per 1,000), with 379 dying in 'accidents' (another 29 committed suicide
while 19 deaths were attributed to alcohol) while 403 deaths were attributed to
disease (Home, 1930). Fleet surgeon W.E. Home (1930: 424), noted the lack of
information and regulatory attention given to these deaths when compared to
the 953 fatalities reported in British factories and workshops and 100 deaths on
British docks reported in the same year.

Just as the devolution of rail operations (separating track, maintenance,
freight and passenger operations into separate –sometimes multiple – entities)
and subcontracting activities like maintenance, undid 150 years of hard
earned safety knowledge in countries like Britain (Baldry and Ellison, 2006)
and Australia, so were some of the hard-won lessons of the nineteenth century
abandoned in the merchant marine. The establishment of 'flags of convenience'
and later second register shipping, using contingent third world crews, was a
calculated and largely successful attempt to evade regulatory standards built up
over many years in relation to safety as well as laws and collective agreements
governing the pay, health, comfort and other conditions of merchant seamen.
It is essentially analogous to outsourcing or subcontracting of land-based
workers (Kathveci and Nichols, 2006).

The health and safety outcomes of the now largely 'regulatory' outsourced and contingently crewed merchant marine have been documented by the Maritime Research Centre at Cardiff University and a series of government inquiries/reports (see for example Roberts and Williams, 2007). A report of Australian federal government's inquiry into shipping safety (Parliament of Australia, 1992) stated it had received evidence of unseaworthy ships, poorly trained and falsely certified crews; deficient safety equipment; beating and abuse of seamen; under-payment (often falsified); inadequate food and poor hygiene facilities; seamen being treated as dispensable; classification societies providing inaccurate information or certifying ships rejected by other societies; careless practices by insurers; and 'flag states'. In Appendix 1 the report listed 45 dry bulk cargo vessels lost between February 1988 and November 1991 – often with all or most of their crew. Endorsing the observation of one witness that 'behind every substandard ship lies a substandard operator' the report found (1992: x) that commercial pressures was the major factor promoting the use of substandard ships and unsafe practices. Like the nineteenth century, the expansion of precarious employment in the global merchant marine since the 1970s via flags of convenience has made the collection and comparison of data on death, illness and injury amongst seamen problematic (Roberts and Williams, 2007: 5).

These problems – a testament to the social consequences of unregulated markets and unfettered competition championed by neoliberalism – are global and they have not improved. The use of 'second' – and second standard – registers by hitherto responsible countries have simply accelerated the literal 'race to the bottom' in terms of safety standards. In 1998 over 20 per cent of the foreign ships checked at UK ports were found to be deficient in food and hygiene standards (Jones, 2006: 295). A study of car-carriers by Kathveci and Nichols (2006) found that the combination of reduced port-turnaround times and staffing levels on ships increased on-board working hours and reduced break-time for seamen (66 per cent of those they surveyed worked more than 72 hours per week). In another parallel with the nineteenth century (where a seaman's past behaviour – recorded in logbooks and discharge certificates – could affect new hiring), the propensity of Philippino and other poor-country crews to endure poor conditions without complaint must be seen in the context of the competition for jobs and fears that an adverse report from an officer to crew agencies will result in no further work.

Conclusion

What would now be viewed as precarious employment – and indeed was sometimes labelled as such at the time – was pervasive during the first Industrial Revolution and it brought with it emiseration and risks to health on a grand scale. As today vulnerable groups of workers such as children, women and foreign workers were concentrated in many (though not all) of these jobs. From the 1970s a deliberate effort was made to reintroduce precarious employment globally through a variety of devices designed to evade or undermine the regulation and polices that addressed these issues. Many of these devices were not essentially new but a repackaging, re-badging or changes to scale in past practices (like subcontracting or putting out work). We now have evidence that like the earlier period of laissez faire capitalism a return to flexible work has brought with it a host of health and safety problems for workers and their families.

While no historical epoch is identical to another, some important lessons can be drawn from evidence pertaining to the earlier period. First, examination of the five groups in this chapter indicated there was contemporary awareness of the health damaging effects of irregular employment (including irregular hours of work and intermittent employment), low or irregular/piecework-based payment systems, and the inability of these workers to protect themselves from work intensification or the most dangerous working conditions. There was also recognition of the exploitative and exacerbating effects of subcontracting (as in the conditions found in sweatshops or the gang system in agriculture) as well as the cascading health effects of low and irregular income which encouraged child labour, poor nutrition, poor quality/overcrowded accommodation and susceptibility to disease (and discouraged reporting of infectious disease). There was also contemporary recognition that these work regimes made it difficult to record injuries and disease exposures. These observations parallel the findings of recent research into precarious employments – both its nature and its health effects (Lewchuk et al., 2008).

Second, at least some groups of workers that were identified as vulnerable in the nineteenth and early twentieth century, such as home-based garment workers, agricultural workers and merchant seamen, occupy the same situation today. Efforts to restrict their exploitation in the twentieth century through a combination of regulation and union organization have effectively been unwound while the long-standing exploitative processes of subcontracting, isolation (as in the case of home-based work) and the like have been extended to new categories of work in the service sector and elsewhere.

Third, one positive lesson to be drawn from historical experience is that social mobilizations and campaigns targeting the inhuman treatment of vulnerable workers were one of the key bridgeheads to securing social reform/ protection. A number of the most critical regulatory and social policy initiatives of the late nineteenth and first half of the twentieth century initiatives were a specific response to the problems experienced by vulnerable workers and modified the 'flexible' labour market conditions that underpinned this. Women and children in particular were the initial target of interventions that were later extended, from the first factory legislation onwards – something conspicuous to early writers and more recently in debates about the gendered character of protection legislation (Price, 1914, 1923). Anti-sweating campaigns and the like played a critical role in the introduction of social protection legislation in the period 1880–1920. This suggests that vulnerable workers can be a mobilization point in the contemporary context and indeed there are some examples of this, notwithstanding some important differences in the current context, especially the more global network of production/service delivery and contingent work (Quinlan and Sokas, 2009).

References

Age 15 and 20 May 1873.

American Journal of Public Health, anonymous articles various issues.

Andrews, J. (1918), Report of Work 1917, *American Labor Legislation Review*, 8: 114–199.

Arlidge, J. (1892), *The Hygiene Diseases and Mortality of Occupations*, Percival and Co., London.

Aronsson, G., Gustafsson, K. and Dallner, M. (2000), 'Sick but yet at work. An empirical study of sickness presenteeism', *Journal of Epidemiology and Community Health*, 54, 502–509.

Baldry, C. and Ellison, J. (2006), 'Off the rails: factors affecting track work safety in the rail industry', *Employee Relations*, 28(3): 255–272.

Balfour, A. (1926), 'Hygiene as a world force', *The British Medical Journal*, 2(3434): 783.

Baron, S. (2005), 'Injuries in child laborers in the informal sector in Mexico City, Mexico, 1997', *Public Health Reports*, 120: 598–601.

Benach, J., Muntaner, C. and Santana, V. and EMCONET (2007), *Employment Conditions and Health Inequalities*, Commission on the Social Determinants of Health, World Health Organisation, Geneva.

Benach J., Muntaner, C., with Solar, O., Santana, V. and Quinlan, M. (2010), *Employment, Work, and Health Inequalities: A Global Perspective*, University of Pompa Fabra, Barcelona.

Bianchi, C. Brollo, A. Ramani, L. Bianchi, T. and Giarelli, L. (2001), 'Asbestos exposure in malignant mesothelioma of the pleura: a survey of 557 cases', *Industrial Health*, 39: 161–167.

Boivin, D. Tremblay, G. and James, F. (2007), 'Working on atypical schedules', *Sleep Medicine*, 8: 578–589.

Brisbane Courier 11 August 1886: 2–3.

Cho, C., Oliva, J., Swertzer, E., Neuvarez, J., Zanoni, J. and Sokas, R. (2007), 'An interfaith workers' centre approach to workplace rights: implications for workplace safety and health', *Journal of Occupational and Environmental Medicine*, 49(3): 275–281.

Collier, P. (1915), *Minimum Wage Legislation in Australasia, Fourth Report of a Factory Investigating Commission, State of New York in Senate No. 43*, Appendix VIII, J.B. Lyon and Co. Albany.

Collingridge, W. (1902), 'Health in the marine service' in Oliver, T., ed., *Dangerous Trades: The Historical, Social and Legal Aspects of Industrial Occupations as Affecting Health, by a Number of Experts*, John Murray, London, 182–189.

Corn, J. (1992), *Responses to Occupational Health Hazards: A Historical Perspective*, Van Nostrand Reinhold, New York.

Debrah, Y.A. and Ofori, G. (2001), 'Subcontracting, foreign workers and job safety in the Singapore construction industry', *Asia Pacific Business Review*, 8(1): 145–166.

Dembe, A. (1996), *Occupation and Disease: How Social Factors Affect the Conception of Work-related Disorders*, Yale University, New Haven.

Dembe, A., Erickson, J., Delbos, R. and Banks, S. (2005), 'The impact of overtime and long work hours on occupational injuries and illnesses', *Occupational and Environmental Medicine*, 62, 588–597.

Derickson, A. (1992), 'Making human junk: child labor as a health issue in the progressive era', *American Journal of Public Health*, 82(9): 1281–1287.

Dew, K., Keefe, V. and Small, K. (2005), '"Choosing" to work when sick: workplace presenteeism', *Social Science and Medicine*, 60: 2273–2282.

Dimich-Ward, H., Kennedy, S., Dittrick, M., DyBuncio, A. and Chan-Yeung, M. (1995), 'Evaluation of the respiratory health of dockworkers who load grain cargoes in British Columbia', *Occupational and Environmental Medicine*, 52: 273–278.

Dong, X. and Platner, J. (2004), 'Occupational fatalities of Hispanic construction workers from 1992 to 2000', *American Journal of Industrial Medicine*, 45: 45–54.

Engels, F. (1976 reprint), *The Conditions of the Working Classes in England*, Panther Books, London.

Flinn, M. (ed.) (1977), *Scottish Population History from the Seventeenth Century to the 1930s*, Cambridge University Press, Cambridge.

Floud, R., Wachter, K. and Gregory, A. (1990), *Height, Health and History: Nutritional Status in the United Kingdom 1750–1980*, Cambridge University Press, Cambridge.

Gihon, A. (1876), 'The need for sanitary reform in ship-life', *Public Health Papers and Reports*, 3: 85–97.

Hoffman, F. (1916), 'Occupational hazards in the American merchant marine', *American Labor Legislation Review*, 6: 69–83.

Home, W. (1910), 'The ventilation of ships, particularly merchant ships', *The Lancet*, 17 September, 176(4542): 880–884.

Home, W. (1924), 'The health of merchant seamen', *The Lancet*, 8 November, 203(5254): 981–982.

Home, W. (1926), 'The deaths of mechant seamen in 1924', *Proceedings of the Royal Society of Medicine*, 28 May, 19(Section of Epidemiology and State Medicine): 95–103.

Home, W. (1928), 'Care of the health of merchant seamen', *The British Medical Journal*, 21 July, 2(3524): 130.

Home, W. (1930), 'The deaths of British merchant seamen in 1928', *The Lancet*, 22 February, 215(5556): 423–424.

Home, W. (1931), 'The health of merchant seamen in 1929', *The Lancet*, 31 October, 218(5643): 994–996.

Home, W. (1932), 'Deaths of merchant seamen', *The British Medical Journal*, 19 November, 2(3750): 945.

Home, W. (1933), 'Death-rate of retired merchant seamen', *The Lancet*, 19 August, 222(5738): 440.

Home, W. (1934), 'Mortality of British merchant seamen', *The Lancet*, 19 May, 223(5777): 1081–1083.

Horrell, S., Humphries, J. and Voth, H. (1998), 'Stature and relative deprivation: fatherless children in early industrial Britain', *Community and Change*, 13(1): 73–115.

Hughes, E. and Parkes, K. (2007), 'Work hours and wellbeing: the roles of work–time control and work–family interference', *Work and Stress*, 21(3): 264–278.

Jones, N. (2006), *The Plimsoll Sensation; The Great Campaign to Save Lives at Sea*, Little Brown, London.

Kathveci, E. and Nichols, T. (2006), *The Other Car Workers: Work, Organisation and Technology in the Maritime Car Carrier Industry*, Palgrave MacMillan, Basingstoke.

Kelley, F. (1902), 'Child labor legislation', *Annals of the Academy of Political and Social Science*, 20: 157–162.

Kirby, P. (1995), 'Short stature among coal-mining children, 1823–1850', *The Economic History Review*, 48(4): 698–699.

Lacey, R., Lewis, M. and Sim, J. (2007), 'Piecework, musculoskeletal pain and the impact of workplace psychosocial factors', *Occupational Medicine*, 57: 430–437.

Legislative Assembly of New South Wales (1914), *Report of the Royal Commission on Mining in Broken Hill in the State of New South Wales*, Government Printer, Sydney.

Lewchuk, W., Clarke, M. and de Wolff, A. (2008), 'Working without commitments: precarious employment and health', *Work, Employment and Society*, 22(3): 387–406.

Lipscomb, H., Kucera, K., Epling, C. and Dement, J. (2008), 'Upper extremity musculoskeletal symptoms and disorders among a cohort of women employed in poultry processing', *American Journal of Industrial Medicine*, 51: 21–36.

Lovejoy, O. (1910), 'Age problems in industrial hygiene', *American Journal of Public Hygiene* 20(2): 233–238.

McWilliam, J. (1862), *On the Health of Merchant Seamen* reviewed in 'Bibliographic Notices', *The American Journal of the Medical Sciences*, 43(2): 510–512.

Montizambert, F. (1898), 'Report of the Committee on Steamship and Steamboat Sanitation', *Journal of the American Public Health Association*, 23(4): 239.

Nelson, T. (1957), *The Hungry Mile*, Waterside Workers' Federation, Sydney.

Nossar, I., Johnstone, R. and Quinlan, M. (2004), 'Regulating supply-chains to address the occupational health and safety problems associated with precarious employment: the case of home-based clothing workers in Australia', *Australian Journal of Labour Law*, 17(2): 1–24.

Oliver, B. (1997), '"Lives of misery and melancholy": the rhetoric and reality of industrial reform in post-world war 1 Western Australia', *Labour History*, 73: 112–116.

Osborne, E. (1919), *Report of Enquiry into the Conditions of Employment of Women Workers in the Clothing Trades*, Industrial Relations Commission of New South Wales, Sydney.

Parliament of Australia (1992), *Ships of Shame: Inquiry into Ship Safety, Report from the House of Representatives Standing Committee on Transport, Communication and Infrastructure*, Australian Government Publishing Service, Canberra.

Parliament of New South Wales (1891), *Report of the Royal Commission on Strikes*, Government Printer, Sydney.

Parliament of Victoria (1900), *Report of the Chief Inspector of Factories, Work-Rooms and Shops for the year ended 31st December 1899*, Government Printer, Melbourne.

Perth Gazette (1874), 22 May 1874: 2.

Piddington, A. (1912), *Report of Royal Commission of Inquiry into the Hours and General Conditions of Employment of Female and Juvenile Labour in Factories and Shops, and the Effect on Such Employees*, Legislative Assembly of New South Wales, Government Printer, Sydney.

Premji, S., Messing, K. and Lippel, K. (2008), 'Broken English, broken bones? Mechanisms linking language proficiency and occupational health in a Montreal garment factory', *International Journal of Health Services*, 38(1): 1–20.

Price, G. (1914), *Administration of Labor Laws and Factory Inspection in Certain European Countries, Report No. 142*, United States Department of Labor, Washington.

Price, G. (1923), 'Administration of labor laws and factory inspection in certain European countries', *Monthly Labor* Review, 16(6): 1153–1171.

Public Health (1931), April 1931: 195–196.

Quinlan, M. (1996), 'Industrial relations before unions', *Journal of Industrial Relations*, 38(2): 269–293

Quinlan, M. (2010a), *Precarious employment and the not so casual health risks of casual labour 1880–1945: Lessons from history*; unpublished paper.

Quinlan, M. (2010b), *Precarious employment, health and the sweated labour debate 1840–1920: Lessons from history*. Unpublished paper.

Quinlan, M. and Bohle, P. (2009), 'Over-stretched and unreciprocated commitment: reviewing research on the OHS effects of downsizing and job insecurity', *International Journal of Health Services*, 39(1): 1–44.

Quinlan, M. and Goodwin, M. (2005), 'Combating the tyranny of flexibility: the struggle to regulate shop closing hours in Victoria 1880–1900', *Social History*, 30(3): 342–365.

Quinlan, M. and Sokas, R. (2009), 'Community campaigns, supply chains and protecting the health and wellbeing of workers: examples from Australia and the USA', *American Journal of Public Health*, 99(Supplement 3): s538–546.

Quinlan, M., Mayhew, P. and Bohle, P. (2001), 'The global expansion of precarious employment, work disorganisation and occupational health: a review of recent research', *International Journal of Health Services*, 31(2): 335–414.

Roberts, S. and Williams, J. (2007), *Update on Mortality for Workers in the UK Merchant Shipping and Fishing Sectors, Report for the Maritime and Coastguard Authority and the Department for Transport, Research Project 578*, School of Medicine, Swansea University.

Rosen, G. (1988), 'Urbanization, occupation and disease in the United States, 1870–1920: the case of New York City', *Journal of the History of Medicine*, 43: 391–425.

Royal Commission (1881), *Royal Commission on Employees in Shops, Second Progress Report, 1883*, Government Printer, Melbourne.

Sargeant, M. and Tucker, E. (2009), 'Layers of vulnerability in occupational safety and health for migrant workers: case studies from Canada and the UK', *Policy and Practice in Health and Safety*, 7(2): 51–73.

Scharnau, R. (1973), 'Elizabeth Morgan: crusader for labor reform', *Labor History*, 14(3): 340–351.

Sheldon, P. (1988), 'Job control for workers' health: the 1908 Sydney rockchoppers strike', *Labour History*, 55: 39–54.

Siefert, A. and Messing, K. (2006), 'Cleaning up after globalization: an ergonomic analysis of the work activity of hotel cleaners', *Antipodes*, 557–578.

Smart, R. (1873), 'On the claims of sick and wounded merchant seamen', *The British Medical Journal*, 19 April, 1(642): 427–429.

Smart, W. (1884), 'On the marine hospital service for sick and hurt merchant seamen of the United States', *The British Medical Journal*, 19 April, 1(1216): 755–758.

Smith, H. (1875), '*Sailors as propagators of disease*', Public Health Reports and Papers Presented at the meetings of the American Public Health Association in the year 1873, 449.

Spooner, W. (1906), 'Sailors' food', *The British Medical Journal*, 6 October, 2(2388): 862–864.

Thackrah, C. (1832), *The Effects of the Arts, Trades and Professions and of the Civic States and Habits of Living on Health and Longevity with Suggestions for the Removal of Many of the Agents which Produce Disease and Shorten the Duration of Life*, 2nd edition, Longman, Rees, Orme, Brown, Green and Longman, Leeds.

The Lancet, anonymous articles various issues.

Toh, S. and Quinlan, M. (2009), 'Safeguarding the global contingent workforce? Guestworkers in Australia', *International Journal of Manpower*, 30(5): 453–471.

Tull, M. (1987), 'Blood on the cargo: cargo handling and working conditions on the waterfront at Fremantle', *Labour History*, 52: 15–29.

United States Bureau of Labor (1910–1913), *Report on Condition of Women and Child Wage Earners in the United States*, 19 vols, Washington, DC, Government Printing Office.

Verdon, N. (2001), 'The employment of women and children in agriculture: a reassessment of agricultural gangs in nineteenth-century Norfolk', *The Agricultural History Review*, 49(1): 43–55.

Vernon, H. (1939), *Health in Relation to Occupation*, Oxford University Press, London, pp. 60–61.

Webb, S. and Webb, B. (1914), *Industrial Democracy*, Longman, Green and Co., New York.

Wesley Bready, J. (1927), *Lord Shaftesbury and Social-Industrial Progress*, Allen and Unwin, London.

Whitaker, W. (1973), *Victorian and Edwardian Shopworkers: The Struggle to Obtain Better Conditions and a Half-holiday*, David and Charles, Newton Abbot.

Williamson, A. (2007), 'Predictors of psychostimulant use by long distance truck drivers', *American Journal of Epidemiology*, 166(11): 1320–1326.

Wohl, A. (1983), *Endangered Lives: Public Health in Victorian Britain*, Methuen, London.

Woodworth, J. (1876), 'The safety of ships and of those who travel in them', *Public Health Reports and Papers*, 3: 79–82.

3

Supply Chains and the Protection of Vulnerable Workers

Philip James and David Walters[1]

Introduction

The utilisation of more de-centred or fragmented forms of labour supply and 'production' has grown dramatically over the last three decades or so across the industrialised world (Marchington et al., 2005). That they have done so can be seen to be the product of a range of different, but often interlinked, developments. Notable among which have been an increased tendency on the part of manufacturers to outsource component production, a more general trend towards employers outsourcing 'internal services' such as maintenance, cleaning and catering activities, the much more widespread use of franchising in the retail sector and the placing of increasing reliance on self-employed and employment agency supplied labour. An important consequence of this move towards more de-centred 'production regimes' has been therefore to undermine Fordist ones based on the direct employment of staff within large, integrated organisational entities (see for example Piore and Sabel, 1984; Harvey, 2005). Another related consequence therefore has been to shift a growing proportion of workers into less secure forms of employment and into organisational contexts in which employment levels and conditions are more directly and immediately influenced by surrounding product market forces.

Unsurprisingly, this growth in outsourcing has formed an important part of current concerns and debates about employment vulnerability in the modern world of work, including those concerning how far workers are

1   Philip James is Professor of Employment Relations at Oxford Brookes University and David Walters is Professor of Work Environment and Director of Cardiff Work Environment Research Centre, Cardiff University.

being exposed to increased risks to their health and safety while going about
the task of earning a living (Walters and James, 2009). At the same time, it is
one that has, somewhat ironically, also spawned a growing interest in the
possibility of using the economic dynamics encompassed within supply chain
relationships to counter the negative consequences they potentially have for
those employed in supplier organisations. This interest can be seen to be most
clearly highlighted by the way in which NGOs, trade unions, governments
and other stakeholders have sought to utilise such chains to protect labour
standards, and hence counter employment vulnerability, within global supply
chains (see for example Rodriguez-Garavito, 2005; O'Rourke, 2003; Rawlings,
2006; Weil and Mallo, 2007; World Bank, 2000).

The present chapter effectively takes this juxtaposition between concerns
about the labour standards implications of outsourcing and attempts to use
supply chains to protect them as its starting point. More specifically, it sets out
to explore in the context of industrialised economics (a) how far it is correct
to view the economic forces embedded in such chains as being problematic
in health and safety terms, and (b) under what circumstances they are used to
exert a positive influence over health and safety standards.

This exploration falls into three main parts. In the first, attention is paid to
the way in which supply chains impact on labour conditions in general within
supplier organisations. The second then moves on to review briefly the existing
evidence concerning the health and safety implications of outsourcing. Finally
the third, again drawing upon existing evidence, examines the circumstances
under which supply chains are sometimes used to positively influence health
and safety management and standards.

Supply Chains and Labour Conditions

Existing evidence demonstrates clearly that purchaser–provider relationships
embodied in supply chains can have important implications for employment
regimes within provider organisations (see for example Scarborough, 2000;
Beaumont et al., 1996; Truss, 2004; Swart and Kinnie, 2003; Wright and
Lund, 2003). It further shows that these implications can be both positive
and negative in nature: indeed, that these different types of effect can occur
alongside each other.

On the more positive side, studies have shown that purchasers can intervene directly to positively shape the management of provider staff, for example, by laying down training requirements, specifying (minimum) pay rates and other conditions of employment, and requiring the introduction of more empowering work systems and processes. On the other, cost, delivery and quality pressures have also been found to more indirectly lead suppliers to revise (detrimentally) working time arrangements and increase their reliance on temporary staff, introduce tighter staffing levels and intensify workloads and reduce pay and other conditions of employment. These different employment effects have, in turn, been identified as being intimately connected to the varying nature of supply chain relationships.

The literature highlights that such relationships vary considerably and can, and often do, extend beyond highly transactional, 'arm's length' ones (Sako, 1992). For example, it highlights how purchasers and suppliers can be involved in the joint development of new products and co-investments in equipment and premises and how the former can also attempt, as the findings referred to above demonstrate, to directly shape various internal aspects of supplier operations.

It further emerges from a range of studies that purchasers are most likely to attempt to intervene in the internal operations of suppliers when such action is seen to be supportive of their business interests. In particular, their findings point to the fact that such attempts are more likely to occur where alternative suppliers of the products or services being purchased are limited, the products or services concerned are of highly critical importance to the purchasing organisation's activities and reputation, and their complex nature means that there is considerable scope for failures in supply to occur (Cousins and Lawson, 2007; Marchington and Vincent, 2004; Heide and John, 1990). In other words, they suggest that closer supply relationships will be sought by purchasers when outsourcing is seen to be associated with substantial business risks and related benefits.

What further appears to be the case is that even where supply chain purchasers have business-based incentives to interfere in the internal affairs of suppliers, it does not follow that they necessarily do so with a view to establishing collaborative relationships embodying a high degree of mutual sharing of business costs, risks and benefits (Cousins and Lawson, 2007). Rather, they can co-exist with a strong focus on cost minimisation, and therefore a strong downward pressure on supplier labour costs. Consequently, such relationships can potentially embody contradictory dynamics whereby purchasers can seek, say for reasons of quality, to shape positively some aspects of employment conditions in supplier organisations, while also indirectly adversely affecting others through a desire to negotiate lower prices.

Such contradictory dynamics can be viewed as an inevitable feature of market-based exchanges. The degree of contradiction involved is, though, variable. In part, because the type of factors identified above as encouraging purchasers to intervene in the affairs of suppliers can, to differing degrees, act to similarly place limits on the scale of cost savings they pursue; for example, because beyond a certain point price reductions could endanger the quality and reliability of supply. In part also because suppliers may be in a position, for example because of a lack of alternative sources of supply or their lack of dependency on a particular purchaser, to resist, albeit to varying degrees, price demands placed on them.

Indeed, studies shedding light on the circumstances supporting the establishment of mutuality-based collaborative relationships between purchasers and supplier serve to highlight these last observations. They show that such relationships are most likely to emerge when they are perceived to support the business interests of purchasers and in a context marked by a substantial degree of mutual dependency between the contracting parties (see for example Sako, 1992). This latter point is well captured by Dore's observation that a partnership approach which seeks to match 'business goals and needs', reconcile 'cultures' and develop the 'right chemistry' is likely to prove challenging and frustrating where contracting is between 'unequals' (Dore, 1996).

In short, on the basis of the wider supply chain business literature, there may be situations in which purchasers seek to positively and directly influence how health and safety is managed within supplier organisations. It also cannot be said that the financial relationships existing between purchasers and suppliers inevitably involve cost (and other) pressures on the latter that indirectly require them to downgrade the resources they devote to health and safety management and to more generally introduce employment regimes that have harmful consequences for the well-being of their staff. What does, however, also emerge from this literature is that in general the former direct source of influence will only arise where such actions fit with the wider business interests of purchasers, while the latter indirect negative ones are most likely to be absent where the ability of purchasers to drive down costs is substantially constrained by countervailing supplier negotiating power.

Supply Chains and Health and Safety Outcomes

The discussion in the previous section has served, then, to indicate that supply chains should not be viewed as inevitably or invariably impacting negatively on health and safety standards. It has further highlighted that their effects on health and safety can flow from a combination of positive and negative forces, the balance between which is likely to vary considerably.

This said, however, a consideration of the structural consequences of outsourcing and its surrounding market dynamics suggests that there are at least four compelling sets of reasons for suggesting that it will be associated, at the aggregate level, with greater health and safety vulnerability (James et al., 2007). In brief these are that:

- Much of the externalisation of work activities has gone to smaller organisations, which possess less adequate and sophisticated systems of risk management than their larger counterparts;

- Problems can arise with regard to the co-ordination of such management in situations where subcontractor and temporary staff work in close physical proximity to in-house personnel, as in the case of many construction projects;

- Work is frequently exported away from organisational settings within which exist well-established channels for the representation of the interests of workers; and

- Cost pressures exerted by purchasers can limit the ability of those organisations engaged in the supply of labour or the provision of manufacturing or other services to invest in preventive health and safety.

Existing empirical findings add much weight to these propositions. For example, there is clear evidence that workplace injury rates tend to vary negatively with both workplace and establishment size (Eurostat, 2002; Nichols et al., 1995; Cully et al., 1999; Stevens, 1999), while the poorer safety performance of small firms has been attributed to a 'general and multifaceted lack of resources' which gives rise to 'structures of vulnerability' (Nichols, 1997, Walters, 2001). A number of studies and official inquiries into the causes of injuries and disasters in chemical plants, and in the rail and offshore oil industries have, meanwhile, drawn attention to the difficulties that can arise with regard to the adequate control and management of workers employed by subcontractors (Wright, 1986; Baldry, 2006; Cullen, 2001; Uff, 2000).

Available evidence regarding the management of the health and safety of temporary workers similarly points to a problematic situation. A British study in 2000, for example, revealed that around half of the recruitment agencies surveyed did not have measures in place to ensure they were fulfilling their legal obligations and a widespread lack of awareness among agencies and host employers that legal responsibility for health and safety is a shared one (Wiseman and Gilbert, 2005). In a similar vein, a parliamentary inquiry in the Australian state of Victoria concluded that the use of 'labour hire' arrangements can complicate the co-ordination of work processes, including occupational health and safety standards, and that weak lines of communication between labour hire worker agencies, and between host employers and employees, can lead to the obfuscation of occupational safety and health responsibilities. It further observed that the cost-sensitive nature of the labour hire industry could lead agencies to compromises or even non-compliance with occupational health and safety duties relating to such matters as induction training and risk assessment (Victoria Parliament Economic Development Committee, 2005).

More generally, numerous studies have shown that the cost and delivery pressures that exist within supply chains can lead suppliers to reduce staffing levels, place a greater reliance on temporary and other forms of contingent employment, increase workloads and more generally create more intense and demanding work regimes (James and Lloyd, 2008). In doing so, they therefore point to their capacity to lead to the establishment of work contexts embodying features that have been found to be associated with a range of adverse work-related health outcomes, including cardiovascular disease, burnout and depression (see for example Ferrie et al., 2002; Kivimaki et al., 2000; Quinlan et al., 2001).

Supply Chains as a Source of Health and Safety Good

In a recent report the authors reviewed some of the main examples of initiatives that have been undertaken to improve health and safety management within supply chains (Walters and James, 2009). The initiatives identified took three main forms. First, the utilisation by purchasers of procurement strategies under which health and safety standards are used as a basis for selecting contractors and the extension of these in some cases to the imposition on those selected of requirements relating to the general management of health and safety, including in relation to the carrying out of risk assessments and communication within multi-contractor/subcontractor work sites. Secondly, industry-level certification schemes aimed at ensuring the competencies of contracting organisations and those working for them. Thirdly, 'product-related initiatives' undertaken by trade/industry bodies, as well as individual supplier organisations.

In examining these various identified initiatives, an attempt was made to trace the factors that had shaped their development, identify evidence relating to their impact, and, where such evidence was found, to explore the factors that had influenced this impact. In general, what emerged from the analysis undertaken is that few of the initiatives examined had been subjected to any systematic evaluation of their effects and that the available evidence similarly shed little light on the contextual factors that had contributed to their development, design and subsequent operation.

A number of examples were, however, identified in which positive health and safety outcomes had been achieved. In particular, clear evidence along these lines was identified in respect of a small number of large-scale construction projects. For example, in the case of the building of the major land works supporting the land/sea link between Denmark and southern Sweden in the 1990s, evidence showed that initiatives on health and safety requirements in procurement had helped to reduce the incidence of occupational accidents (EU OSHA, 2000). In a similar vein, controls on subcontracting adopted by Renault in building a new industrial plant in France in the 1990s were found to have achieved a much improved accident frequency when compared to the French construction industry as a whole (EU OSHA, 2000: 89–94), Similarly again, agreements between stakeholders involved in the supply of labour and services in the construction of the facilities for the Sydney Olympics, led to marked improved OHS performance compared to the construction industry more generally and also to OHS outcomes in the previous construction of such facilities (Webb, 2001). The same picture emerges, as shall be seen below, with regard to the impressive safety performance achieved during the construction of Heathrow Airport's Terminal 5.

Such examples consequently suggest that supply chains can be used to positive effect. However, the evidence relating to them also suggests that the positive outcomes concerned were the product of a combination of internal business motives and external pressures which served to raise the profile of health and safety as an issue meriting attention. Or to put it another way, pointed to the fact that the initiatives arose as a result of a range of factors that extended beyond narrow, market-based considerations and which acted to make them somewhat atypical in nature.

This atypicality is highlighted in what follows by juxtaposing evidence concerning health and safety management within subcontracting in the British construction industry in general with the findings of a recent analysis of the labour-management context within which the construction of Terminal 5 occurred undertaken by Deakin and Koukiadaki (2009). This focus on Terminal 5 is adopted because it not only provides a good demonstration of the positive use of supply chains in relation to workplace health and safety, but also demonstrates how such usage is dependent on a surrounding institutional context that acts to counter an exclusive focus on short-term and narrow market-based objectives.

SUB-CONTRACTING AND HEALTH AND SAFETY MANAGEMENT IN THE BRITISH CONSTRUCTION INDUSTRY

The British construction industry consists of around 168,000 firms and employment in it, prior to the recent recession, stood at close to two million people (Department for Business, Enterprise and Regulatory Reform, 2007). Of those working in the industry, at least 40 per cent are self-employed, or effectively treated as such for tax purposes (Donaghy, 2009). More generally, as these figures clearly indicate, the vast majority of firms in the industry are relatively small.

Construction employment in Britain is therefore highly fragmented. Larger-scale projects are, as a consequence, invariably carried out through complex, multi-tiered systems of subcontracting. As a result, labour conditions, including standards of health and safety, in the sector are inevitably strongly influenced by the processes of procurement that underlay this subcontracting.

That this is the case is amply demonstrated by existing British and international evidence. Onsite subcontracting, for example, has been found to be associated with those working for subcontractors receiving lower levels of supervision and training than directly employed workers, and dangerously poor levels of communication between client managers and contracted personnel (see for example Rebitzer, 1995; Kochan et al., 1994 and more generally Donaghy, 2009). In a similar vein, studies have shown it to lead to both workers and their managers being unclear about the division of responsibilities for health and safety and to give rise to subcontractor and agency workers being substantially less well-informed on health and safety matters than workers of the principle contractor on the same construction site (Dawson et al., 1985).

There is additionally clear evidence that such features of health and safety management within subcontracting do lead to adverse health and safety outcomes. A case in point is the study of subcontracting in the British and Australian residential building industries undertaken by Mayhew and Quinlan (1997) which found health and safety standards in both countries to be 'compromised in tandem with the increase in outsourced labour'.

In the case of Britain, statutory provisions, in the form of the Construction (Design and Management) Regulations, do admittedly lay down requirements relating to the management of health and safety in such situations of subcontracting. Research on procurement practices in construction, however, suggests that the impact of these regulations, as well as supporting guidance, is highly qualified in terms of their acting to ensure that matters of health and safety are accorded adequate priority.

A survey by Davis Langdon (2007) on public sector construction procurement, for example, showed clients to be familiar with setting contractual requirements on health and safety in the procurement of services but also demonstrated them to be far less engaged with efforts to monitor compliance or undertake post-completion reviews of such arrangements. It additionally indicated that the frequently observed late appointment of contractors meant that they often had little engagement with design decisions that might have OHS implications. In other words, this study suggested that opportunities to monitor and improve supply chain influence were generally being overlooked by public sector clients in the UK construction industry – despite its comparatively tight regulation.

Other evidence suggests that this is not just a problem of the British public sector. For example, in a detailed research study into fatal accidents in the UK construction industry a range of procurement issues were identified that it was believed contributed to their relatively high incidence, as the following quote illustrates:

The principal area of uncertainty, of concern across all workshops, related to policy level approaches to contracting strategy. Increased outsourcing contractorisation etc. ... means contracting forms and strategies deserve attention, particularly as the workshops indicated there was generally little effective attention to health and safety in contractor selection, within contract terms or as part of contract monitoring (BOMEL 2003: 118).

The research literature more generally on selection issues in the procurement of contractors in construction and key criteria for assessing subcontractors' eligibility for tender invitation and award, and subsequent performance at the construction stage, bears this last point out. Thus, while findings from an early study (Hatush and Skitmore, 1997) indicated that the most common criteria considered by procurers during the pre-qualification and bid process were 'those pertaining to financial soundness, technical ability, management capability, *and the health and safety performance of contractors*' (our italics), most studies show that quality record, contractor experience and company reputation are the most influential criteria for selecting subcontractors at the pre-qualification stage, with tender price exerting the most significant influence in the subcontract award (Jennings and Holt, 1998).

LABOUR MANAGEMENT AT TERMINAL 5

The construction of Terminal 5 at Heathrow airport was a massive undertaking. It was done over a six-year period from September 2002 to March 2008, and at any one time involved the employment of 8,000 workers. At a number of levels, the building of the terminal has been widely judged to have been a major success. It was, for example, completed on time and within budget. It also, more relevantly for this chapter, was successful in the goal set of achieving an above average health and safety performance. Thus, during the course of construction, two lives were lost against an expectation of six deaths for a project of its size and in employee surveys more than 75 per cent of the workforce felt that T5 was the safest site they had worked on and more than 60 per cent thought it was a good place to work (Doherty, 2008).

These outcomes, according to the analysis offered by Deakin and Koukiadaki (2009), would seem to have been intimately connected to the establishment at the outset of the project of a system of stakeholder governance and a related focus on labour–management partnership. Features that, among other things, involved the British Airports Authority (BAA), as the client, accepting that 'residual risk' would remain with it, the creation of mechanisms for the sharing of liabilities that encouraged collaborative approaches to inter-firm problem solving, and the establishment of framework collective agreements which included the following principles: the negotiation of local (labour) agreements that were no less favourable than existing national and sectoral ones; the use of direct labour in preference to other forms of employment, with only limited provision for agency work to meet peaks in demand; limits on overtime working; the cascading of agreed terms and conditions and employment quality standards to second-tier subcontractors and suppliers, coupled with arrangements for the monitoring of their performance; and the setting and meeting of exemplary levels of health and safety protection.

In effect therefore BAA sought to put in place a governance structure for the Terminal 5 project based on risk sharing and collaborative working with the contractors involved and hence one that encompassed supply relationships embodying a substantial degree of joint mutuality. That is relationships that entailed a 'move away from the lowest initial cost tendering to long term value with suppliers who are able to invest in people, innovation, research and development and equipment' (Lane et al., 2002, cited in Deakin and Koukiadaki, 2009: 386).

In tracing the evolution of these features of the project, Deakin and Koukiadaki note that from the outset of it BAA 'saw itself as particularly vulnerable to the risks arising from late completion', recognised that 'as a leading company on the FTSE 100 share index [it was] subject to intense scrutiny by its shareholders and city analysts', and 'took the view that it needed to deal with', in the words of Doherty (2008), 'the risk that individual suppliers would adopt differing terms of employment and possibly result in unstable industrial relations or employee relations'; outcomes that it is further observed could have 'potentially negative impacts on BAA in terms of corporate reputation and labour costs'. In addition, and more generally, the authors point to the fact that, as a public utility, BAA faced regulatory pressures for service improvements, while the budget for the project was equivalent to two-thirds of BAA's then capital value and therefore represented 'a risk to the very viability' of the company.

The impressive health and safety performance achieved during the construction of Terminal 5, then, cannot simply be viewed as a product of the arrangements put in place to manage health and safety. Rather it must be seen as more broadly stemming from the wider strategies that were adopted towards the overall governance of the project, and, in particular, the contractual arrangements put in place in relation to labour management and relationships with subcontractors and suppliers. Furthermore, the adoption of these strategies can, in turn, be seen as having been informed by a more fundamental set of concerns that BAA had regarding reputational and regulatory risks, costs and corporate survival.

As a result, the backcloth against which the construction of Terminal 5 was planned and undertaken meant that the client, BAA, had a number of drivers prompting it to accord the issue of occupational health and safety a high priority. And ones that, in doing so, also supported the establishment of governance arrangements for the project which encompassed a high level of management–union collaboration, and comprehensive arrangements for managing and monitoring the activities of subcontractors that differed markedly from those found in the British construction industry more generally.

Conclusions

This chapter commenced by observing that the growth in outsourcing that has occurred over the last three decades or so has formed an important part of current concerns and debates about employment vulnerability in the modern world of work, including those concerning how far workers are being exposed to increased risks to their health and safety. Against this background, it has consequently explored, in the context of industrialised economics, how far it is correct to view the economic forces embedded in supply chains as being problematic in health and safety terms and under what circumstances they are used to exert a positive influence over health and safety standards.

The analysis provided lends considerable weight to the concerns about the employment-related consequences of outsourcing. In particular, it has drawn attention to a range of evidence pointing to the fact that it (a) tends to relocate employment into contexts – smaller organisations and agency and other more peripheral forms of employment – marked by poorer standards of health and safety management, and (b) encompasses economic dynamics that serve to create more intense and less secure working conditions that are prone to give rise to a range of adverse health effects.

At the same time, the analysis provided has indicated that the health and safety implications of outsourcing are very much contingent on the nature of the supply chain relationships that are established. Indeed, it cannot simply be assumed that all supply chains act to generate adverse consequences for those employed in supplier organisations in terms of an increased risk of work-related injuries and ill health.

The wider supply chain literature reviewed, for example, suggests that the purchasers of goods and services can have incentives to intervene to positively shape the internal management and operations of supplier organisations, including in relation to health and safety at work. It also indicates that supplier organisations can at times be in a position, because of a relatively low position of dependency, to resist cost and delivery pressures from purchasers that have potentially detrimental consequences for their existing employment arrangements and ability to invest in health and safety.

It is impossible, of course, to judge with any precision how common these 'qualifying conditions' are. Both, though, seem likely to be relatively uncommon.

In the case of the first, it would seem on the basis of the evidence reviewed that such situations will be generally restricted to those where poor health and safety management on the part of suppliers has the potential to generate problematic reputational, regulatory or more general business risks. Moreover, even where such risks exist and do encourage attempts to directly influence health and safety management within supplier organisations, there are good grounds for believing that they can occur alongside the imposition of cost pressures that indirectly act to generate revisions to employment conditions within such organisations that are, in health terms, problematic.

As regards the second of the above 'qualifying conditions', it is difficult to see how suppliers will generally be in positions of 'low dependency'. For such situations logically can only arise in contexts where alternative sources of supply are limited and market competition therefore constrained – situations which, insofar as they exist, are ones anyway that are likely to provide less favourable outsourcing contexts because of the business risks they involve (Williamson, 1975).

Given this, 'success stories' of 'positive supply chain influence' must, it is argued, be seen to relate to relatively exceptional cases. In fact, this would seem to be the only sensible description that can be applied to the much lauded case of the construction of Terminal 5 discussed earlier, given the wider evidence reviewed on how subcontracting operates in the construction industry more generally and the factors that influenced it.

It is therefore, on the basis of the evidence reviewed in this chapter, impossible not to conclude, from a health and safety perspective, that the trend towards outsourcing is one that is acting, at the aggregate level, to generate greater employment vulnerability. It is also difficult, in the current recessionary economic environment, to see this linkage between outsourcing and employment vulnerability as doing anything other than intensifying.

For those who see this (intensifying) linkage as unsatisfactory, the question inevitably arises as to what can be done to counter, or at least, ameliorate it. There is, in our view, no simple answer to this question. In the face of evidence that narrow business logics of themselves will not provide a solution, it is clear, however, that regulatory action, of some form or other, offers a potential way forward (James et al., 2007; Heckscher, 2006; Weil, 2009).

In the space available, it is not possible to discuss in detail how such action can best be formulated. However, it would seem clear that to be effective it needs to both stimulate powerful actors in supply chains to actively support health and safety management within them and to encompass the establishment of a framework of collective and individual employment standards that limits the capacity of supply chain dynamics to drive down labour cost and conditions. Indeed, in this last regard, it is argued that there is much to learn from the experiences detailed above with regard to the construction of Terminal 5. The same is true of those relating to attempts to protect labour standards in global supply chains and, in particular, the way in which these have been created and operationalised via 'constellations of interests' in civil society encompassing NGOs, trade unions and activist groups.

References

Baldry, C. 2006. 'Off the rails: Factors affecting track worker safety in the rail industry', *Employee Relations*, 28 (3), 255–272.

Beaumont, P., Hunter, L. and Sinclair, D. 1996. 'Customer–supplier relations and the diffusion of employee relations change', *Employee Relations*, 18 (1), 9–19.

BOMEL. 2003. *Factors and Causes Contributing to Fatal Accidents 1996/97–2000/01, Technical Support*. Health and Safety Executive: London (unpublished).

Cousins, P. and Lawson, B. 2007. 'Sourcing strategy, supplier relationships and firm performance: An empirical investigation of UK organisations', *British Journal of Management*, 18 (2), 123–137.

Cullen, Lord. 2001. *The Ladbroke Grove Rail Inquiry Report*. Health and Safety Executive: London.

Cully, M., Woodland, S., O'Reilly, A. and Dix, G. 1999. *Britain at Work as Depicted in the 1998 Workplace Employee Relations Survey*. Routledge: London.

Davis Langdon LLP. 2007. *Health and Safety in Public Sector Construction Procurement*. HSE Books: Sudbury.

Dawson, S., Clinton, A., Bamford, M. and Willman, P. 1985. 'Safety in construction: Self regulation, industrial structure and workforce involvement', *Journal of General Management*, 10 (4), 21–38.

Deakin, S. and Koukiadaki, A. 2009. 'Governance processes, labour–management partnership and employee voice in the construction of Heathrow Terminal 5', *Industrial Law Journal*, 38 (4), 365–389.

Department for Business, Enterprise and Regulatory Reform. 2007. *Construction Statistics 2007*. The Stationery Office: London.

Doherty, S. 2008. *Heathrow's T5: History in the Making*. John Wiley and Sons: Chichester.

Donaghy, R. 2009. *One Death is too Many: Inquiry into the Underlying Causes of Construction Fatal Accidents*, Cm 7657. Stationery Office: London.

Dore, R. 1996. 'Goodwill and market capitalism', in P. Buckley and J. Michie (eds), *Firms, Organisations and Contracts: A Reader in Industrial Organisation*. Oxford University Press: Oxford, pp. 359–384.

EU OSHA. 2000. *Occupational Health and Safety in Marketing and Procurement*. Office for Official Publications of the European Communities: Luxembourg.

Eurostat. 2002. *European Social Statistics: Accidents at Work and Health-related Problems – Data 1994–2000*. Luxembourg: Statistical Office of the European Communities.

Ferrie, J., Shipley, M., Stansfield, S. and Mamot, M. 2002. 'Health effects of chronic job insecurity and change in job security on self-reported health, minor psychiatric morbidity, physiological measures and health related behaviours in British Civil Servants. The Whitehall II Study', *Journal of Epidemiology and Community Health*, 56 (6), 450–454.

Harvey, D. 2005. *A Brief History of Neoliberalism*. Oxford University Press: Oxford.

Hatush, Z. and Skitmore, M. 1997. 'Criteria for contractor selection', *Construction Management and Economics*, 15 (1), 19–38.

Heckscher, C. 2006. 'Organisations, movements, and networks', *New York Law School Review*, 50, 313–336.

Heide, J. and John, G. 1990. 'Alliances in industrial purchasing: The determinants of joint action in buyer–supplier relationships', *Journal of Marketing Research*, XXVII, 24–36.

James, P., Johnstone, R., Quinlan, M. and Walters, D. 2007. 'Regulating supply chains to improve health and safety', *Industrial Law Journal*, 36 (2), 163–187.

James, S. and Lloyd, C. 2008. 'Too much pressure? Retailer power and occupational health and safety in the food processing industry', *Work Employment and Society*, 22 (4), 1–18.

Jennings, P. and Holt, G. 1998. 'Prequalification and multi-criteria selection: a measure of contractors' opinions', *Construction Management and Economics*, 16 (6), 651–660.

Kivimaki, M., Vahtera, J., Pentti, J. and Ferrie, J. 2000. 'Factors underlying the effect of organisational downsizing on the health of workers: a longitudinal cohort study of changes in work, social relationships and health behaviours', *British Medical Journal*, 320, 971–975.

Kochan, T., Smith, M., Wells, J. and Rebitzer, J. 1994. 'Human resource strategies and contingent workers: The case of safety in the petrochemical industry', *Human Resource Management*, 33 (1), 55–77.

Lane, R., Lepardo, V. and Woodman, G. 2002. 'How to deal with dynamic complexity on long, large projects', in W. Sproule and S. Jansen (eds), *Designing, Constructing, Maintaining and Financing Today's Airport Projects*, CD-ROM. ASCE: Reston, VA.

Marchington, M. and Vincent, S. 2004. 'Analysing the influence of institutional, organizational and interpersonal forces in shaping inter-organizational relations', *Journal of Management Studies*, 41 (6), 1029–1056.

Marchington, M., Grimshaw, D., Rubery, J. and Willmott, H. (eds) 2005. *Fragmenting Work: Blurring Organizational Boundaries and Disordering Hierarchies*. Oxford University Press: Oxford.

Mayhew, C. and Quinlan, M. 1997. 'Subcontracting and occupational health and safety in the residential building industry', *Industrial Relations Journal*, 28 (3), 192–205.

Nichols, T., Dennis, A. and Guy, W. 1995. 'Size of employment unit and industrial injury rates in British manufacturing', *Industrial Relations Journal*, 26 (1), 45–56.

Nichols, T. 1997. *The Sociology of Industrial Injury*. Mansell: London.

O'Rourke, D. 2003. 'Outsourcing regulation: Analysing non-governmental systems of labour standards and monitoring', *The Policy Studies Journal*, 31 (1), 1–29.

Piore, M. and Sabel, C. 1984. *The Second Industrial Divide*. Basic Books: New York.

Quinlan, M., Mayhew, C. and Bohle, P. 2001. 'The global expansion of precarious employment, work disorganisation, and consequences for occupational health: A review of recent research', *International Journal of Health Services*, 31 (2), 335–414.

Rawlings, M. 2006. 'A generic model of regulating supply chain outsourcing', in C. Arup, P. Gahan, J. Howe, R. Johnstone, R. Mitchell and A. O'Donnell (eds), *Labour Law and Labour Market Regulation*. Federation Press: Sydney, pp. 520–541.

Rebitzer, J. 1995. 'Job safety and contract workers in the petrochemical industry', *Industrial Relations*, 34 (1), 40–57.

Rodriguez-Garavito, C. 2003. 'Global governance and labor rights: Codes of conduct and anti-sweatshop struggles in global apparel factories in Mexico and Guatemala', *Politics and Society*, 33 (2), 203–233.

Sako, M. 1992. *Prices, Quality and Trust: Inter-firm Relations in Britain and Japan.* Cambridge University Press: Cambridge.

Scarborough, H. 2000. 'The HR implications of supply chain relationships', *Human Resource Management Journal*, 10 (1), 5–17.

Stevens, G. 1999. 'Workplace injuries in small and large manufacturing workplaces 1994/5–1995/6', *Labour Market Trends*, 107, 19–26.

Swart, J. and Kinnie, N. 2003. 'Knowledge-intensive firms: The influence of the client on HR systems', *Human Resource Management Journal*, 13 (3), 37–55.

Truss, C. 2004. 'Who's in the driving seat? Managing human resources in a franchise firm', *Human Resource Management Journal*, 14 (4), 57–75.

Uff, J. 2000. *The Southall Accident Inquiry Report.* Health and Safety Commission: London.

Victoria Parliament Economic Development Committee. 2005. *Inquiry into Labour Hire Employment in Victoria.* Melbourne: Government Printer.

Walters, D. 2001. *Health and Safety in Small Enterprises.* Peter Lang: Brussels.

Walters, D. and James, P. 2009. *Understanding the Role of Supply Chains in Influencing Health and Safety at Work.* Institution of Occupational Safety and Health: Leicester.

Webb, T. 2001. *The Collaborative Games.* Pluto Press: Sydney.

Weil, D. 2009. 'Rethinking the regulation of vulnerable work in the USA: A sector based approach', *Journal of Industrial Relations*, 51, 411–430.

Weil, D. and Mallo, C. 2007. 'Regulating labour standards via supply chains: Combining public/private interventions to improve workplace compliance', *British Journal of Industrial Relations*, 45 (4), 791–814.

Williamson, O. 1975. *Markets and Hierarchies: Analysis and Antitrust Implications.* Free Press: London.

Wiseman, S. and Gilbert, F. 2000. *Survey of the Recruitment Agencies Industry*. HSE Books: Sudbury.

World Bank. 2000. *Company Codes of Conduct and International Standards: An Analytical Comparison*. World Bank, Washington, DC.

Wright, C. 1986. 'Routine deaths: Fatal accidents in the oil industry', *Sociological Review*, 34 (1), 265–289.

Wright, C. and Lund, J. 2003. 'Supply chain rationalization: Retailer dominance and labour flexibility in the Australian food and grocery industry', *Work, Employment and Society*, 17 (1), 137–157.

4

Precarious Work in Times of Crisis: Regulatory Discourses and Labour Standards in the New EU Member Baltic States

Charles Woolfson[1]

Introduction

The increase in labour precariousness which has accompanied the global economic and financial crisis is itself part of a longer term historical trend towards the increasing vulnerability of labour. This has two elements that are relevant:

1.   The impacts of crisis on regulated labour standards in general.

2.   The role of crisis-induced migration flows in accelerating labour precarity on a European and transnational scale.

Both of these need to be seen against fundamental changes in the architecture of European labour rights and the diminishing regulatory reach of labour law as it seeks to accommodate the competitiveness agenda of the European Commission in promoting greater labour 'flexibility' and an 'individualisation'

1   Charles Woolfson is Professor of Labour Studies at the Institute for Research on Migration, Ethnicity and Society (REMESO) at Linköping University, Sweden. He was previously a full-time Marie Curie Chair in the Baltic States (2004–2007) during which period he researched labour standards in the new accession EU member states. The author wishes to acknowledge funding support from the Visby Programme of the Swedish Institute for the project 'East-West labour migration, industrial relations and labour standards in a Swedish-Baltic context' which enabled completion of the current work.

of employment rights. Yet the contemporary political economy of capitalism, not least its spectacular regulatory failure in the current global economic and financial crisis, has placed the issue of the renewal of regulation back on the agenda of governments and supranational agencies. If capital needs regulation to control its financial excesses, an inescapable conclusion that the European Union and its governments recognise, the need is at least equal for regulation to control the harms which capital directly perpetrates on labour at both a national and supra-national level. In this context, claims for effective labour standards pose a public policy imperative of devising protective regulatory strategies to counter precarity, not least those aspects of precarity heightened by the crisis. The challenge is to address the socially imperative task of 're-protecting' the 'un-protected' in an increasingly globalised and insecure labour market.

The New EU Member States

Nowhere has the debate concerning regulation and its appropriateness been more testing and tested than in the new European Union member states which have had to align their regulatory frameworks to conform to requirements of EU accession and, at the same time, create a regulatory environment conducive to domestic business while attracting inward foreign investment on favourable terms. The new EU member states therefore represent a paradigmatic case study with respect to the vexed problems of securing decent labour standards which counter labour precarity.

In the process of both EU enlargement and of market-making the European Commission has proved a less than ardent champion of labour protection and regulation, arguing that such matters fall primarily within the competence of national governments. Many point the finger of blame for the European Commission's reluctance to regulate in the sphere of labour rights at the era of deregulation, promoted in particular by a neoliberal agenda. But the picture is more complex than a simple trajectory of politically inspired deregulation. The true thrust of the regulatory agenda has been a complex mixture of deregulation and re-regulation in which the ultimate aim has been to manage risk in order to preserve system integrity, but to do so in the least intrusive manner possible from the point of view of capital. This is the policy agenda of so-called 'better regulation', or 'smart regulation' (Burrows and Woolfson 2000). It is also encapsulated in allied discourses of 'new modes of multi-level governance', 'soft' law, 'responsive' and 'reflexive regulation' (Aalders and Wilthagen 1997). The objective has been not simply crude 'capture' of the regulatory process or its avoidance, but the relocation of the centre of gravity of regulatory oversight from the state (seen as command-and-control) to private interests (and stakeholders) who take ownership of regulation. The actual trajectory of regulation has been from the public to the private sphere, in other words, an ongoing privatisation and diffusion of governance and the consequential dilution of regulatory efficacy under the guise of self-regulation. The ultimate purpose has been to expand the arena of self-regulation in order to promote Europe's competitiveness in which business is the lead actor, with the state, at best, a secondary onlooker and democratic accountability to interests such as those of labour, a peripheral concern.

In the new EU member states this business-friendly agenda has played out in very particular ways which directly increase labour precarity. This is not only a basic issue of labour standards but is also relevant in assessing the transferability of a European social model to the new EU member states, and the implementation or otherwise, of the social *acquis*. The prescription for the new EU member states that has been on offer by its neoliberal advisors also warrants scrutiny. The US-based Cato Institute, for example, in a discussion document originally hosted on a European Commission web site, has advocated the creation of a dual standard regulatory environment for safety and health in the workplace for the new EU member states, arguing that excessive regulation emanating from within the EU will reduce labour flexibility and impose an economic burden on business producing 'sub-optimal growth' (Tupy 2003). It has suggested that over-regulation of conditions of employment will diminish the comparative advantage that CEE workers enjoy over their more highly paid western counterparts. The Cato Institute has expressed its concern over the fact that 'the EU explicitly rejects the possibility of different levels of safety and health protection of labour within the Union' and instead, emphasises 'the need to harmonize health and safety standards *irrespective of the different needs of the member states*' (sic). Such policies, Cato's spokesperson has warned 'do not contribute to alleviation, but to worsening of the workers' lot' by 'creating an artificial increase in labour costs'. Indeed, the *un*protecting of labour or its differential access to the right to a safe and decent working environment is seen by such commentators as the necessary price of transition to market discipline from the over-protected world of the former state socialist system. Market-driven policy prescriptions such as these, with their brutal implications for the protection of employees at work, have found a ready audience among domestic entrepreneurial elites in the new EU member states, but take little cognisance of actually existing working conditions.

Take evidence concerning working environment from the three Baltic states of Estonia, Latvia and Lithuania. The latest data from the European Foundation's Fifth Working Conditions Survey (2010) reveal the *highest* percentages of respondents in the Union reporting 'work negatively affects your health' (q67) with the partial exception of Greece at 40.8 per cent (Estonia 42.5 per cent, Latvia 52.5 per cent and Lithuania 38.6 per cent, as against an EU27 average of 25 per cent). When asked to indicate if 'very satisfied' with working conditions in their main job (q76), the *lowest* percentages of respondents are to be found here (Estonia 16.2 per cent, Latvia 11.2 per cent and Lithuania 11.9 per cent, as against an EU27 average of 25 per cent). Quantitative evidence, albeit statistically imperfect, is also useful in suggesting a deteriorating work environment. For example, in Estonia, the rate of major injuries is among the highest in the EU. In neighbouring Lithuania today the rate of workplace fatalities is twice the European Union average (four times the rate for France) and has remained highest in the EU over a number of years, although showing signs of recent improvement. In Latvia, where the rate of fatalities at work is also high, the official statistics do not record those incidents among the self-employed, despite the fact that many workers in this category are in real terms employees, and engaged in sometimes highly hazardous occupations such as forestry work and construction.

Latvia had previously adopted a Labour Protection Law, inspired by the requirements of EU *acquis* conformity. Ironically, it has been one of the few recent pieces of legislation which has not caused intense discussion and protests either at the time of adoption, or later on implementation. There are several reasons for this lack of controversy. As an authoritative report from the European Foundation notes, employers regard an ideal health and safety system which complies fully with all the relevant legislation as expensive, and therefore impossible to provide by almost all companies in Latvia. The report adds:

> *Many employers thus implement the law only incompletely, in order not to damage the operation of the company. Their employees, in whose interests the health and safety system operates, agree to their rights being violated in order to maintain their jobs (European Foundation 2004).*

This was the situation in the working environment, be it noted, *before* the onset of crisis and economic recession.

The Crisis in the Baltic States

The scale of the crisis should be acknowledged. At a European level GDP fell by 4 per cent in 2009, industrial production dropped back to the levels of the 1990s and 23 million people – or 10 per cent of the labour force – became unemployed. As the European Commission has put it: 'The crisis has been a huge shock for millions of citizens and it has exposed some fundamental weaknesses of our economy' (CEC 2010, p. 5). However, nowhere has the shock of the recent global crisis been more intense than in Eastern Europe. Fundamental weaknesses of the neoliberal economic development adopted for the last two decades in the Baltic states have been exposed in recession, which in relative if not absolute terms, has experienced the impact of the crisis in probably the most drastic form in the entire globe. Let us recall that the so-called Baltic tiger economies during 2000–2007 produced average yearly growth of GDP exceeding 8 per cent in Estonia and Latvia, and in Lithuania it reached around 7.5 per cent, at a time when the EU27 average was less than 2.5 per cent. The unwelcome corollary of high GDP growth rates was that it was largely based on the unsustainable development of economic sectors such as speculative property development, rather than investment in productive manufacture.

The predictable hard landing finally came in the second half of 2008 when the asset bubble burst. From their previous elevated title of Baltic tigers, almost within a matter of months they experienced the shock of near catastrophic economic slowdown. By the spring of 2009 the European Commission economic forecast for the Baltic States was gloomy, with the economic downturn predicted to be 'deeper and more protracted than previously assumed' (CEC 2009a: 80). Already in 2008 compared to 2007, Estonia and Latvia had witnessed decreasing GDP. By the fourth quarter of 2009 compared to the previous year, GDP had decreased 17.9 per cent in Latvia, 13.2 per cent in Lithuania and 9.4 per cent in Estonia (the three most significant declines in the EU, with the only other countries in Eastern Europe, Bulgaria at 6.2 per cent and Romania at 6.9 per cent, approaching these figures. The EU27 average GDP decline for this same period was 2.7 per cent (Eurostat 2010).

An economic shock on the scale of the current crisis has had immediate and massive impacts on labour market. In 2009, official unemployment rates in Baltic countries equalled the highest in the EU after Spain, reaching 17.6 per cent in Latvia, and 14 per cent in Lithuania and Estonia according to Eurostat (2009a). Youth unemployment reached over 30 per cent in Latvia and Lithuania, and 28.5 per cent in Estonia (Eurostat 2009b). Currently, unemployment has more than doubled since the onset of the crisis in all three Baltic States. But the impacts of the crisis go well beyond the appearance of perhaps the highest mass unemployment since independence from the USSR, with the possible exception of the years immediately following the collapse of communism.

Among significant changes in the labour market has been acceleration in the use of part-time and temporary contracts and informal payment systems. In Estonia for example there has been a doubling of the number of part-time contracts in the labour force within the space of a year. However, a rapid heightening of precarity in the Baltic States needs to be seen against a background of already existing deteriorated working conditions and employee disempowerment in which a substantial measure of informalisation has previously been the norm (Woolfson et al., 2008). According to the Eurobarometer survey on undeclared work of 2007 (that is, well before the onset of the crisis), Latvia at 15 per cent of the labour force ranked the highest among the Central and East European new EU member states for so-called undeclared work, perhaps the most telling proxy for informal or precarious employment (CEC 2007a; Hazans 2009). Some estimates suggest as much as 25–40 per cent of GDP is generated in the shadow economy (Schneider 2002).

Many pathways to such forms of regulatory avoidance exist. For example, employers can claim that they only recruited and employed workers that very day and they will comply with the law by recording their employment at the State Revenue Service local office by the fifth day of the following month. As a result, employers can employ staff without an employment contract and avoid fiscal obligations. Curiously, one of the Latvian government's crisis response measures was to place the State Revenue Service engaged in combating tax evasion and fraud and the front line agency in fiscal compliance, at least temporarily, on a reduced working week. At the same time, a 2009 survey of Latvian employees during the crisis suggested that more than half of the workforce would now accept envelope wages in the form of unofficial payments comprising a greater or lesser proportion of their income (*The Baltic Course* 2009).

This kind of payment system also has important negative effects on employee rights to social security, sickness benefits and pension entitlements. Paradoxically, during recent years in the Baltic States, the prevalence and social acceptability of envelope wages was beginning to be challenged by workers who recognised the negative impacts on their rights and labour standards (Woolfson 2007). The national labour inspectorate of Lithuania had introduced a telephone hotline for workers to complain about employers seeking to impose such envelope payment systems. The Latvian labour inspectorate even had a policy of naming and shaming errant employers. Anecdotal evidence suggests however that, with the advent of crisis, there has been a resurgence of forms of unofficial wage payment, as workers fear for their employment and employers seek to intensify utilisation of labour resources at the lowest cost and avoid social insurance obligations. Indeed, a recurrent demand of the trade unions in their campaigns against government austerity measures has been prevent illegal working and the informal economy (LPSK, Lithuanian Trade Union Confederation 2010).

The fight against undeclared work or, as it is termed in the Baltic States, illegal work, is now a policy priority at both ILO and EU levels (CEC 2007b; European Parliament Committee on Employment and Social Affairs 2008; ILO 2009, 2010a; Williams and Renooy 2009). At the level of individual member states, especially in conditions of constrained fiscal revenues, the issue of the balance between traditional occupational health and safety enforcement and the search for illegal forms of work and illegal workers has become a central one. The Latvian Labour Inspectorate, in collaboration with the Ministry of Welfare, is developing a plan for 2010–2013 to improve the inspectorate's capacity to reduce the incidence of illegal employment (Vega 2009: 10). Thus, perhaps the most concerning aspect of the impact of the crisis on the role of labour inspection has been a tendency towards diversion from enforcement of safety and health regulation.

At one level this shift in priorities is perhaps predictable, if regrettable. The impact of the crisis on the operational capacities of the labour inspectorates in the Baltic states has been significant. As part of the huge cuts in public spending, the budget of the State Labour Inspectorate (SLI) has been reduced in Latvia by over 50 per cent and in Lithuania by 34 per cent from 2008–2010, or from 18.6m Litas (€5.3m) to12.3m Litas (€3.5m). In Lithuania the SLI had government permission for an establishment of 199 inspectors, but the budget now only allows for a staff of 180. Higher-level employees have lost some 30 per cent of their salaries while inspectors are paid some 10–20 per cent less. Some inspectors have left for jobs in the private sector or gone abroad. Supporting resources have also been reduced. Inspectors are no longer reimbursed for the use of personal cars to make inspection visits, and many SLI cars have been sold. In Vilnius for example there is a pool of only 4–5 cars to share between 50 inspectors. Only inspectors whom the SLI deems to require their use have been allowed to keep their laptops and mobile phones. From 2006–2008 companies could apply for subsidies for occupational health and safety improvements from the State's social insurance fund, but these have been deleted from the budget. The level of inspection has also been reduced. The SLI inspected health and safety conditions of some 16,000 – or 6 per cent – of the workplaces in 2008 and 2009. In 2010 the total will be more like 10,000 because of staff reductions and of lack of transport. Cuts on a similar or even more extensive scale have been introduced in the other Baltic states.[2] In this manner, the inspection and enforcement capacities of the regulatory agency have been undermined by financial constraints.

In the case of Latvia, a new labour inspection regime (Law of 19 June 2008 on State Labour Inspection) had recently been adopted in response to a critical audit of the national inspectorate by the International Labour Organisation (Albracht and Campbell 2006). The new legislation, inter alia, provided for more rights for the State Labour Inspectorate to act and suspend the operation of an enterprise that is in breach of occupational safety and health rules and standards and general labour legislation. It also provided for more rights for the inspectorate to supervise labour law compliance on private construction sites (Vega 2009). While formal response to external criticism had been initiated, in the heat of crisis the governing party has now admonished state regulators to suspend occupational health and safety regulation.

Elsewhere, similar pressures are being applied by governments, and not just in the newer EU member states. This suggests a longer-term trend towards the erosion of regulatory regimes *intensified by* and not just in response to economic recession. The impact of the global economic and financial downturn has encouraged pressures towards what in the new regulatory discourse is termed a lighter regulatory touch. The European Commission, for example, has argued: 'The importance of reducing unnecessary administrative burdens increased with the economic crisis', since small- and medium-sized enterprises in particular 'need quick relief' (CEC 2009b: 4). The crisis of 2008–2009 therefore has provided the perfect pretext to intensify an assault on regulated labour standards within the European Union, both by national governments and by the Commission itself, under the banner of reviving European economies and stimulating further flexibility in labour markets as part of its 'strategy for smart, sustainable and inclusive growth' (CEC 2010).

Meanwhile, the European Commission has pursued its wider ongoing agenda of lifting the burden of regulation from business. In a Communication

---

2   I am grateful to Kaj Frick for this information based on interviews conducted with the State Labour Inspectorate of Lithuania in 2010.

from the Commission in October 2009, working environment is identified as one of 13 priority areas for action. The Commission has proposed to exempt small firms from risk-assessment requirements (the most difficult sector in which to ensure effective occupational health and safety). This proposed exemption is complemented by a further proposal to 'facilitate lighter transpositions by Member States of the Health and Safety of Workers Framework Directive' (CEC 2009b: 102). The compliance thrust of the Commission's proposals is revealed in the following suggestion to modify the enforcement practices of national labour inspection authorities: 'While inspections are essential to achieve safety and health at work, they should be made less time-consuming for businesses and compliant employers (for example in low risks enterprises) [and] should be rewarded by fewer inspection visits' (CEC 2009b: 103). The full implications for labour inspection and enforcement have still to be assessed, but the commentary above does not bode well for more effective labour protection and the preservation of decent standards in the European workplace.

Thus, the ILO's watchdog committee, the Committee of Experts on the Application of Conventions and Recommendations (CEACR), has recently expressed concerns over ongoing trends in various member states, not just in Eastern Europe, which have skewed the primary regulatory objectives of labour inspection. In particular, ILO has expressed its unease over 'the compatibility of additional functions which may entrusted to inspectors', specifically in the pursuit of undeclared work and relatedly, illegal immigration. With regard to the former, CEACR has reminded the Belgian Government in its application of the convention on labour inspection in agriculture:

> that the primary function of the labour inspection system in agriculture should be ... to secure the enforcement of the legal provisions relating to conditions of work and the protection of workers while engaged in their work. The monitoring of illegal employment and undeclared work would therefore appear to be an additional function and, as such, it should ... not ... interfere with the effective discharge of the primary duties (emphasis added) (ILO 2010b).

In regard to so-called illegal migration in the sphere of agricultural work, CEACR has requested that the Italian government respond to its concerns regarding initiatives to combat clandestine and illegal labour:

> even though there may be no doubt that measures are necessary to put a stop to the phenomenon of illegal migration, the role assigned to labour

inspectors in this regard at the workplace can severely jeopardize the realization of the prime objective of the Convention, namely, to ensure the protection of workers *against the imposition of conditions of work which are contrary to the relevant legal provisions. The Committee therefore requests the Italian Government ... to ensure that labour inspectors working in the agricultural sector* refocus their action on the duties defined by the Convention *and to limit their collaboration with services responsible for monitoring immigration* (emphasis added) (ILO 2010c).

A recent ILO review of labour inspection activities again suggests that specific pressures on national governments during the crisis may have created a further 'imbalance' in the priorities of labour inspection:

> *the urgency of the crisis has in many respects limited the labour inspectorates' scope of action. Inspectors have understandably focused their efforts on certain aspects related to the crisis (for example mass redundancies) with the result that inspection visits have not been conducted in the normally comprehensive or balanced way. The impact of this imbalance should be evaluated carefully because it could have a negative effect on other elements of working conditions (for example the impact of stress at work), which may be neglected at the expense of crisis-specific issues (Vega 2009: 16).*

ILO expressed concerns that would seem to be well-founded, or at least worthy of further research. Yet the basic issue of the need to interrogate effective forms of labour protection remains, precisely because the crisis has undermined many previously seemingly assured labour standards and enforcement procedures. The following *discussion* of unequal burden-sharing allows us to view the more profound consequences of the crisis for working environment in a wider theoretical perspective.

Unequal Risk-burdening

With the arrival of economic recession has come renewed impetus and further inventiveness in regulatory discourses. While errant capital and excessive spending on social services by profligate governments is to be carefully monitored in a new regime of austerity controls, the exact opposite would appear to be the case in respect of the elaboration of socially protective regulation. Financial and economic turmoil and its attendant harms to global capitalism resulting from systemic regulatory failure to control excessive risk-taking, can be contrasted with hesitant regulatory response to ongoing excessive *risk-burdening*, resulting in real harms to workers in the extended supply chains of the global economy (Woolfson and Likic-Brboric 2009). Yet underlying most forms of risk assessment are calculations of the costs and benefits of regulation and control. These imply certain assumptions which are highly questionable and go beyond a simple critique of the technical accuracy of the criteria of quantitative risk assessment or of the standard cost model when applied to the financial impact of regulation (Vogel 2010). The costs of the burden of regulation on business can be counterposed to those real risk burdens *imposed* upon workers who are ultimately held responsible (responsibilized) for their own misfortunes (Gray 2009). Not only are workers to be unprotected, they are themselves to blame for the consequences in terms of injury and harm. At issue is the notion of accountability, in the form of a realistic structure of penalties for managerial failure, in this case to prevent harm to employees in the workplace. In the context of crisis the absence of accountability presents an opportunity to employers to intensify work demands upon their employees regardless of the outcomes. 'Accidents' just happen, and in the end, no-one is responsible and questions of accountability remain unresolved.

The hidden dimension of much that passes for impartial regulation and a balanced jurisprudence draws our attention to the fact that behind the measures and formal standards of legal appraisal stand real human beings, who are socially *sub*ordinated or *super*ordinated in ongoing structures of embedded inequalities and social *injustice*. There are winners and losers, where the sense of natural justice collides with naturalised inequality, or more precisely, with *structures of legally enforced* inequality and *unequal and excessive risk-burdening*. In real-world terms, the global supply chains of multinational capital, exploiting the advantages of differential regulatory stringency and the capacity to indulge in regime shopping offer vivid proof of the displacement mechanisms of unequal risk-burdening from north to south and from west to east. The paradox of law (and of politics) is to reconcile these uncomfortable real-world facts of social differentiation as competing claims to legitimacy are advanced, while at the same time, appearing to remain neutral and *above* class interests.

We have seen this most recently in the impartial rulings of the European Court of Justice in favour of market freedoms in the *Laval* and *Viking* cases, occasioned by the unscrupulous use of workers from the Baltic States to undermine labour standards in the older member states. These judgments together with others have effectively reinstated the country of origin principle of the original Bolkenstein services directive. There are profound implications, not least in Sweden for its largely voluntaristic labour market model, concerning the capacity of trade unions to preserve existing labour standards in the face of the threat of wage dumping from lower-cost East European labour (Woolfson, Thörnqvist and Sommers 2010). Meanwhile, the state regulatory authorities in the form of *Skatteverket* tax agency or the Swedish Working Environment Authority do not have the institutional resources to secure compliance, while the Swedish trade unions have reduced collective bargaining resources with which to enforce at workplace level the appropriate labour standards that conform to those previously achieved in the context of Sweden's advanced social democracy.

This clash of labour standards between the new Europe and the old, realised in differentiated labour regimes is precisely that – socially reproduced advantage and disadvantage – configured on a transnational basis. At the same time, it is legally entrenched in the formations and practices of *class* society, not least in those institutions of its jurisprudence, organised both on a national and increasingly, on a European-wide basis. One conclusion is that the posted workers directive should be seen to all intents and purposes as an archaic survival of a previous Delors-era of EU cohesion-building labour policy that now has little to offer workers, either from abroad or for that matter in Sweden, by way of enforceable labour standards. Both Swedish workers and those migrants who arrive to work on either a short- or long-term basis whether documented or not, have become significantly more unprotected.

Thus, even where intra-EU migration is documented, in reality documented migration has important homologies (similar characteristics due to relatedness) to that of the undocumented, at least so far as real access to employment rights, social insurance and labour markets are concerned. In other words, legal documentation of migrant workers, strictly defined, may not provide adequate pointers as to where the impetus towards more gross forms of exploitation, social inequities and deleterious impacts on labour standards are in fact occurring. So-called documented migrants may be becoming more similar to the undocumented than previously considered. This poses the reverse question, of how to make the documented less undocumented, and raises important public policy concerns which have so far hardly been addressed by social and political actors. Paradoxically, it may be that labour migration is becoming the stalking horse of the *re*-informalisation of the European work space rather than its renewal.

Nor is this challenge to labour standards simply a theoretical possibility or an abstract academic conjecture. Faced with the sudden end of the post-communist dream, Baltic Latvia and Lithuania in particular have seen both violent social unrest (the first instances in the new EU member states) and now emigration on an unprecedented scale, at least since independence from the Soviet Union in the early 1990s. The migration in the case of Lithuania for instance can be described as symptomatic of massive social disillusion. It has brought social disaffection to a critical level. With 8,000–10,000 Lithuanians leaving each month, including significant numbers of those still in employment joining the outward migration, the issue has risen to the top of the political agenda. The total forecast for 2010, following record figures in 2009, is in the region of 78,000–80,000 emigrants out of a population of 3.4 million. It may be that as many as 150,000 have left in the last two years alone (somewhere in the region of 5 per cent of the population or 10 per cent of the labour force).

This haemorrhage of population – migration as a societal *dis*location – raises key issues for future sustainable development of the country, against a background of serious demographic decline and a prognosis for eventual economic recovery that is at best uncertain. Yet the most profound cost is not quantifiable. It is levied in the desolidarisation of society, the loss of a social dimension to human existence in a raw free-for-all world of new capital accumulation (Reiter 2007). Post-communism exemplifies marketisation without limits in which precarity becomes the existential norm. The new member states therefore provide a rather problematical context for the eventual harmonisation of European labour standards, even as those standards are themselves being reconfigured in the backwash of crisis. The implication of a lack of harmonisation is the creation of a reservoir of low-cost/high-hazard cheap labour in the East, to be drawn upon or discarded as the economic cycles of European capital require. In terms of precarity in the working environment of the Baltic states, the effects of the crisis may produce the paradoxical outcome of a short-term improvement in accident rates, as the number of employees in the labour force declines, and hence also aggregate risk exposure. In the longer term however, there is likely to be an accelerated trend of injuries as the economy revives in a working environment of heightened risks and eroded regulatory regimes.

Conclusion

Today, an ailing capitalism having patently failed to self-regulate is supported by state and supranational interventions of unprecedented magnitudes with scant regard to the question of accountability for manifest failure. It is therefore legitimate to ask whether the present conjuncture has opened a window of opportunity for new regulatory momentum to reinforce labour standards and protect the most vulnerable sections of labour, however defined. Is there renewed legitimacy in the call for a regional or global governance regime of effective social rights and labour standards, or in the aftermath of crisis, will it simply be business as usual?

Thus the debate over precarious labour requires urgent reframing in the context of the crisis and indeed of the post-crisis: how do we address the socially imperative task of re-protecting the unprotected and devising effective regulatory strategies to *counter* precarity? The call for decent work now advanced by the ILO and by the EU, and endorsed by the international trade union movement, must be tested against the realities of the faltering political project of wider European integration. Symbolic declarations alone will be insufficient in the face of absent national, regional, supranational, or far less global governance and the effective regulation of labour standards. It is necessary to prevent regularised migration transmuting into the irregularisation of the shadow economy in a post-crisis context where there are powerful economic drivers to informalisation and intensified precarity. The search for values and practices of social solidarity, inclusion and the (*re*)protection of workers from market forces implies the reinstatement of a regulatory discourse with the purposive enforcement of labour standards as its core assumption.

References

Aalders, Marius and Wilthagen, Tom (1997) 'Moving beyond command-and-control: reflexivity in the regulation of occupational safety and health and the environment', *Law and Policy*, 19(4): 415–443.

Albracht, Gerard and Campbell, Stewart (eds) (2006) *Labour Inspection Audit: Tripartite Audit of the Labour Inspection System of Latvia, 3–14 October 2005*. Geneva: International Labour Office.

Balibar, Etienne and Wallerstein, Immanuel (1991) *Race, Class and Nation: Ambiguous Identities*. London and New York: Verso.

Baltic Course, The (2009) '52% of Latvian residents would not mind working under the table', 1 June edition, http://www.baltic-course.com/eng/analytics/?doc=14390.

Burrows, Noreen and Woolfson, Charles (2000) 'Regulating business and the business of regulation; the encouragement of business friendly assumptions in regulatory agencies' in Laura MacGregor, Tony Prosser and Charlotte Villiers (eds) *Regulation and Markets Beyond 2000*, pp. 319–340, Aldershot: Ashgate.

(CEC) Commission of European Commission (2007a) *Undeclared Work in the European Union. Report: Special Eurobarometer 284*, by Arnold Riedmann and Gabriele Fischer. Brussels: European Commission.

CEC (Commission of the European Communities) (2007b) *Stepping up the Fight Against Undeclared Work*. Brussels: European Commission.

CEC (Commission of the European Communities) (2009a) *Economic Forecast Spring 2009*. Brussels: Directorate-General for Economic and Financial Affairs, 4 May, http://ec.europa.eu/economy_finance/publications/publication15048_en.pdf.

CEC (Commission of the European Communities) (2009b) *Communication from the Commission to the Council and the European Parliament. Action Programme for Reducing Administrative Burdens in the EU Sectoral Reduction Plans and 2009 Actions*. Brussels, 22 October, COM (2009) 544 final, http://hesa.etui-rehs.org/uk/newsevents/files/com_2009_544_main_en.pdf.

CEC (Commission of the European Communities) (2010) *Communication from the Commission, EUROPE 2020 A Strategy for Smart, Sustainable and Inclusive growth*, Brussels, 3 March, http://ec.europa.eu/eu2020/pdf/COMPLET%20EN%20BARROSO%20%20%20007%20-%20Europe%202020%20-%20EN%20version.pdf.

European Foundation for the Improvement of Living and Working Conditions (2004) *Latvia – Legislation Strengthens Institutional Basis for Health and Safety – EIRonline Report*, http://www.eiro.eurofound.eu.int/2003/08/inbrief/lv0308101n.html.

European Foundation for the Improvement of Living and Working Conditions (2010) *European Working Conditions Survey – Mapping the Results*, http://www.eurofound.europa.eu/ewco/surveys/ewcs2010/results.htm.

European Parliament Committee on Employment and Social Affairs (2008) *Draft Report on Stepping up the Fight Against Undeclared Work, 2008/2035(INI)*. Brussels: European Parliament Committee on Employment and Social Affairs.

Eurostat (2009a) *Newsrelease, Euroindicators, 121/2009*, 24 August, http://epp.eurostat.ec.europa.eu/cache/ITY_PUBLIC/4-24082009-AP/EN/4-24082009-AP-EN.PDF.

Eurostat (2009b) *Newsrelease, Euroindicators, 112/2009*, 31 July, http://epp.
eurostat.ec.europa.eu/cache/ITY_PUBLIC/3-31072009-BP/EN/3-31072009-
BP-EN.PDF.

Eurostat (2010) *First Estimates for the Fourth Quarter of 2009, Euroindicators,
34/2010*, 4 March, http://epp.eurostat.ec.europa.eu/cache/ITY_PUBLIC/2-
04032010-AP/EN2-04032010-AP-EN.PDF.

Gray, Garry C. (2009) 'The responsibilization strategy of health and safety:
neo-liberalism and the reconfiguration of individual responsibility for risk',
British Journal of Criminology, 49: 326–342.

Hazans, Michael (2009) *Undeclared work and envelope wages in Latvia: Prevalence
and perspectives*, unpublished paper. Riga: University of Latvia.

ILO (International Labour Organisation) (2009) *Labour Inspection and Labour
Administration in the Face of Undeclared Work and Related Issues of Migration
and Trafficking in Persons: Practices, Challenges and Improvement in Europe.
Towards a Labour Inspection Policy*, National Workshop on Labour Inspection
and Undeclared Work, October. Budapest: International Labour Office.

ILO (International Labour Organisation) (2010a) *Labour Inspection in Europe:
Undeclared Work, Migration, Trafficking, Working Document Number 7, Labour
Administration and Inspection Programme LAB/ADMIN*. Geneva: International
Labour Office.

ILO (International Labour Organisation) (2010b) *CEACR: Individual Direct
Request Concerning Labour Inspection (Agriculture) Convention, 1969 (No. 129)
to Belgium (ratification: 1997)*, Submitted: 2010.

ILO (International Labour Organisation) (2010c) *Individual Observation
Concerning Labour Inspection (Agriculture) Convention, 1969 (No. 129) to Italy
(ratification: 1981)*, published: 2010.

LPSK (Lithuanian Trade Union Confederation) (2010) Naujienos. Gana
Skurdinti Žmones! Svarbiausia – Darbo Vietų Kūrimas ir Ekonomikos
Augimas! http://www.lpsk.lt/, accessed 5 October 2010.

Reiter, Herwig (2007) 'Non-solidarity and unemployment in the '"New West"',
in Nathalie Karagiannis (ed.) *European Solidarity*, pp. 164–185, Liverpool:
Liverpool University Press.

Schneider, Freidrich (2002) *Size and Measurement of the Informal Economy in 110
Countries around the World*, Washington, DC: World Bank.

Tupy, Marian L. (2003) *EU Enlargement Costs, Benefits, and Strategies for Central
and Eastern European Countries. Policy Analysis No. 489*, Washington, DC: Cato
Institute, http://www.cato.org/pubs/pas/pa489.pdf.

Vega, Maria Luz (2009) *The Global Economic and Social Crisis and its Impact on Labour Inspection Systems. Negotiating out of the Crisis.* Turin: International Training Centre of the ILO, http://www.ilo.org/labadmin/what/pubs/lang--en/docName--WCMS_123770/index.htm.

Vogel, Laurent (2010) *Better Regulation: A Critical Assessment.* Brussels: European Trade Union Institute.

Williams, C. Colin and Renooy, Piet (2009) *Measures for Combating Undeclared Work in 27 European Union Member States and Norway,* Dublin: European Foundation for the Improvement of Living and Working Conditions.

Woolfson, Charles (2007) 'Pushing the envelope: the "informalisation" of labour in post-communist new EU Member States', *Work, Employment and Society,* 21(3): 551–564.

Woolfson, Charles, Calite, Dace and Kallaste, Epp (2008) 'Employee "voice" and working environment in post-communist New Member States: an empirical analysis of Estonia, Latvia and Lithuania', *Industrial Relations Journal,* 39(4): 314–334.

Woolfson, Charles, Thörnqvist, Christer and Sommers, Jeffrey (2010) 'The Swedish model and the future of labour standards after *Laval*', *Industrial Relations Journal,* 41(4): 333–350.

Woolfson, Charles and Likic-Brboric, Branka (2009) 'Migrants and the unequal burdening of "toxic" risk: towards a new governance regime', *Debatte: Journal of Contemporary Central and Eastern Europe,* 16(3): 291–308.

All URLs checked 14 September 2011 unless otherwise stated.

5

Work Organisation, New Forms of Employment and Good Practices for Occupational Health and Safety: Evidence from Italy within the European Context[1]

Maria Giovannone and Michele Tiraboschi[2]

Introduction

THE PRINCIPLE OF EQUAL TREATMENT AND THE FORMAL PROTECTION OF NON-STANDARD WORKERS

There is general consensus on the fact that European legislation has played a crucial role in reforming EU countries' regulatory framework for OHS. An example in this connection has been the adoption of a series of provisions (individual Directives) as laid down by the Framework Directive No. 391/1989/EEC[3], according to which risk assessment has a significant impact on hazard prevention. Subsequently, Directive No. 91/383/EEC[4] was issued, stating that

---

1 English language reviser: Pietro Manzella.
2 Maria Giovannone is Research fellow at ADAPT – 'Marco Biagi' International and Comparative Study Centre of the University of Modena and Reggio Emilia (Italy). Michele Tiraboschi is Full Professor of Labour Law at the University of Modena and Reggio Emilia (Italy) and Director of the 'Marco Biagi' International and Comparative Study Centre.
3 Council Directive 89/391/EEC of 12 June 1989 on the introduction of measures to encourage improvements in the safety and health of workers at work.
4 Council Directive 91/383/EEC of 25 June 1991 supplementing the measures to encourage improvements in the safety and health at work of workers with a fixed-duration employment relationship or a temporary employment relationship.

protection should be granted to all categories of workers, with special reference to those regarded as more vulnerable, because of the nature of their employment relationship, viz. precarious and temporary workers.

Regarded as complementary to Directive No. 89/391/EEC, Directive No. 91/383/EEC lays down special safeguards for temporary workers aimed to provide them with the same level of protection granted to standard workers. A definition of 'temporary agency work' is also provided, that is a tripartite form of employment, where a company (temporary work agency), assigns a worker to a company customer (the user). In this connection, Article 5 of the Directive is significant, as entrusting Member States with the right to resort to temporary agency workers for those activities requiring special medical surveillance, in order to comply with national legislation. Temporary workers should receive ad hoc medical surveillance, also to be provided once the employment relationship has terminated. Before starting work, agency workers have also the right to be informed about any risks they might face while carrying out their activities, and, if necessary, to receive adequate training. In this light, an evaluation of their professional qualifications is also highly advisable.

Although laying down significant preventive measures, Directive No. 91/383/EEC has been more announced than implemented. It has not produced, according to statistics for the year 2004 made available by the European Commission, consistent results in practical terms. Nevertheless, there are two main principles laid down by the Directive that are worthy of note: the principle of equal treatment between standard and non-standard workers and the risk prevention to be assessed considering workforce diversity resulting from a number of factors (nationality, expertise, psychosocial issues). Equally important is the implementation of special and supplementary medical surveillance, and information and training based on workers' needs.

Before the passing of Legislative Decree No. 81/2008[5] and its later amendments, which was the means of transposition of Directive No. 91/383/EEC into Italian legislation, there were a number of difficulties to be faced before implementation could be finalised.[6]

In the context of this chapter it seems worth pointing out that the definition of 'traditional work' in Italian labour law encompasses paid employment performed

---

5   The so called 'Consolidate Act' on health and safety at work.
6   To know more about the process of transposition, see M. Tiraboschi (1996, 1997; Javilier et al. 1996).

on a full-time and on a permanent basis, which is still the most common form of work in the country. However, Italy has witnessed major changes within the labour market over the years, especially because of a process of modernisation and flexibilisation resulting from new contractual arrangements. A significant contribution in this connection has been provided by the so-called 'Biagi Law' (Law No. 30/2003, and Legislative Decree No. 276/2003), which, in order to fulfil the need for flexibility, redesigned existing employment contracts (part-time work, quasi-subordinate employment) and introduced new forms of employment (staff-leasing, temporary agency work), also giving priority to issues related to OHS as involving a considerable number of employees.[7]

In 1996,[8] the transposition into national law of Directive No. 91/383/EEC was accompanied by strong reservations about its effectiveness, regarded as partial, and as putting employees on a fixed-term contract at a disadvantage in terms of health and safety compared to those employed on a permanent basis. Since no reference was made to the obligation on the part of the employer to assess risk by considering workforce diversity, the transposition of the Directive only focused on the need for equal treatment between standard and non-standard workers at a formal level.

In 1997, the Italian Ministry of Labour and Social Policies carried out a survey on the relationship between temporary work, accident prevention and safety measures, pointing out that a number of risks were associated with factors such as isolation, communication and training issues, lack of organisation and expertise. The report also argued that questions of this kind called for significant changes

---

7   Labour-market reform in Italy has been an incremental process over more than a decade, but the two main provisions have been the Treu and Biagi reforms of 1997 and 2003, respectively. The 'Treu package' (September 1996), named after then-Labour and Social Policies Minister Tiziano Treu, aimed to increase employment, particularly among the young, with special measures for the economically depressed south (the Mezzogiorno). It eased regulation of new apprenticeships and work-training contracts, and created incentives for on-the-job training, temporary work via private agencies and intra-regional labour mobility. It also legalised worker-dispatching services for the first time and reduced disincentives for the use of fixed-term contracts. Marco Biagi was a labour law professor who drafted the law, one of the most controversial reforms of the Italian labour market. Its aim was to increase employment among youth, women, older workers and job-seekers, particularly in the Mezzogiorno. The new measures included allowing private employment agencies to compete in the full range of services with public ones; promoting apprenticeships; improving conditions for the use by firms of part-time work; and offering greater opportunities to use other non-standard forms of employment. If previous labour-market policies tended to reflect an overriding concern with the protection of employed 'insiders', these reforms sought to create greater opportunities for new entrants and other labour-market 'outsiders'. Both these reforms (as well as a number of other changes to labour legislation adopted in between) were driven by EU-related policy considerations.

8   Legislative Decree No. 242 of 19 March 1996.

in legislation in general terms – therefore not simply reconsidering provisions in health and safety – in compliance with EU Directives, in particular Directive No. 91/383/EEC. A number of proposals have also been put forward at a European level. In France, for instance, it has been demonstrated that temporary workers can be protected by ensuring parity of treatment between this group and those employed on a permanent basis. Other proposals – implemented in June 1997[9] – aimed at identifying those occupations requiring special surveillance measures, inclusion of OHS in different levels of education and training and ad hoc initiatives safeguarding workers classified as 'unusual'. Therefore, at both national and international levels, there was a mounting recognition of the OHS problems posed by labour market restructuring and the changes in work organisation, as well as of the need to reconsider regulatory strategies.[10]

Further provisions dealing with OHS for atypical workers are laid down in the Biagi Law, which is of considerable importance in the modernisation of the labour market because it represents a legislative intervention aimed at liberalising the emerging forms of atypical contracts, as well as facilitating the national implementation of Directive No. 91/383. Before the entry into force of this provision, health and safety at the workplace mainly dealt with traditional employment relationships. Today, by promoting cooperation between health and safety authorities and labour market actors, the aim is for the Biagi Law to combat joblessness, and to promote access to regular and quality employment, in accordance with the Community goals laid down in the Lisbon Strategy. Although no specific reference has been made to OHS, the Decree has provided a definition of 'worker'[11] according to which protection granted to traditional workers has been extended also to those who have already exited the labour market, or to those employed under new forms of contract (agency work, intermittent work, job-sharing, outsourcing, quasi-subordinate employment and so on). As for quasi-subordinate employment, the law provides that workers operating within the employer's premises are entitled to full protection in line with case law decisions, whereas a more detailed definition for OHS is provided for agency workers, especially referring to obligations on the part of the user enterprise. In terms of health and safety, the awareness of special needs for some categories of workers, as well as the adoption of new criteria in the definition of the employment status, represent the first significant attempt to provide effective safeguards to atypical workers.

---

9   Law No. 196 of 24 June 1997, called 'Treu package'.
10   Quinlan and Mayhew (1998).
11   Article 2 par. 1 sub. J.

TACKLING PERSONAL FACTORS OF VULNERABILITY

There are usually four personal factors to consider while analysing workers' vulnerability in Italy: age, sex, nationality and physical condition, with the regulatory approach mainly oriented towards policies aimed at controlling, preventing and prohibiting discriminatory practices at a systematic level. Such policies usually deal with working time patterns, skills development and maintenance, access-to-work programmes and hazardous tasks, with workers who need to be instructed and further trained about their equipment, machinery and personal safety, especially regarding the exposure limits to dangerous substances (in accordance with Directive No. 92/85/EEC[12] and Directive No. 94/33/EC[13]). It should be pointed out, however, that risk assessment processes identify hazards that result from personal factors de facto, classifying them as 'particular risks', for which further measures have been adopted in relation to organisational issues, equipment, emergency situations and so on. Significantly, no special provision applies to workers with disabilities, even though the employer is under the obligation to ensure their health and safety and work accessibility (through staircases, showers and so on). In this respect, although introducing a number of innovative measures, domestic safety legislation has been regarded as affected by major shortcomings in the implementation of provisions at a practical level.

It should worth pointing out that psychosocial factors, such as mobbing (discriminatory behaviour directed in a systematic manner by the empoyer towards an employee resulting in psychological abuse) and burnout, have been largely neglected by safety legislation, with relevant case law showing that such phenomena have been dealt with by resorting to general provisions included in the Civil Law Code (Article 2087). However, special attention has been given to work-related stress, for which ad hoc guidelines have been adopted by the Ministry of Labour and Social Policies, as a result of the transposition of the European Framework Agreement into national law.[14]

---

12 Council Directive 92/85/EEC of 19 October 1992 on the introduction of measures to encourage improvements in the safety and health at work of pregnant workers and workers who have recently given birth or are breastfeeding (tenth individual Directive within the meaning of Article 16 (1) of Directive 89/391/EEC).

13 Council Directive 94/33/EC of 22 June 1994 on the protection of young people at work.

14 See Italian Ministry of Labour and Welfare (2010).

A New Approach to Health and Safety Culture

THE CONSOLIDATED ACT

In compliance with Community Directives, the passing of the Consolidated Act on occupational health and safety has resulted in a major overhaul of relevant legislation, with its implementation being rather difficult due to the fact that the preventive measures that needed to be adopted called for a review of labour organization models *in toto*, and also because of a rise in non-standard employment relationships. In this connection, the enactment of Legislative Decree No. 81/2008 raised awareness of the issue, as an instrument to identify atypical workers' needs regardless of contractual arrangements, and to modernise the labour market in organisational terms. In fact, while applying to those categories of workers that are characterised by high rates of occupational injuries, the Decree also makes provision for individuals engaged in apprenticeship and voluntary work, as well as to those performing under more flexible forms of work (quasi-subordinate employment), provided that they operate at the employers' premises.

RISK ASSESSMENT

In the context of the new law the risk-assessment process is of fundamental importance in identifying the areas of vulnerability[15] and their related occupational hazards at the workplace and the adoption of preventive measures to safeguard workers' health and safety.[16] The new structure of risk assessment is based on a workforce diversity management approach.[17] In particular, according to Article 2, par. 1, sub. Q of Legislative Decree No. 81/2008 such processes aimed at 'providing an overall and certified evaluation of work-related risks within the establishment they operate, in order to put in place appropriate preventive measures and draw up guidelines with the view to improving health and safety in the workplace'. This definition consists of three phases: assessing the risks, identifying effective safety policies and improving workers' protection through legislation. Accordingly companies need to face the new issue of vulnerability by implementing new policies in terms of work organisation and the environment, also increasing public awareness of the

---

15 For further information on the new approach to risk assessment in Italy, see Ferrua, Giovannone and Tiraboschi (2009).
16 See Court of Justice of the European Communities (2001) which deals with the employer obligation to assess particular risks within the Italian framework.
17 European Agency for Safety and Health at Work (2009).

issue, moving beyond stereotypical views and promoting safety training in any stage of life.

It is also advisable to improve job satisfaction by means of specific training and retraining initiatives designed also to consider differences among workers – making use of personalised programs and small study groups – which will result in higher levels of productivity, innovation, occupational development and mobility between companies. In light of the above, there is a need for innovation in cultural terms to be carried out by all actors involved in the labour market, and to reconsider links between environment, health and age in the workplace over the entire working life. In this light, apart from the draft of the ordinary risk-assessment report it was also established that in cases of contracting, subcontracting, supply and installation of materials and provision contracts, the principal employer promotes cooperation and coordination with the contractor and drafts a Unified Interference Risk Assessment Document (DUVRI) which must be dated and must contain the following compulsory elements:

- a report on the assessment of all health and safety risks, which specifies the criteria adopted for the assessment;

- indication of the prevention and protection measures implemented and the personal protective equipment adopted;

- the programme of measures necessary to improve safety levels over time;

- identification of the procedures to implement the measures to be taken and the roles of the company that must apply these procedures;

- the name of the prevention and protection service manager, the workers' safety representative;

- the identification of the tasks that expose workers to specific risks, which require recognised professional know-how, specific experience, adequate training and preparation.[18]

18   See Castriotta, Grosso and Papale (2009).

Vulnerable Workers[19]

The new risk-assessment process is the key for the definition of vulnerability, both at the personal and contractual level. The definition adopted for vulnerable workers in the context of occupational health and safety (OHS) refers to those workers who are more likely to suffer from industrial injuries as a result of environmental, physiological and personal factors (for example young people, people over 50, women and migrant workers), though this does not necessarily depend on the type of employment contract. It will be useful here to provide an overview of relevant legislation in order to frame the issue. Pursuant to Legislative Decree No. 81/2008 (Article 28, par.1, as amended by Legislative Decree No. 106/2009), it falls to the employer to assess the employees' level of protection, especially for those who are more vulnerable, viz.:

- workers suffering from work-related stress;

- pregnant women;

- workers who are discriminated against because of their age, gender, nationality and employment status.

WORKERS EXPOSED TO RISKS ARISING FROM GENDER INEQUALITIES AND PREGNANT WORKERS

As mentioned earlier, Legislative Decree No. 81/2008 (Article 28, par.1, as amended by Legislative Decree No. 106/2009), sets forth that the process of risk assessment should inter alia consider gender inequalities and hazards that are specific to some categories – for example pregnant women – as also laid down by Legislative Decree No. 151 of 26 March 2001.[20] The aim is to provide women with employment protection that also considers their commitment to family and children, taking into account differences with male workers. For example, exposure to chemicals, vibrations and radiation has a different impact on women and men's health.[21] Therefore, while identifying preventive measures and good practices to be adopted to safeguard working women, the employer should take such diversity into account. Among the aspects to consider for a *women-friendly* approach in terms of health and safety, mention should be made of the following:

---

19 For further information on the different degrees of vulnerability, Sargeant (2009).
20 The so Called Consolidated Act on the protection of maternity and paternity at work.
21 European Agency for Safety and Health at Work (2005).

- certain hazards are specific to certain occupations;

- women and men are clearly different, especially in terms of reproduction;

- they take responsibility for different household chores, with women regarding them as an extra working activity.

Women should be granted safeguards in terms of work–life balance, and protected as human beings in all different stages of life (pregnancy, maternity and so on).[22] In this connection, a number of actions should also be taken, especially concerning work organisation, in order to provide women with flexible working time and better career prospects. In addition, equal opportunities should be granted to women in terms of adequate training, career advancement, fair remuneration and measures to prevent them from experiencing direct and indirect discrimination. Special attention should also be paid to measures adopted to tackle discrimination on the grounds of sex, together with offensive and persistent behaviour leading to sexual harassment. With reference to pregnant workers and their legal protection, Article 11 of Legislative Decree No. 151/2001 states that it is up to the employer to assess risks for women employees during pregnancy, considering their exposure to chemicals and biological agents and other factors: the results of such evaluation are to be communicated to workers and their representatives. Measures of this kind might include the assignment of the worker to another task, if necessary at a lower level in terms of the employment grade, especially if an adjustment to working hours is not possible, with the employer being under the obligation to provide notice of the new assignment to the inspectorate of the Ministry of Labour in writing. Otherwise, the Provincial Labour Office (Direzione Provinciale del Lavoro) might provide for parental leave lasting three months prior to and seven months following the expected date of childbirth.

Furthermore, working women, both during pregnancy and up to seven months following childbirth, cannot be employed in hazardous tasks that are physically demanding and that require the lifting of heavy loads, pursuant to Article 7 of Legislative Decree n. 151/2001. They must be immediately reassigned to a new task, regardless of the risk assessment. Jobs defined as dirty, demanding and dangerous are listed in Article 5 of Presidential Decree No. 1026 of 25 November 1976 on support of women workers' conditions,

---

22 For further details on risks arising from gender inequalities, see Legislative Decree No. 198 of 11 April 2006 which regulates the Code of Equal Opportunities between men and women.

also appearing in Annex A of Legislative Decree 151/2001, while Annex B of the Decree provides a list of those tasks deemed to be hazardous due to their exposure to chemicals and unsafe working conditions.

Measures of this kind should also be adopted in the event that an inspection carried out by the Ministry of Labour – on its own initiative or upon the party's request – certifies that working and environmental conditions pose serious health risks to working women. In addition, they should not be employed in the event of poor state of health, also in the event of complications in pregnancy, or when a new assignment is not available. Hence, they are required to communicate their medical condition to the employer by providing a medical certificate. If the employee does not present the medical certificate within the required time period, the implementation of the measures mentioned above can be delayed until such certification is provided.

Article 8 of Legislative Decree n. 151/2001 deals with exposure to ionising radiations, setting forth that 'pregnant workers cannot be engaged in activities involving a significant risk for the child to be born', with the provision also applying to breastfeeding mothers. In this case, women are under the obligation to submit a declaration of pregnancy to the employer, who has to promptly assign them a new task, more compatible with their health status. If this is not possible, the worker is prohibited from performing the current working activity.

Further measures have been introduced to protect health and safety of pregnant workers, dealing with night work, that is from midnight to 6 a.m. In this connection, they cannot be assigned to night shifts during pregnancy, or for 12 months following childbirth. In addition, the following categories are exempt from performing night work:

- female and male workers with care-giving responsibilities with children younger than three years old;

- primary carers with children younger than 12 years old.

The provisions mentioned above dealing with night work are included in Article 11 of Legislative Decree No. 66/2003on the revision of working time arrangements, also specifying that failure to comply with such measures may result in a two- to four-year prison sentence and a fine of between €516 and €2,582.

RISKS ASSOCIATED WITH MIGRANT WORKERS

People working overseas face major challenges, particularly related to language barriers and a reduced perception of occupational risks. They are also more likely to take up hazardous and unskilled jobs, characterised by unfavourable working conditions, excessive working hours and unsocial shifts resulting in mental and physical fatigue that undermines alertness levels. It is also relevant that rotating shift workers, as well as night workers, tend to underperform their dayshift counterparts because of an attenuated brain response, with lack of sleep resulting in a general fatigue and tiredness often leading to occupational injuries. Poor language skills are another major issue, representing an obstacle to adequate training opportunities in OHS. Migrant workers often come from countries with low levels of awareness of risks in the workplace, developing a different approach to occupational hazards. Therefore, the focus should be on information and training as a way to improve migrants' capacity to assess risk. As mentioned earlier, Legislative Decree No. 81/2008 (Article 28, par. 1) specifies that immigrant workers are classified as being more vulnerable: employers should take responsibility for their health and safety and adopt specific measures to safeguard them. Article 36, par. 4 of the decree also makes provision for the workers' right to be informed properly about health and safety risks at work, setting forth that content must be easily accessible to workers – especially migrants – enabling them to gain necessary knowledge. Article 37 also lays down that the onus is on the employer to provide occupational and language training, with par. 13 reasserting that the content should be understandable by all workers. In addition to assessing language skills, measures should be adopted to increase awareness of workers' rights and duties in terms of OHS, also by way of the implementation of good practices.

Finally, there is a need to take into great consideration occupational risks involving the followers of Islam, especially during Ramadam, the Islamic month of fasting according to which participants refrain from eating and drinking from 5 a.m. to 5 p.m. In this light, the employer should provide more flexible time arrangements in order to safeguard their health and safety, as well as their freedom of religion.

AGE-RELATED RISKS

Pursuant to Article 28, par. 1, of Legislative Decree No. 81/2008, the burden is on the employer to assess and adopt measures to prevent risks associated with age for both young and older workers. In this connection, Law No. 977/1967 – as amended by Legislative Decree No. 345/1999, which was itself supplemented by Legislative Decree No. 262/2000 – lays down special provisions for minors. In particular, Article 7 sets forth a number of factors to be considered while assigning them a new task, such as their physical development, lack of expertise, low risk perception and the need for health and safety training and information. Young workers face additional challenges because, unlike older workers, they are unfamiliar with the working environment, and unaware of risks and their rights and duties. Also, the working conditions and the employment status they operate in are often on a temporary basis with inadequate safety training (a case in point is young people working in call centres). In addition to being precarious, young workers – especially those aged 15 to 24 years – are more likely to undertake physically demanding jobs and to work to tight deadlines and at very high speed and this may result in musculoskeletal disorders. In addition, young workers are also more likely to take on jobs characterised by repetitive motion, rapid movement, vibration, the handling of toxic chemicals, exposure to high temperature and, as newly hired, to harassment and bullying. In order to cope with those questions, the employer needs to adopt a set of measures in terms of health and safety, training and information, also appointing mentors within the company to help newly hired workers in their routine activities.

In order to safeguard young people the company must disseminate relevant information on potential risks and preventive measures before they start work, as statistics show that in the first month of work they are five times more likely to suffer from occupational injuries than their older counterparts.

Furthermore, supervisors should oversee their work to evaluate the effectiveness of training programmes and to make sure they carry out their tasks properly. Supervisors should also be provided with adequate training themselves, and be instructed on what actions need to be taken in the event of injuries suffered by young workers. More specifically, their task consists of:

- ensuring the implementation of good practices in terms of health and safety;

- making sure that safety measures have been designed also in practical terms;

- promoting a strong culture of health and safety;

- reporting any changes and problems;

- providing advice for younger workers.

In the same way, young workers must report to their supervisor any perceived risks, comply with OHS rules and regulations, and be instructed and trained properly about their equipment, machinery and personal safety devices.

A case can be made for the inclusion of risk education as part of educational programmes. In this respect, schools and colleges need to play a major role in increasing the awareness of hazards among young people, and in the planning of specific measures to be adopted in the years to come. Specific risk assessment should involve also older workers, due to their vulnerability arising from lower levels of adaptability and reduced physical strength.

WORKERS EXPERIENCING STRESS AT WORK

Legislative Decree No. 81/2008 (Article 28, par. 1) sets forth that work-related stress is a factor to be considered in the evaluation of occupational risks. In doing so, reference is made to the Autonomous Framework Agreement of 8 October 2004, which was transposed on 9 June 2008 by way of an inter-business collective agreement between employers' associations and trade unions. The main goal of the Agreement is to provide employers and workers with an instrument to identify, prevent and manage issues associated with work-related stress, therefore contributing to the improvement of employees' efficiency and working conditions, with a considerable impact also in economic and social terms. However, the Agreement does not envisage any measure to deal with workplace bullying, harassment, and post-traumatic stress disorder, therefore disregarding phenomenon such as mobbing and straining (a work-related disorder which takes place over a long period of time as a result of stress negatively affecting the individual's work). As a result, the focus is on work-related stress,that is defined as a medical condition – accompanied by physical, psychological or social complaints or dysfunctions – resulting from individuals feeling unable to keep up with the requirements expected of them. Individuals may be well adapted to cope with short-term exposure to pressure, which can be considered as positive, but have greater difficulty in coping with prolonged exposure to intense pressure. Moreover, different individuals can react differently to similar situations and the same individual can react differently to similar situations at different times of their life. It should be pointed out, however, that work-related stress does not include all manifestations of stress at work, although stress originating outside the working environment can lead to changes in behaviour and reduced effectiveness at work. In this connection, the employer is under the obligation to provide protective measures only with regard to work organisation, working conditions and environment. This entails the identification of those factors that are stress-inducing and actions to be taken to reduce them, with the duty to report and evaluate the results on a regular basis.

In addition to the risks mentioned above, reference should be made also to those associated with precarious employment, as workers engaged in precarious jobs – characterised by low income, inadequate opportunities in terms of training and career advancement – usually operate in more dangerous working conditions, without necessarily receiving training in occupational safety and health, and with higher levels of stress due to uncertainty over the continuity of employment.

In this connection, it is up to the employers to prevent, reduce or eliminate issues arising from work-related stress. They should work to determine appropriate measures to be implemented together with workers and their representatives. Such measures might also include an overall process of risk assessment, or ad hoc initiatives aimed at identifying stress factors. Furthermore, measures in terms of management and communication, such as those clarifying the company's objectives and the role of workers, should be adopted, ensuring suitable management support for individuals and the team, matching responsibility and control over work, and improving work organisation and processes, working conditions and environment. This should also be followed by adequate training for both managers and workers, awareness-raising campaigns aimed at increasing understanding of the issue and how to deal with it, and the adoption of an award system for those complying with health and safety regulations. In addition, a number of actions should be taken to address questions dealing with:

- working hours;

- participation and management;

- workload;

- work content;

- role within the organisation;

- working environment;

- career prospects.

Once implemented, anti-stress measures should be reviewed on a regular basis to assess their effectiveness, in order to verify their appropriateness.

With reference to the employer's obligation to evaluate risks associated with work-related stress, Legislative Decree No. 207/2008, converted into Law No. 14/2009, deferred the date of the enforcement of this obligation to 16 May 2009.

Subsequently, Legislative Decree No. 81/2008 (in particular Article 28, par. 1) was amended by Legislative Decree No. 106/2009, which specifies in this regard that, from 1 August 2010, the assessment of the risks linked to work-related stress should be carried out in compliance with the conditions laid down by the Advisory Panel on Health and Safety at Work. This obligation, applying to both the public and the private sector, was further deferred to 31 December 2010.

The guidelines on risk assessment, which are normative in character, were issued by the Advisory Panel on Health and Safety at Work set up by the Italian Ministry of Labour and Social Affairs on 18 November 2010. In order to comply with European legislation, and to deal with questions arising from its interpretation, Article 28, par. 8 of Legislative Decree No. 81/2008 specifies that the assessment of risk must be carried out also considering work-related stress. With the issuing of par. 1-*bis*, the Panel was also entrusted with the task of performing an advisory function, helping employers, advisers and supervisors to fulfil the necessary requirements not later than 31 December 2010, also backed by a tripartite committee. Far from being taken for granted, the issuing of the guidelines on 2 November 2010 was the subject of a heated debate between the government, the social partners, experts in the field and inspection bodies at a local level. In this connection, strong reservations were expressed about the transposition into national law of the Framework Agreement via the inter-business Agreement of 9 November 2008, to which Legislative Decree. 81/2008 referred, as methodology to assess the risk is subject to a variety of interpretations. Furthermore, considerable doubts were raised about the adoption of mandatory minimum standards to be reliable, fair in evaluating the individual's state of health and cost-effective for the companies, who pay for the medical surveillance.

The long-awaited much-discussed provision was the result of months of talks among the actors involved, and aims to meet everyone's interest and provide employers with minimum requirements to be improved on a voluntary basis.

OCCUPATIONAL RISKS ASSOCIATED WITH CONTRACTUAL ARRANGEMENTS

Legislative Decree No. 106/2009, which amended Legislative Decree No. 81/2008, makes provision for the risks associated with the nature of the employment relation, focusing particularly on atypical workers and temporary workers, who are more exposed than others groups to hazards. This is due to a number of factors: the short duration of the assignment, job insecurity, inadequate training, the nature of the tasks to be carried out, low bargaining power and low levels of union and legal protection.[23] The new provision is in this regard an attempt to safeguard those workers who are more vulnerable in contractual and individual terms. The categories of workers who are more likely to suffer from occupational risks (for example young people, women and migrant workers) are often employed under these forms of contracts, although the individual risk is not necessarily associated with the type of employment contract.

The Role of Information and Training

Decree No. 81/2008 codified the notions of training and information by fully embracing the current case law and doctrinal standpoint; it also introduced the fundamental principle that every subject playing a role related to safety and security in a company needs a training path, tailored to their responsibilities and tasks within that specific organization.[24] The latter statement clearly extends the duty of training and information on safety and security to managers and other roles in the company (it is not solely for employees). As for training, it has been defined as the educational process through which employees (and other subjects of the safety and security system) acquire knowledge and procedures that are useful in performing their duties in security and to identify, reduce and manage risks.

The initial aspect of stress is that of the educational process: as mentioned in the law it is not of a generic kind (that is, general skills concerning safety and security), rather it is specific in the sense that it comprises the risks, procedures and actions relative to the office carried out by the employee in his company. This point relates to a fundamental condition to evaluate the adequacy of the training process.

---

23 Messineo et al. (2006), see also Kompier et al. (2009).
24 See Werquin (2007) and ECOTEC (2007).

Other rules tend to further reinforce the concept of specific training as a mandatory requisite to tackle factors of vulnerability by a specific approach. The result is that, for instance, the mere participation of employees and other roles in basic and generic courses on safety and security, without any reference to the real situation of the company and the specific tasks carried out, makes the training process extremely inadequate, because it does not provide the necessary skills to prevent accidents and professional illness.

Descending from this principle, the employer not complying with this duty, as defined by the law, is liable both from the penal standpoint (for inadequate training) and from the contractual standpoint. An employee not adequately trained (for example one who only attended a course of a few hours and only about general topics), can refuse to carry out his office (Articles 15, 18 and 44), in compliance with the principle of self-protection, and he keeps the right to remuneration and to preserve his position of employment. He can also resign 'for good reasons', according to Article 2119 of Civil Code. Among the inadequacy parameters of the training process, we can certainly include 'undifferentiated training', that is, the fact that heterogeneous groups of workers, of different office, sex and age, can attend the same lesson. Another inadequacy parameter is the planning of the training process that does not take into account the behavioural aspects and the specific needs of the trainee. An inadequate training process is moreover one that lacks proper interaction and collaboration with the local Organismo Paritetico (joint bodies), and training courses to migrant workers, performed without an evaluation of their level of understanding of the language.

Another relevant point is the teacher's qualification: Article 106 of Decree 2009 has appointed to the Advisory Panel on Health and Safety at Work set up by the Italian Ministry of Labour and Social Affairs the task of identifying a list of criteria to assess teacher's qualification. It was recently discovered that teachers were too young and/or lacked any experience on the specific topic themselves. The result was that the lessons were carried out as a formality, rather than being of any substance. It is surely relevant to our study that risk evaluation should comprise all risks for employees. On the other hand, the Ministry of Labour is working on the redesign of training subjects and tools in order to include new risks and organisational models.

The Participatory Model

One of the leading principles in the new regulatory context is the strengthening of the role of workers' representatives and the revisiting in the role of third parties, as a means to give stronger voice to vulnerable workers.

This has been an important precondition for the generalisation of the participatory model of worker representation, deepening the roots of the principle of tripartism, stated by the International Labour Organisation, which implies an involvement of representative organisations (not only employers but also employees).

Legislative Decree No. 81/2008 is distinguished by particular cultural openness to the participatory model, knowing that participation, even more than consultation, is a relationship model, a style of confrontation and constant relation.

Recently there have been a number of signs of openness towards greater attention to collective protection, in particular through the consolidation of the thought that recognises the legitimacy of unions as the civil party in trials related to violations of accident prevention regulations, the liability for workplace accidents and occupational diseases and the liability for sexual offences in the workplace.

In the same connection there is the innovative provision which recognises that trade unions hold the power to exercise rights on behalf of the person offended by the crime of manslaughter or offences.

The desirability of a trade union's involvement in a criminal trial is meaningful as long as they are able to make a contribution to what is being informed to the court. As has been recognised, the new role of the union should move organisations toward less conflictual behaviour and onto a greater focus on a new style of industrial relations, to affirm the viability of an increase of safeguards, including the increase of protection levels.

The participation of workers and their representatives is invoked in many regulations concerning the management of safety and security prevention; starting with the general measures of protection; the obligations of the employer and the manager, with particular attention to risk assessment and its implementation modes; the obligations of the competent physician, related to innovative work contracts, up to the organisation of prevention services, regular meetings, training of workers, of their representatives, and of those responsible for checking the implementation of effective models of organisation and management of safety and security.

Participation takes the form of information, consultation, right of access and concerns – mainly the representatives of workers' safety, the joint bodies and in some cases bilateral bodies and trade unions. For the workers' representatives the new law enhances the role of workers and their representatives.

The criteria followed were the revision of requirements and safeguards, and the functions of subjects in the company prevention system, with particular reference to the strengthening of the role of representatives of workers for territorial security and the introduction of the concept of a safety representative on the production site. This concept was developed in two directions: on the one hand, guaranteeing a certain figure of reference for employees for each working reality (company representative/area/production site), on the other hand strengthening the powers of the workers' representative for safety and security. This means that the figure of a specialized occupational health and safety workers' representative (or representation) at enterprise, unit and local level is now very clearly defined with a strategic role and with specific professional abilities and competencies focused on occupational health and safety issues. All this makes him/her different from the general workers' representative.

These measures meant renewed emphasis on the participatory philosophy, which is stipulated in European law. This particular Italian law is an implementation of the European law, which deems it essential that workers and their representatives are able to contribute with balanced participation in the adoption of the necessary preventive measures.

Best Practices and Future Evolution: Certification of Labour Contracts and Qualification of Enterprises

With the prospect of a dynamic evolution of the regulatory framework, the Consolidated Act introduced the principle of consolidation of best practices development and dissemination, as a soft law mechanism to improve health and safety standards. Indeed the definition of good practice varies between Member States due to different OHS systems and legislation, culture, language and experiences. In addition different groups with different interests and levels of knowledge have different points of view on good practice in the workplace.

In the past the EU-OHSA has highlighted the difficulty in finding an exact definition of good practice, but gave the following definition: Good practice information should provide persons with OHS duties the information to allow them to reduce the health and safety risks to workers at enterprise level in the EU.[25] This information should be of sufficient quality and quantity to produce, following an appropriate assessment of the hazards and risks present, a permanent and verifiable reduction in the whole potential to cause harm to all person affected by the enterprise and ensure that relevant occupational health and safety legislation is met. The information should be relevant, ethical and effective, focusing where possible on preventing exposure to hazards at source. It is implemented most effectively with the strong involvement of all relevant parties and in particular those workers and their representatives who will be directly affected by the action taken.

In Italy the concept of good practice was established for the first time by the Consolidated Act (Article 2) as

> *organisational or procedural solutions, which are compliant with current legislation and employ good technique; are adopted voluntarily and are aimed at promoting occupational health and safety by reducing risks and improving working conditions; are developed and collected by the regions, the National Institute for Occupational Safety and Prevention (ISPESL), the National Institute for Insurance against Occupational Accidents and the joint bodies; they are approved by the Permanent Consultative Committee as per Article 6, subject to a technical review by ISPESL, which ensures its broadest possible dissemination.*

In this light the Advisory Panel on Health and Safety at Work set up by the Italian Ministry of Labour and Social Affairs is also working on behalf of the law (Article 27) on the definition of a system of qualifications of enterprises as a means of selection of virtuous employers within the market. Obviously OHS standards are at the top of the selection criteria. This system is based on the identification of economic sectors and the set organisational criteria which should be based not only on formal compliances and certifications, but on the constant application and monitoring of requisites of professional capacity in terms of: training activities, effective respect of sectoral collective agreements,

---

25 European Agency for Safety and Health at Work (2000).

use of genuine individual labour contracts and tenders, accompanied by the certification set in the Biagi Law.

The system has immediately focused on vulnerable sectors which included construction, temporary agency work and work in call centres. In the field of construction this instrument has been defined as a sort of licence which assigns the employer and the enterprises a score based on the application of the previous standards. This score is subject to deduction in cases of OHS violations and related crimes, up to final elimination from the market. Furthermore, in contracting and subcontracting all the stakeholders in value chains associated with these requisites will receive preferential treatment with regards to access to public tenders and public funding.

In cases of private contracting and subcontracting purchasers, apart from the traditional documental requisites, they are obliged to check the tenure of these requisites for the selection of contractors, subcontractors and self-employed workers engaged for their activities.

The Biagi Law certification is going to be the cornerstone and the most innovative element of the system. It is a voluntary administrative process conducted by the Commissions of Certification (neutral public bodies established within public universities, the local labour inspectorates and bilateral bodies) whose task, as is clear from the wording, consists of a reduction of the use of litigation in labour law matters. On the basis of a preliminary investigation of the formal content of the contract and an eventual investigation on its development in practice, a judgment is issued by the same Commissions of Certification. This judgment, which can be positive or negative, aims to check and test the genuineness of the contracts. It has a legal effect in case of litigation on labour matters even if not binding. At a certain stage it can also stop and postpone the inspections in the workplace. Certification of labour contracts is an Italian legal procedure whose main function is to reduce legal disputes concerning the qualification of labour contracts.

With reference to the Italian labour law system, the correct qualification of a labour contract is a process of great importance, as different contracts provide considerably different levels of protection to the worker; in other words, the qualification has direct impact on the worker's salary. This explains why, within the Italian labour law system, contractual qualification continually gives rise to a considerable amount of litigation.

In fact, qualification is excluded, by law, from the contractual terms under the power of variation of the parties and, therefore, may not be waived or altered by agreement. This is because qualification is mandatory and expressly established by law. Following from this, not even Certification is entitled to endorse variations of mandatory provisions, pursued or introduced by the agreement of the parties. Nonetheless, Certification, by attesting the lawfulness and the correct qualification of the labour contract, is the institutional and legal means available to the parties to reduce uncertainty and ensure compliance with the regulatory framework. In legal literature this concept is widely expressed: Certification, in fact, is exclusively regarded as a form of 'assisted consensus ad idem', and is therefore not viewed in terms of 'assisted variation' to mandatory rules.

Thus, Certification meets the need for certainty felt and expressed by interested parties who seek to perform flexible labour relations or to externalise stages of the production process by means of supply chain contracts (independent contractors). The subjects in charge of Certification are appointed by law. These certifying bodies are called Commissions/Boards for Certification (Article 76, Legislative Decree No. 276/2003).

Commissions for Certification (from now on: Commissions) shall be set up:

- by each territorial body of Ministry of Labour (Direzione Provinciale del Lavoro, Provincial Labour Direction (4);

- by the Ministry of Labour;

- by provinces, as expression of the local and territorial autonomies;

- by universities and university foundations, under the supervision of a professor of labour law;

- by bilateral bodies (unions and employers associations);

- by the Professional Association of the Labour Advisors.

The law (Article 79, Legislative Decree No. 276/2003) establishes that the legal effects of Certification, which enforce the qualification and the regulation between the parties and toward third parties (that is, Social Security Authorities as regards social security contributions), persist unless the judge of labour overturns Certification declaring it void.

The Provincial Labour Direction is the territorial organ of the Ministry of Labour. So, they are part of the Government, and not organs of the local administration. The province, which is the territorial partition where they have competence in, corresponds to a district, and consists of a chief town with its surrounding territory. Because Certification is an administrative act, the requirement of motivation is established by the general law for administrative acts Law 241/1990 (Article 2.4 entitlement to issue administrative orders for the re-qualification of labour contracts retrospectively to the starting date of work), produce the same legal effects between the parties and before third parties. Certification, though, has a legal impact upon inspectors, who cannot re-qualify a certified contract. Where there is a doubt about the correctness of its qualification or of its execution, they can appeal to a judge of labour for a review of the decision handed down by the Commission. In the meanwhile, the certified contract still produces its legal effects.

Because of this and the close examination already carried out by the Commissions, with the General Directive of 18 September 2008, the Minister of Labour has requested the inspectors of labour to focus their inspections on non-certified contracts, unless a written claim is filed by workers complaining about a violation of rightful labour protections, or where the incorrect actual execution of the contract is immediately ascertained.[26]

Certification seeks to enforce labour standards through a proper use of contractual models, to manifest the true intention of the parties and fully suit their interests. Certification is addressed from a regulatory perspective. First, all labour and supply chain contracts are eligible for certification. Although apparently different, these contracts share a common origin: the global process of 'vertical disintegration' of the firm. Secondly, certification is a form of labour market regulation, which does not fall among compulsory provisions nor is the expression of pure self-regulation. It rather represents an enforced self-regulation, or better a 'co-regulation' willingly undertaken by the parties, availing of and relying on the competence and expertise of the members of the board of certification, who act impartially. Employers are not compelled by law to defer their contracts to the board of certification, but if they do so and receive positive feedback, certification gives the contract a legal presumption of fairness, certifying its conformity to the principles of law so as to prevent future disputes. The theoretical framework of the paper views certification as a tool to promote regulatory compliance and responsibility, along with a more conscious use of contractual models.

---

26 A deeper analysis on certification is provided in Bizzarro et al. (2009).

As for OHS this new system, which is to be developed and implemented by the Permanent Consultative Committee (a Ministerial body), could bring an extension of voluntary certification systems of labour contracts and tenders, as introduced by the Biagi Law (Legislative Decree No. 276/2003) in the field of OHS organisation standards. This could lead to the implementation of quality in OHS management standards, where it remains the case that a preponderant role should be assigned to risk assessment and specific training of collective and individual protection for use by workers.[27]

In a broad sense it can be also be interpreted as a modern and soft law mechanism to validate from the outside the quality of policies and product of a company in terms of customer orientation and satisfaction, professional reliability, economic stability leadership, staff policies, corporate reputation and better management. This evolutionary perspective of the managerial model of labour relations applies a management process that has the characteristics of transparency and of the absence of negative externalities for the worker. Therefore a certification of concentric circles could be hypothesised – to use an image dear to those who, like Marco Biagi, envisaged the establishment of a 'Worker's Statute' – which, starting from the analysis of compliance with the rules of law and the collective agreement applications (minimum standard of legal and formal coherence), would extend to measures in successive circles and therefore beyond mere legal requirements, although the compliance with certain standards of quality and optimal management of staff along the lines of certification of excellence and good practice is evidently still to be defined. Or, on the contrary, one could imagine the reverse path, enabling the achievement of excellence only to companies that perhaps matches the certification of a limited number of reports that have embarked on a path of change.

Finally with regards to the criminal prosecution prospect; the new law has revised the pattern of offences and penalties, on the other hand it introduced, for the first time in our system, the principle of corporate social responsibility and the voluntary adoption of compliance programmes in the field of occupational health and safety. The implementation of this regulatory pattern is supposed to be strengthened within the context of the system of qualification of enterprises.

---

27   On the evolution of certification in OHS field see Barboni et al. (2009).

Conclusions

From the analysis of above mentioned indicators (risk assessment, participatory models, information and training and consolidation of best practices), it is evident that risks related to precariousness and vulnerability must be faced, not only through the recognition of equal treatment between vulnerable and non-vulnerable workers and traditional compensation/social security systems. Equal treatment must be balanced by including age, sex, nationality, psychosocial conditions and contractual position in a special mandatory process of risk assessment and by the use of special training programmes.

At the same time, all these organisational instruments must be accompanied by legal instruments of quality certification of labour contracts and models of organisation of work, and the enforcement of compliance systems.

References

Barboni, A., Bizzarro, C., Giovannone, M., Pasquini, F. and Tiraboschi, M. (2009) Mutamento dei modelli di organizzazione del lavoro, gestione della sicurezza, certificazione [The change of organizational models, occupational health and safety certification], in M. Tiraboschi and L. Fantini (eds), *Il Testo Unico della salute e sicurezza sul lavoro dopo il correttivo* [The Consolidated Act on Health and Safety at work after the amendment] (d.lgs. n. 106/2009), Giuffrè ed., Milan, pp. 67–94.

Bizzarro, C., Pasquini, F., Tiraboschi, M. and Venturi, D. (2009) Certification of labour contracts: a legal instrument for labour market regulation in Italy, paper presented at the International Society for Labour and Social Security Law, XIX World Congress, 1–4 September 2009, Sydney, Australia.

Castriotta, M., Grosso, F. and Papale, A. (2009) The European Campaign on risk assessment: a new concept for a successful model, *Prevention Today*, 5(1/2), 3–8.

Court of Justice of the European Communities (2001) C-49/00, 15 November 2001.

ECOTEC (2007) *European Inventory of Informal and Non-formal Learning*, ECOTEC, Birmingham.

European Agency for Safety and Health at Work (2000) *Guidelines on the Collection, Evaluation and Dissemination of Good Practices Information on the Internet*, European Agency for Safety and Health at Work, Bilbao, July.

European Agency for Safety and Health at Work (2005) *Mainstreaming Gender into Occupational Safety and Health*, European Agency for Safety and Health at Work, Bilbao.

European Agency for Safety and Health at Work (2009) *Workforce Diversity and Risk Assessment: Ensuring Everyone is Covered*, European Agency for Safety and Health at Work, Bilbao, October.

Ferrua, S., Giovannone, M. and Tiraboschi, M. (2009) Gruppi di lavoratori esposti a rischi particolari e tipologie di lavoro flessibile: la valutazione del rischio [Groups of workers exposed to special risks and atypical labour contracts: risk assessment], in M. Tiraboschi and L. Fantini (eds), *Il Testo Unico della salute e sicurezza sul lavoro dopo il correttivo* [The Consolidated Act on Health and Safety at work after the amendment] (d.lgs. n. 106/2009), Giuffrè ed., Milan, pp. 569–584.

Italian Ministry of Labour and Welfare (2010) *Indicazioni della Commissione consultiva per la valutazione dello stress lavoro-correlato* [Guidelines on the assessment of work-related stress by the Permanent Consultant Committee on health and safety at work], published 18 November 2010, http://www.lavoro.gov.it/Lavoro/Notizie/20101118_stresslavorocorrelato.htm.

Javilier, J.C., Neal, A., Weiss, M., Saloheimo, J., Runggaldier, U. and Tinhhofer, A. (1996) Lavoro atipico/temporaneo e tutela della salute: la trasposizione della Direttiva n. 91/383 in Francia, Regno Unito, Germania, Finlandia e Austria [Atypical and temporary work and occupational health and safety: the transposition of the EU directive n. 91/383 in France, Uk, Germany, Finland and Austria], *Diritto delle Relazioni Industriali*, 3, 35–50.

Kompier, M., Fekke Ybema, J., Janssen, J. and Taris, T. (2009) Employment contracts: cross-sectional and longitudinal relations with quality of working life, health and well-being, *Journal of Occupational Health*, 51, 193–203.

Messineo, A., Bruschi, A., Di Martino, G., Imperatore, A., Rossi, O. and Serretti, N. (2006) I lavori atipici: rilievi di attualità, sorveglianza sanitaria, vigilanza [Atypical work: actuality, medical surveillance and inspectorate issues], *GIMLE*, XXVIII, 3, 307.

Quinlan, M. and Mayhew, C. (1998) The implications of changing labour market structures for occupational health and safety, paper presented to Policies for Occupational Health and Safety Management Systems and Workplace Change Conference, Amsterdam 21–24 September 1998.

Sargeant, M. (2009) Health and safety of vulnerable workers in a changing world of work, Working Paper ADAPT, n. 101, 27 November 2009, http://www.adapt.it/acm-on-line/Home/Pubblicazioni/docCatWorkingPaperAdapt.1796.1.15.3.html.

Tiraboschi, M. (1996) Lavoro atipico e ambiente di lavoro: la trasposizione in Italia della direttiva 91/383/CEE, *Diritto delle Relazioni Industriali* [Atypical work and workplace conditions: the transposition of directive 91/383/EC into the Italian system], Giuffrè ed., Milan, n. 3, 57.

Tiraboschi, M. (1997) La trasposizione della direttiva n. 91/383/CEE nei principali paesi dell'Unione Europea e l'anomalia del caso italiano [The transposition of EU directive 91/383/EC in some EU member states and the peculiar caase if Italy], in *Diritto e Pratica del Lavoro, IPSOA*, Wolters Kluwer Group ed., n. 18, 1284.

Werquin, P. (2007) *Activity on Recognition of Non-Formal and Informal Learning Italy Country Background Report*, OECD.

6

Occupational Health and Safety of Migrant Workers: An International Concern

Mark Boocock, Zeenobiyah Hannif, Suzanne Jamieson, J. Ryan Lamare, Felicity Lamm, Christophe Martin, Nadine McDonnell, Cathy Robertson, Peter Schweder and Boaz Shulruf

Introduction

While it is estimated that over 175 million or 3 per cent of the world's population live outside their country of origin, there is a lack of documented evidence on the health and safety of migrant workers. In response to this, an international, collaborative research team has begun to investigate the health and safety of migrant workers and in particular to address the inherent methodological issues, by undertaking a number of exploratory studies focusing primarily on small businesses located in different countries and within different jurisdictions. The examples presented here indicate that migrant workers are more likely to be located in small, subcontracting businesses in most all sectors, including service (particularly, hospitality, cleaning and retail), construction and manufacturing as well as in the agricultural sector. We argue that it is more useful to begin at the level of the individual and the workplace and from there develop a research design model that can be applied to further studies located within other jurisdictions and settings. By undertaking research at the level of the worker and the workplace, it is hoped that deficiencies in the management of the health and safety of migrant workers will be exposed.

The health and safety of migrant workers is at the centre of a number of intersecting issues, including the increasing international movement of people, the often vulnerable position in which many migrant workers find themselves and the lack of regulatory and social support mechanisms associated with documented and undocumented labour. International research shows that migrant workers are over-represented in precarious employment (United Nations 2002, 2006; CARAM, 2007; OECD, 2007). There is also evidence to show that migrant workers are frequently exposed to hazardous, life-threatening conditions and not surprisingly have higher rates of injury and illness compared to non-migrant workers in standard employment (McKay et al., 2006; Quinlan et al., 2010). However, it is difficult to gauge the extent of occupational illness and injury amongst migrant workers because government databases rarely capture statistics on the occupational injury, fatalities and compensation claims of precariously employed migrant workers. A further impediment to obtaining workers' compensation by migrant workers is the rigorous measures needed to determine the causal factors linking employment, residency status and occupational health and safety (OHS) (Tinghög et al., 2007; Anya, 2007; Lay et al., 2007; Passel, 2007; Mirsky, 2009).

This chapter, therefore, attempts to widen our understanding of the OHS of migrant workers in precarious, non-standard employment, often located in small businesses. Based on an international comparative research project on the OHS of migrant workers, we will present an overview of the universal themes and highlight key differences in the treatment of migrants within each jurisdiction. Methodological issues around capturing meaningful and rigorous data from this so-called 'invisible population' raised at two recent colloquia are also discussed here. Moreover, we argue that this research stream has both national and international implications and dovetails with concerns of the rights of other vulnerable workers. Before commencing, however, it is necessary to first establish a working definition of 'migrant worker' and to present a brief overview of the literature as well as the research questions driving this research.

Occupational Health and Safety of Migrant Labour

Although there are a number of nuanced definitions of 'migrant worker', we have adopted Sargeant and Tucker's (2009) definition:

> *workers who have migrated to another country to take up work but who*
> *currently do not have a permanent status in the receiving country ...*
> *The migrant category ... includes both workers who have obtained a*

legal right to enter and work, as well as those who have entered and are working without legal authorisation. It also includes temporary foreign workers (TFWs) whose right to work is time-limited from the outset, as well as foreign workers who have a more open-ended right to remain but have not yet obtained permanent status (Sargeant and Tucker, 2009: 51).

Sargeant and Tucker's definition of 'migrant worker' is useful in that it describes the layers or structures of vulnerability and the risks faced by migrant workers. Their description of migrant workers allows for an analysis of the risks faced by these workers. Both the description and analysis are at a level which the authors describe as a macro or political economic level, rather than micro or personal level. Thus the definition not only serves as a starting point, but also involves investigation at a level of abstraction. In particular, their layers of vulnerability include (Sargeant and Tucker, 2009: 605):

- *Layer 1 – receiving country factors*: socio-economic conditions in the receiving country, sectors in which migrant workers are employed; access to, and strength of, collective representation; access to, and strength of regulatory protection; social inclusion/exclusion; living on employer's premises; urban/rural location; role of unions/civil society groups, for example Church and community groups.

- *Layer 2 – migration factors*: this encompasses migration security, such as the existence of legal status in receiving country, visa or non-visa status, and whether status is tied to a contract of employment as well as the duration and conditions of right to remain. The role of recruitment agents and employers in the migration process and the treatment of migrants are also acknowledged.

- *Layer 3 – migrant worker factors*: reasons for migrating, such as socio-economic conditions in the home country and the need to send remittances home. The level of education, language and skill levels of the migrant are also important considerations as well as the availability of and access to decent work.

In terms of the extent of the problem, studies show that employing migrant labour is common and widespread, particularly in industries where non-standard, precarious employment and the use of unregulated, contingent labour is the norm (McLaren et al., 2004; McDowell et al., 2008; see also European Commission 2007; International Labour Conference 2004; WHO 2007).

Migrant workers are required to work longer and more unsociable hours than many non-migrant, full-time workers in standard employment (Loh and Richardson, 2004; Quinlan et al., 2010) with these vulnerable workers facing greater job insecurity and having access to fewer entitlements compared to those in more secure positions (Quinlan and Mayhew, 2001; Tucker, 2002; McLaren et al., 2004; Nossar et al., 2004; Siddiqui, 2006; Schenker, 2008; Goldring et al., 2009; Sargeant and Tucker, 2009). Research shows that migrant workers are frequently exposed to hazardous, life-threatening conditions and not surprisingly have higher rates of injury and illness than workers in standard employment (see McKay et al., 2006). In the US for example, while the proportion of migrant employment increased by 22 per cent between 1996–2000, the proportion of fatal work injuries for this population increased by 43 per cent, at a time when the overall number of fatal work injuries in the US declined by 5 per cent (Loh and Richardson, 2004: 42).

Having lost much of the economic and social safety net they had in their country of origin, migrant workers are often marginalised, falling between the economic and social cracks in their new country. The effect of this is that many migrants are, to a large extent, 'invisible' on many levels of society, including being overlooked in government health statistics (see Schenker, 2008). In their report, Abrahams et al. (2004: 56) note that contingent migrant workers face pervasive exclusion from the so-called 'primary' labour market and instead are concentrated in the 'secondary' labour market of mostly low-paid minorities which in turn places these groups at a distinct disadvantage in terms of income, wealth, social mobility, housing, training, participation in social life and a number of other dimensions (also see Cheung, 2006; Siddiqui, 2006). Castells (2000: 376) rightly notes that the borderline between social exclusion and daily survival is increasingly blurred for a growing number of people, including migrants. Workers in precarious employment share many labour market characteristics – poor, hazardous working conditions, low and insecure income, and so on – with migrant workers (Benach and Muntaner, 2007: 276). This has both short and longer-term health and safety consequences for these workers.

The other central theme in this research – namely cultural diversity – is complex and value laden. The examination of cultural diversity tends to be sidestepped in the OHS discourse on migrant labour and instead the focus is on other OHS explanations, such as individual behaviour or miscommunication. However, research on the influence different cultural attributes, such as communication styles and so on on OHS outcomes is mixed. On one hand there is some evidence that the junction between the migrant and the non-migrant can expose differences in attitudes, perceptions and beliefs regarding safety (Fiske, 2002). On the other hand, based on a review of published literature on the topic, Mearns and Yule (2009) conclude that there are no consistent predictors of risk-taking behaviour and safety performance across cultures. They point to Spangenbergen et al.'s (2003) study as being significant because it provided a unique opportunity to study workers of similar (yet distinct) national backgrounds involved in exactly the same tasks on the same project over the same time period. They add that although basic national values were not measured in this study, data from the cultural dimension research by Hofstede and others (see http://www.geert-hofstede.com/), would seem to indicate that Norway and Sweden share similar dimensions in terms of power-distance, masculinity and individualism, yet the safety performance of the two national groups was significantly different. Spangenbergen et al. (2003) attribute this to varying levels of planning and education between the two countries and also differences in the work compensation systems – thus revealing an intersection between national and organisational environmental/cultural factors (Mearns and Yule, 2009). It is clear, therefore, that comparing OHS differences across distinct cultures is a complicated task.

In spite of the growing interest in this research topic, examining the extent of the work-related injury and illness among the migrant worker population is still largely absent from the discourse on globalisation, which focuses primarily on trade and capital flows within specific political and economic paradigms. At the same time, those who are working on international health issues often fail to look beyond a strictly medical paradigm to consider the larger social, cultural, political and economic contexts in which health issues are embedded (CARAM Asia, 2007; Siddiqui, 2006; Lay et al., 2007). Moreover, there are a number of specific gaps in the extant research. First, most of the studies on the topic are located within a limited number of industries, namely textile and clothing manufacture, retail and call centres, which have a tradition of exploitation and tend to employ vulnerable workers, such as women and/or new migrants on a casual basis. Second, it is difficult to gauge the extent of occupational illness and injury amongst migrant workers because government databases rarely capture statistics on the occupational injury, fatalities and compensation claims of these workers. Further research is needed to determine the causal factors and to establish more rigorous measures (Tinghög et al., 2007; Anya, 2007; Lay et al., 2007; Passel, 2007; Mirsky, 2009). Finally, there is still little research on the well-being of migrant workers, particularly the psychological stress of being a foreign worker, who are frequently both isolated and subjected to exploitation.

In sum, as the literature is dispersed amongst multiple discourses, it is necessary and more useful to adopt a multidisciplinary approach in order to understand the complexities of the topic. Moreover, this project is not only about measuring the extent of work-related injuries and illnesses among migrant workers, it is also necessary to develop the methodological tools in order to give a voice to a group of vulnerable people and improve their health outcomes.

Methodological Issues

The consensus within the literature is that there is a need for a suite of effective research methods to address the methodological issues associated with migrant workers for a number of reasons. First, migrant workers are difficult to reach, the employers are often hostile to intrusion and the workforce is typically contingent, mobile and frequently hidden (McKay and Winkelmann-Gleed, 2005; Banton, 2008). Secondly, the application of orthodox single-method, survey-based, experimental, randomised, control research designs are unlikely to capture sufficient viable data on the topic, particularly in the context of the OHS of migrant labour located in the small business sector. In addition, studies in many recipient countries on new migrants are typically located within a limited number of industries, large businesses and focus on young, professional migrant workers in standard employment. Thirdly, it is difficult to gauge the extent of occupational illness and injury amongst migrant workers because government databases are frequently incompatible and data collection mechanisms rarely capture injury and illness data of precariously employed, migrant workers. The lack of data at a national level or macro level is also troubling as information is needed to develop an understanding of the larger issues and institutional context for OHS of migrant workers. Even in the absence of resources to undertake studies at a national level, investigation of the OHS of migrant workers at the micro/individual and enterprise level serves to provide an entry point for the study of the issues and, possibly, a means of pressuring government agencies to gather data at the national level. Fourthly, there are ethical implications for both the researcher and the participants of the study that need to be resolved prior to launching into fieldwork. These issues include the ethics of investigating workers who may be employed illegally. Another ethical issue arises as the research itself may change that which is being investigated. That is, by investigating the OHS culture of so-called 'invisible workers', these workers are no longer invisible and their status is changed to 'visible' (albeit vulnerable) workers. Therefore, given that the migrant workers are geographically scattered, often mobile and difficult to reach, innovative methodological approaches are required.

The methodology adopted for this study is a form of action research involving a dialectical and reflexive process (Kemmis, 2008: 595). The term 'action research', although possibly contentious, is appropriate as OHS research generally aims to improve the lives of working people by making work healthier and safer. While action research is understood as qualitative methodology, the proposed methods include both quantitative and qualitative instruments. Decisions about the appropriate method, the ways and means of collecting the data (whether qualitative or quantitative), are a part of that planning and provide information for further description and analysis. The appropriate method ensures that sufficient data are gathered so as to develop better description and analysis – and possibly a solution for the social problem being investigated.

While the limited government data on migrant workers and review of the literature will provide some of the information needed to begin the analysis, in reality, the challenge will be in obtaining field data. The difficulties in investigating OHS amongst migrant workers at a low level of abstraction are acknowledged above. These methodological issues were debated at two recent colloquia in which transcripts of the discussion reveal that there were convergent views regarding the importance of setting minimum OHS standards, yet how these standards are operationalised within small, culturally diverse workplaces generated a great deal of debate. It could be suggested that the comments at the colloquia were also shaped by the individuals' cultures and ethnicities. For example, one participant argued that it is important to first begin with research on the different ways OHS is perceived and then identify what are the influences that change the individual perceptions of OHS. His concern was that cultural differences were perceived as both good and bad. These comments reflected a research approach at an individual/enterprise level of abstraction and ideas about the social benefits of immigration. Before an investigation can begin at the individual level the factors shaping OHS for migrant workers at a structural level need to be clarified. There was consensus amongst the participants, however, that migrant workers are more likely to be located in small, subcontracting businesses in the service (particularly, hospitality, cleaning and retail), construction, manufacturing and agricultural sectors, therefore representing both rural and urban settings (Hannif and Lamm, 2005; McDowell et al., 2008).

In terms of operationalising the research, the project has been divided into three stages: (1) description; (2) analysis; and (3) planning. At the first stage, the researchers have begun to identify industry sectors and businesses within each sector where migrant workers are employed in significant numbers. Identifying and following through a cohort group of migrant workers before they leave their country of origin and within their host country as well as locating groups of migrant workers within their employment and social settings will also be a point of difference from other more orthodox approaches. The information gathered will be analysed to assess its reliability and to provide the basis for development of the second stage of the investigation, which will involve gathering field data using a range of instruments, such as semi-structured interview schedules and participant observation as well as incorporating individual narratives. The interview schedule will be constructed in such a way as to elicit as much data on the broad experiences of being a migrant worker as well as possible cases of injury or disease. The underpinning epistemology is drawn from Fuller's (2002) social epistemological approach in that while the attention on the method is important, the choice of method and how it is imposed and used on the community is equally critical. The conclusion of the second stage will occur when sufficient data are gathered to support an assessment of the OHS issues within the identified sector. The third stage is expected to involve further sectoral investigation and analysis in order to evaluate information and assess whether the sectoral analysis might be applicable to other sectors. At each stage, part of the objective is to develop contacts, techniques and models that might be used to assist investigation of OHS and migrant workers in a variety of sectors. The overall objective remains, however, to develop a holistic understanding of the issues related to OHS of migrant workers and, if necessary, to offer suggestions as to how their work situations may be made safer and healthier.

International Comparisons

To illustrate that the global diaspora of migrant workers is not only unprecedented, but that there are differences and similarities in the classification and treatment of migrant labour, examples of migrant law and key issues surrounding their employment in five countries is presented below. Although the selected counties have similar migrant categories, there are significant differences in terms of how migrant labour is perceived and the level of legal protection provided, ranging from Kuwait, which has immature migrant and employment legislation and represents one end of the spectrum, to Antipodean countries, which have more mature and liberal employment legislation, at the other end of the scale.

AUSTRALIA

Australia is a land of migrants, with 25 per cent of the current population (or 5.5 million people) originating from overseas. Between 2008 and 2009, 62 per cent of the total population growth (406,100) was accounted for by net migration (Australian Bureau of Statistics, 2009). Nevertheless, large-scale immigration has been a post-war phenomenon. After 1949, Australia made agreements with Britain, some European countries and the International Refugee Organisation to encourage levels of migration, particularly from war-torn European regions. Since that time, migration policies have been widened significantly, with the most important changes occurring after the 1970s abandonment of the notorious White Australia Policy which precluded non-whites/Europeans from obtaining long-term permanent residency and citizenship (Kelley and Schmidt, 2007).

While almost 50 per cent of the current population originating from overseas are from a European background, this figure has declined over the last decade, with an increasing number of immigrants originating from countries where English is not the first language (Australian Bureau of Statistics, 2009). In the 2008–2009 financial year, Oceania (19.0 per cent) was the largest contributor to settler arrivals followed by Europe (18.5 per cent), southern Asia (16.4 per cent), South East Asia (13.3 per cent) and North East Asia (13.3 per cent) (Department of Immigration and Citizenship [DIMC], 2009). Recent figures suggest that the fastest growth has been in migrants arriving from the Middle East and Africa, many of whom have done so as part of Australia's refugee and humanitarian programme (DIMC, 2009). These immigrants experience a number of challenges in the employment sphere, including cultural and language barriers, leading to considerable integration issues.

Overall, immigrants to Australia have mainly settled in the largest cities, currently comprising 39 per cent of the population of Sydney and 35 per cent of the Melbourne population (Australian Bureau of Statistics, 2009). Australia has a wide range of working permits. Amongst the principal working visas are those available to full-time students who are restricted to 20 hours of paid work per week although there are increasing numbers of these students working illegally (that is above the permitted 20 hours per week) due to increasing student fees and cost of living. These students often find themselves in precarious working arrangements with poor pay and conditions due to being unaware of their workplace rights or the standard award rates in their industry (Unite, 2009).

In addition, there are various employer-sponsored working visas, especially where there are identified labour shortages. An example of an employer-sponsored scheme is the Temporary Business Long Stay Visa (subclass 457) which allows an immigrant to stay in Australia between 6 months and 4 years. However, it has attracted criticism, especially from the trade union movement because of the number of cases that have emerged of exploited migrant workers who are on this scheme (Australian Manufacturing Workers Union, 2010). The cases include foreign temporary workers being paid below market rates and experiencing considerable difficulties when trying to access basic OHS rights and entitlements (Toh and Quinlan, 2009). The immigration picture in Australia is further complicated by the fact that the 160,000 migrant workers who are permitted to enter Australia annually are also accompanied by their spouses, children and elderly relatives who typically reside outside the formal labour market (Kelley and Schmidt, 2007; Miller, 1999).

While there is some concern over the number and ethnicity of immigrants to Australia, a great deal of the current public debate centres on the arrival of non-documented refugees by boats from South East Asian ports and the large numbers of people regularly overstaying their visitor visas and who are presumably working illegally. It has been estimated that as of 30 June 2009, around 48,700 people were unlawfully residing in Australia, of which approximately 80 per cent are of working age. It is also estimated that most 'over-stayers' are frequently being employed in the agriculture, forestry, fishing (fish farming), accommodation, cafes, restaurants and construction industries (DIMC, 2009b).

Except under extreme situations of hardship, new migrants to Australia are ineligible for most forms of social security payments in their first two years of domicile. It is not surprising that the employment outcomes in terms of wages and conditions of migrants from non-English speaking backgrounds are likely to be poorer compared to English-speaking non-migrants (Teicher et al., 2002). Where migrants are working illegally (that is, in contravention of their visa category) it would seem unlikely that they would access workers' compensation entitlements in the event of injury or disease in order to remain undetected by immigration authorities (Guthrie and Quinlan, 2005). Guthrie and Quinlan (2005) also report that illegal workers working in Australia are frequently exposed to unsafe work practices and are particularly prone to exploitation and violence. The debates surrounding OHS regulatory protection for migrant workers will become more prominent as Australia moves to single national approaches to both workers' compensation and general OHS laws (Purse and Guthrie, 2008).

FRANCE

The central feature in the French discourse on OHS of migrant workers is how one defines 'migrant'. At the broadest level, the National Institute of Statistics and Economic Studies (INSEE), categorises the immigrant population as those not born in France and whose parents were 'foreigners' (that is, not of French ancestry). An individual is considered as belonging to the immigrant population even if they are born in France and/or hold French citizenship. Migrants are also classified by the status of their residency and work permits. Work permits are typically issued to migrants with trade skills needed in France and restricted to a period of one year or less. Currently there are approximately 30 essential trades listed. Temporary work permits are issued to workers undertaking seasonal work for a period of three years. Seasonal workers are able to undertake contract work for no more than 6 months per job, over a period of 12 consecutive months. Other temporary work permits can be issued to workers with expertise in the sciences, or arts or sports. Similar to other EU countries, employees of foreign companies that have a branch in France can also be issued with a French work permit. Finally, foreign students are able to undertake limited periods of work while studying.

By 2005, there were approximately five million immigrants residing in France (INSEE, 2005). While most migrants (45 per cent) hail from other European countries, a significant proportion of migrants originate from the continent of Africa (39.3 per cent). Migrants from Asia make up 12.7 per cent of the migrant population and migrants from America and Oceania constitute 3 per cent of migrants in France (INSEE, 2005). There are over 2.4 million legal or document migrants workers, representing 8.6 per cent of the French labour force (INSEE, 2005). The undocumented or illegal immigrant population is huge and continues to increase. Although it is very difficult to calculate, it is estimated that the number of illegal or undocumented migrant workers entering France annually is in the region of 30,000 to 40,000 per year (Sénat, 2006). The industries with the most infringements under migrant law are the building, hospitality and agriculture sectors (Sénat, 2006).

Migrant workers are typically concentrated around the building sector (14.9 per cent), business services (10.3 per cent) and services to private individuals (15 per cent) (INSEE, 2008). Recent government reports show that generally the migrant population is more vulnerable than French nationals, with migrant unemployment rates twice that of the French domestic labour force (INSEE, 2008). Additionally, four out of ten migrants are in unskilled jobs and more than a third of women migrants are employed in part-time work (INSEE, 2008).

With regard to OHS matters, there have been a number of recent studies to show that the contingent migrant labour force in France is characterised by significant work-related health and safety problems. For example, an investigation carried out by the French government agency DARES (2009) on the working conditions of migrant workers highlights the fact that migrant workers, and in particular new migrants, are exposed to more hazardous, monotonous and isolated working conditions than the rest of the French working population. In particular, low wages and poor working conditions are prevalent among migrant labour in the building sector and among maintenance and domestic migrant workers. Specific issues for migrant workers identified in the report were also constant surveillance and communication problems.

Emerging research also indicates that migrant workers in the building industry are rarely informed of their rights under OHS and employment law and most have no idea of the correct procedures if they become injured (Berretima, 2009). Interviews with migrant workers in the building industry show that typically they are precariously employed and undertake strenuous work for little remuneration. OHS injury surveillance data indicates that migrant workers in the building industry have a higher rate of occupational injury and fatalities than French construction workers, with fatalities being higher for African workers than for European foreigners (Berretima, 2009). Finally, the rate of return to work for the migrant population after an occupational injury or disease is lower than the non-migrant population, especially in the small business sector.

KUWAIT

Currently, the population of Kuwait is almost 3 million of which 34 per cent are Kuwaitis and 66 per cent expatriate workers employed entirely in the private sector. Private sector expatriate or migrant workers come from all parts of the world and are employed in a range of occupations from oil engineers to domestic and construction workers. The labour market is divided along ethnic lines with Europeans tending to be employed in professional occupations, such as engineering, IT, logistics, human resources and education. The less skilled and manual occupations tend to be dominated by workers from Middle

Eastern, African and Asian countries, such as Egypt, Jordan, India, Syria, Pakistan, Bangladesh, Philippines, Malaysia, Korea, Nepal, China, Sudan and Ethiopia. There is also a propensity to employ workers from Muslim countries as labourers and domestic workers.

Workers in Kuwait are covered by three branches of employment law: (1) the Kuwait Public Sector Law (which covers only Kuwaiti nationals); (2) the Oil Sector Law (which applies to both Kuwaiti and Gulf nationals); and (3) Private Sector Labour Law (which applies to all migrant labour regardless of whether they work in the oil industry or other industries in private sector). On 21 February 2010 a new Private Sector Labour Law was gazetted which is designed to improve the wages and working conditions of migrant workers, *except* domestic workers (cleaners, cooks and male chauffeurs). This means that because domestic workers are not officially registered as migrant workers, they are not afforded protection under the Private Sector Labour Law. This is a significant issue given that over 36,000 migrants or 19 per cent of the migrant labour force are employed as domestic workers and that approximately 70 per cent of Kuwait households employ at least one domestic worker. Currently domestic workers can only lodge a complaint against their employer through the Department of Immigration, which in turn can refer the matter to the contract labour hire agents to deal with, or the police if the complaint involves physical or sexual violence. However, it is rare for the government agencies or labour-hire agents to support the complainant which in turn has led to growing pressure to include these workers under an amendment to the Private Sector Labour Law.

The catalyst for employment reforms in Kuwait has been the rights of migrant contingent workers, and in particular, concerns over their OHS in which international human and labour rights organisations have played a significant role. The ILO and the Kuwait authorities have had an ongoing relationship since the 1980s, resulting in the Kuwaiti Government ratifying a total of 19 ILO Conventions. However, Private Sector Labour Law has not been that effective in reducing the number of work-related injuries and fatalities among migrant workers and it is still the case that very few injured employees receive workers' compensation. Historical government statistics show that the majority of workers involved in occupational injuries and fatalities were migrants employed precariously in the construction industry (Kartam et al., 2000; Abdul-Aziz 2001; Tabtabai 2002). In 2002, on average there were 98 reported serious work-related injuries and one fatality per month the Kuwaiti construction industry (Tabtabai 2002). These figures, however, must be treated with caution as the official statistics are incomplete and unreliable due to significant under-reporting of work-related injuries and illnesses to the Kuwait Municipality, the official reporting body for all industries. In short, the exact number of work-related injuries, illnesses and fatalities in Kuwait is unknown.

Finally, there are social, cultural, legal and political constraints that impact on the OHS of migrant workers in Kuwait. Recent Kuwaiti Government's attempts to increase the Kuwaiti labour force, particularly in senior positions, has resulted in pressure to fire migrant workers or to reduce their working conditions, thus pushing migrant workers into even more marginalised, less visible and hazardous jobs than before. Moreover, while the maltreatment of migrant workers in Kuwait has received a great deal of international attention, it is very difficult to obtain reliable evidence. For example, it is very difficult to obtain interview data from migrant workers in the domestic service and construction industries where most are located, as employers will rarely give permission to interview their employees or as in the case of the construction industry, the complex web of subcontractor relationships means that it is difficult to ascertain who exactly is responsible for the health and safety of the migrant worker.

NEW ZEALAND

As with other OECD countries, New Zealand's immigration laws provide different types of work visas, covering a range of periods of stay, from temporary work visas for short periods (1–3 years duration) to permanent residency visas. Specific schemes under the temporary work visas category, namely the Transitional Recognised Seasonal Employer Scheme (TRSE) scheme and the Variation of Conditions (VoC) were created in response to scarce labour in the primary sector and allow employers to employ seasonal workers for short periods of time. Individuals who have entered the country on a student visa are also allowed to work for limited periods of time.

The 2006 census revealed that New Zealand's migrant population was 927,000, of which over one-third of the people born overseas had been living in New Zealand for four years or less (Department of Labour, 2010). Applications for residency in New Zealand have declined in the past two years by 7.5 per cent with 27,215 migrants granted residency between July 2009–Feburary 2010. In Auckland, New Zealand's largest city, over 60 per cent of the population are now migrants (Auckland City Council, 2007). While traditionally most migrants to New Zealand originated from northern Europe, especially from Great

Britain, more recently the most common countries of origin of documented migrants are the People's Republic of China, India and Samoa.

Workers from Pacific nations constitute a substantial proportion of New Zealand's labour force, with Auckland having one of the largest concentrations of Pacific Island workers in the world. Samoans constitute the largest Pacific ethnic group in New Zealand, comprising 131,103 or 49 per cent of the resident Pacific population (265,974) (Statistics New Zealand, 2010). Typically Pacific Island workers are employed in low-paid, precarious, hazardous work that often has little chance of advancement. There is also some evidence that Pacific Island workers in New Zealand are over-represented in the work-related injury and illness government statistics (Allen and Clarke, 2006). Moreover, the rate of work-related injury and illness throughout the Pacific Islands is high (Statistics New Zealand, 2008).

Casual, migrant workers also make up a significant proportion of New Zealand's primary sector labour force, with estimates of 40,000 seasonal jobs, 30,000 of which are located in the forestry and horticulture sectors, and 10,000 in sheep shearing (Timmins, 2008). Labour is mainly drawn from Pacific countries, including Vanuatu, the Solomon Islands and Vietnam and is typically employed under the TRSE and VoC schemes. Students on overseas student visas provide a supplementary source of labour, with findings indicating that many of these workers exceed the legal limit of paid work (Anderson and Naidu, 2010). Further, the paid piece work rate for seasonal work is between NZ$8 and NZ$15 per hour, although as a result of a surplus of labour last year there were reports that the labour-hire contractors were illegally paying their workers as little as NZ$6 an hour, less than half the statutory minimum wage, and were also reducing their working conditions (Ross and Rasmussen, 2009).

Not only is there disquiet over reduced wages of seasonal migrant workers but there has been ongoing concern over their health and safety, given that the primary sector has one of the highest recorded level of occupational injuries and fatalities (Department of Labour, 2009). New Zealand also has the dubious reputation of being the highest user per capita of dioxins in the world, ranging from phenoxy herbicide 2,4,5-T to pentachlorophenol (PCP) timber treatments, all of which have been linked to numerous diseases. It is unlikely, however, that seasonal migrant workers will complain to the Department of Labour or receive workers' compensation for a number of reasons. First, there is general ignorance over the regulations covering occupational health and safety and workers' rights. Secondly, the language and cultural barriers make lodging a complaint difficult for migrant workers. Thirdly, there is reluctance to report breaches of the employment law as the Department of Labour is not only responsible for enforcing the occupational health and safety regulations but is also responsible for issuing and enforcing visas. In addition, given that there are only approximately 150 occupational health and safety inspectors covering more than 500,000 business, the chance of a workplace being randomly visited by an inspector is highly unlikely (Quinlan et al., 2010). Finally, it is difficult for casual workers who work on multiple jobs and sites in a year to establish a causal link between an injury or disease and exposure to a specific work hazard that occurred at a particularly time and location. Without that link, obtaining compensation is problematic.

In sum, New Zealand represents a unique microcosm of what is occurring internationally. Unfortunately, the fate of injured migrant workers has been largely ignored by successive governments. Nonetheless, a number of trade unionists, activists and researchers are raising concerns over the fate of injured and ill migrant workers and are beginning to highlight the short-, medium- and long-term implications of ignoring the health and safety and compensation and rehabilitation issues of migrant workers.

UNITED STATES OF AMERICA

Within the United States characterising migrant workers is not particularly easy, given the heterogeneity of these workers and their dispersal across a variety of industries. Governance and jurisdictional considerations further complicate the issue, whereby individual states may be seen as more or less friendly to migrant workers, depending, for instance, on their specific immigration laws. Arizona has recently elucidated the paramount importance of state-wide governance structures to migrants by proposing Senate Bill 1070, which allows for police officers to verify the immigration status of any person who may be suspected of being an illegal immigrant, a unique authority granted to police by the state of Arizona which pertains to no other regions of the country.

Even defining the term 'migrant worker' proves difficult. For instance, those generally termed 'migrant workers' are often referred to as 'foreign workers' in the US, particularly by federal data collection agencies such as the Bureau of Labor Statistics. However, there are some data available that provide a useful picture of foreign workers in the United States. According to the Bureau of Labor Statistics, there are about 21,239,000 foreign-born workers employed in the US (this estimate is current as of March 2010) and equates to an employment rate of approximately 60.7 per cent of all foreign-born civilians. However, it is not clear to what extent these workers are employed legally or illegally. Of those employed, about 12,501,000 are males, while 8,739,000 are females. The unemployment rate for foreign-born US workers is a full percentage point higher than that for native-born workers, at 11.0 per cent as of March 2010. Although the population of foreign-born citizens is increasing (the data show a rise of over 300,000 between March 2009 and March 2010), the number of those who are employed appears to be remaining constant, thus significantly increasing the overall unemployment rate for this group over the past year (Bureau of Labor Statistics, 2010a).

The demographic information related to foreign-born workers in the US is also worth consideration as it shows that this group is widely dispersed geographically, with foreign workers constituting a significant portion of the population of each region within the US. However, there is evidence that the highest number of foreign-born workers is found in the west (24.1 per cent of the labour force as of 2008), while the midwest has the lowest relative population of foreign workers at 7.8 per cent of the labour force (Bureau of Labor Statistics, 2009). Further, there are clear distinctions between foreign and native workers when it comes to occupational choices, even though foreign workers are employed in a wide variety of industries in the US. According to the Bureau of Labor Statistics (2010b), foreign-born workers were more likely than native-born workers to be employed in traditionally blue-collar sectors such as construction, services, maintenance, production and transportation. On the other hand, native workers were more likely to occupy white collar jobs (managerial or professional positions) than those born in foreign countries (Bureau of Labor Statistics, 2010b). Finally, the educational attainment of foreign workers in the US is worth mentioning; according to the Bureau of Labor Statistics's Current Population Survey (2008), those workers who were born in foreign countries are less likely to complete high school (27.4 per cent) than those born in the US (6.0 per cent).

One of the largest immigrant groups in the US are Latinos. The Bureau of Labor Statistics (2010b) projects that Latinos will comprise 16 per cent of the US workforce by 2014, becoming the most populous minority worker group. However, over the past two decades, the rate of work-related fatalities for Latinos has exceeded the rate for all US workers by nearly 35 per cent during the period 2003–2006, and was particularly high in the construction industry (Howard, 2010). Of concern is the suspicion that there is significant under-reporting of non-fatal occupational injuries and illnesses by Latino workers and a lack of detailed data identifying the ethnicity of injured workers (Howard, 2010). In a recent summit on the OHS of Latino workers, the Director of the National Institute for Occupational Safety and Health (NIOSH) argued that one of the main reasons for the reported disparities in injury rates was due to the disproportionately high participation rate for Latinos in very hazardous, precarious employment which in turn made it difficult for government agencies to reach these workers and to enforce the health and safety regulations (Howard, 2010).

Discussion and Conclusion

By drawing on the extant literature and examples from five countries outlined above, several common themes can be identified. First, governments have tended to treat migrant labour as a disposable commodity, acquiescent in times of low unemployment and high labour shortages but punitive when there is a surplus of labour and growing rates of unemployment. It is also evident from the synopsis of immigration and employment laws and practices of each of the countries that there is a strong political and social desire to maintain homogenous populations in which the class dichotomy of migrant and non-migrant is maintained. Moreover, as illustrated in the five examples, migrant workers are over-represented in sectors that have a prevalence for precarious and hazardous employment. There is also considerable sectoral consistency across the countries, with migrant workers most often found in low-wage, blue-collar industries such as construction and manufacturing, as opposed to managerial positions.

Secondly, in spite of differences in the OHS and employment laws of each of the illustrative countries, migrant workers are significantly over-represented in the work-related injury, illness and fatality rates. The question is: 'Are the reasons for the migrant workers being over-represented in work-related injury, illness and fatality rates the same for each country?' Although there are some (albeit very rudimentary), basic legal human rights for migrant workers evident in all the examples, there are nonetheless apparent differences in the legislative sophistication and protection covering vulnerable workers, including migrant labour. At one end of the spectrum is Kuwait which is only now implementing basic workers' rights under the ILO conventions, their OHS legislation remains piecemeal, confusing and lacks universal coverage or workers' participation mechanisms. At the other extreme are the western nations – namely the US, France, Australia and New Zealand – who have had over a century of developing and refining their employment and OHS laws. In spite of the fundamental differences, the plight of migrant workers and in particular their work-related health and safety encompasses transnational political, legal, economic and social imperatives. That is, the reasons why migrant workers are driven to leave their country of origin to take up dangerous and tedious employment in foreign countries need to be included in the discussion on OHS of vulnerable workers.

Finally, research and the examples indicate that migrant workers, particularly undocumented or illegal workers, tend to operate within the so-called 'secondary' or peripheral labour market, where precarious, non-standard employment is routine and where small, subcontracting businesses are the primary employer. The theoretical explanations for this form of employment and use of labour are, of course, rooted in the discourse of labour market flexiblity and in particular the flexible firm which divides the workforce between the core workers and 'periphery' or disposable workers (Atkinson, 1984). The vigorous debate around the concepts of the flexible firm and labour market flexibility (see for example Collins, 2002), is, to a large extent, the result of the difficulties inherent in researching those 'invisible' workers on the periphery of the labour market, which in this instance comprises the OHS of migrant workers. This lack of access and visibility of migrant workers creates a number problems for both government agents and researchers. That is, what are the most effective research tools to provide an accurate picture of the extent of the problem (in particular, what are the rates of work-related injury, illness and fatality among migrant workers); how best to capture data on the working and OHS experiences of migrant workers; and how and what are the most effective ways of responding to the OHS needs of migrants workers in the immediate and long-term?

References

Abdul-Aziz, A.-R. (2001). Foreign workers and labour segmentation in Malaysia's construction industry. *Construction Management and Economics* (19): 789–798.

Abrahams, D., Haigh, F. and Pennington, A. (2004). *Policy Health Impact Assessment for the European Union: a Health Impact Assessment of the European Employment Strategy Across The European Union, Health Impact Assessment (HIA) of the European Employment Strategy*. Brussels: European Union.

Allen and Clarke Consultancy (2006). *Occupational Health and Safety in New Zealand. Technical Report Prepared for the National Occupational Health and Safety Advisory Committee: NOHSAC Technical Report 7*. Wellington: National Occupational Health and Safety Advisory Committee.

Anderson, D. and Naidu, K. (2010). The land of milk and honey? The contemporary working lives of contingent youth labour. *New Zealand Journal of Employment Relations*, 35(1): 61–79.

Anya, I. (2007). Right to health care for vulnerable migrants. *The Lancet*, 370(8): 827.

Atkinson, J. (1984). *Flexibility, Uncertainty and Manpower Management, IMS Report No. 89*. Brighton: Institute of Manpower Studies.

Auckland City Council (2007). *Auckland's Economy*. www.aucklandcity.govt.nz.

Australian Bureau of Statistics (2009). *Perspectives on Migrants*, Catalogue Number 3416.0. Canberra: Australian Bureau of Statistics.

Australian Manufacturing Workers Union (2010). website www.amwu.org.au/ campaigns, accessed 26 April 2010.

Banton, M. (2008). What the study of migration might contribute to the study of community. *International Journal of Social Research Methodology*, 11(2): 117–120.

Benach, J. and Muntaner, C. (2007). Precarious employment and health: developing a research agenda. *Journal of Epidemiology and Community Health*, 61: 276–277.

Berretima, A. (2009). The site of medical expertise: the health of immigrant workers in question. *Mouvements*, 58, May, http://www.mouvements.info/ Du-chantier-a-l-expertise-medicale.html.

Bureau of Labor Statistics (2008). *Educational Attainment of Foreign-born Labor Force*, 1 April, http://www.bls.gov/opub/ted/2008/mar/wk5/art02.htm.

Bureau of Labor Statistics (2009). *Foreign-born Workers by Region, 2008*, 31 March, http://www.bls.gov/opub/ted/2009/mar/wk5/art02.htm.

Bureau of Labor Statistics (2010a). *The Employment Situation – March 2010*. 2 April, http://www.bls.gov/news.release/archives/empsit_04022010.pdf.

Bureau of Labor Statistics (2010b). *Labour Force Characteristics by Race and Ethnicity, 2009*, http://www.bls.gov/cps/cpsrace2009.pdf.

CARAM Asia (2007). *State of Health of Migrants 2007: Mandatory Testing*. Kuala Lumpur: CARAM Asia Berhad.

Castells, M. (2000). *End of Millennium*, 2nd edn. Oxford: Blackwell.

Cheung, L. (2006). *Living on the edge: Addressing employment gaps for temporary migrant workers under the live-in caregiver program*. Masters Thesis, Simon Fraser University.

Collins, M. (2002). *Problems of Flexible Working Research and Theory in the New Economy*, European Commission's IST Programme, The Key Action II Annual Conference, http://www.cheshirehenbury.com/ebew/index.html.

DARES (2009). The working conditions of migrant workers in 2005. *Premières Synthèses*, 09/02, http://www.travail-emploi-sante-gouv.fr/IMG/pdf/2009.02-09.2.pdf.

Department of Immigration and Citizenship (2009). *Fact Sheet 2 – Key Facts in Migration*, http://www.immi.gov.au/media/fact-sheets/02key.htm, accessed 22 April 2010.

Department of Immigration and Citizenship (2009a). *Immigration Update 2008–2009*, http://www.immi.gov.au/media/publications/statistics/immigration-update/update-jun09.pdf, accessed 20 April 2010.

Department of Immigration and Citizenship (2009b). *Fact Sheet 87 – Initiatives to Combat Illegal Work in Australia*, http://www.immi.gov.au/media/fact-sheets/87illegal.htm, accessed 20 April 2010.

Department of Labour (2009). *Summary of Evaluation Findings from Recognised Seasonal Employer (Rse) Policy, First Season (2007–07)*, research@dol.govt.nz.

Department of Labour (2010). *Monthly Migration Trends February 2010*, http://www.dol.govt.nz/publications/general/monthly-migration-trends/10feb/mmt-feb10.pdf.

European Commission (2007). *Health and Migration in the EU: Better Health for All in an Inclusive Society*, http://www.insa.pt/sites/INSA/PortuguesPublicacoes/Outros/Documents/Epidemiologia/HealthMigrationEU2.pdf.

Fiske, A.P. (2002). Using individualism and collectivism to compare cultures – a critique of the validity and measurement of the constructs: comment on Oyserman et al. (2002). *Psychological Bulletin*, 128(1): 78–88.

Fuller, S. (2002). *Social Epistemology*, 2nd edn. Bloomington, IN: Indiana Univesity Press.

Goldring, L., Berinstein, C. and Bernhard, J.K. (2009). Institutionalizing precarious migratory status in Canada, *Citizenship Studies*, 13(3): 239–265.

Guthrie, R. and Quinlan, M. (2005). The occupational safety and health rights and workers' compensation entitlements of illegal immigrants: an emerging challenge, *Policy and Practice in Health and Safety*, 41–62.

Hannif, Z. and Lamm, F. (2005). When non-standard work becomes precarious: insights from the New Zealand call centre industry, *Management Review*, 16(3): 324–350.

Hofstede, G. (1991). *Cultures and Organizations: Software of the Mind*. New York: McGraw-Hill.

Howard, H. (Director) (2010). Opening Address, National Action Summit for Latino Worker Health and Safety, National Institute for Occupational Safety and Health (NIOSH), http://www.osha.gov/latinosummit/speech_drhowardcumbre_04-14-10.html.

INSEE (2005). *Studies and Analysis, Immigrants in France*, Insee références, http://www.insee.fr/fr/ppp/comm_presse/comm/hcdplmmfra05.pdf.

INSEE (2008). Studies and analyses: the activity of immigrants in 2007, *Insee Première*, 1212, October, http://www.insee.fr/fr/ffc/ipweb/ip1212/ip1212.pdf.

International Labour Conference (2004). *Towards a Fair Deal for Migrant Workers in the Global Economy*, www.ilo.org/public/standards/relm/ilc92/pdf/rep-vi.pdf.

Kartam, N.A., Flood, I. and Koushki, P. (2000). Construction safety in Kuwait: issues, procedures, problems and recommendations. *Safety Science*, 36: 163–184.

Kelley, A. and Schmidt, R. (2007). Modelling the role of government policy in post-war Australian immigration, *Economic Record*, 55(2): 127–135.

Kemmis, S. (2008). Critical theory and participatory action research, in Reason, P. and Bradbury, H. (eds) *Action Research: Participative Inquiry and Practice*, 2nd edn, pp, 121–138. London: Sage.

Lay, B., Nordt, C. and Rossler, W. (2007). Mental hospital admission rates of immigrants in Switzerland, *Social Psychiatry and Psychiatric Epidemiology*, 42: 229–236.

Loh, K. and Richardson, S. (2004). Foreign-born workers: trends in fatal occupational injuries, 1996–2001, *Monthly Labor Review*, 12(6): 42–53.

McDowell, L., Batnitzky, A. and Dyer, S. (2008). Internationalization and the spaces of temporary labour: the global assembly of a local workforce, *British Journal of Industrial Relations*, 46(4): 750–770.

McKay, S., Craw, M. and Chopra, D. (2006). *Migrant Workers in England and Wales: An Assessment of Migrant Worker Health and Safety Risks*. London: Working Lives Research Institute London Metropolitan University.

McKay, S. and Winkelmann-Gleed, A. (2005). *Migrant Workers in the East of England*. London: London Metropolitan University.

McLaren, E., Firkin, P., Spoonley, P., Dupuis, A., de Bruin, A. and Inkson, A. (2004). *At the Margins: Contingency, Precariousness and Non-standard Work*. Research Report, Massey University, Palmerston North.

Mearns, K.J. and Yule, S. (2009). The role of national culture in determining safety performance: challenges for the global oil and gas industry, *Safety Science*, 47: 777–785.

Miller, P. (1999). Immigration policy and immigrant quality: the Australian Points System, *The American Economic Review*, 89(2): 192–197.

Mirsky, J. (2009). Mental health implications of migration: a review of mental health community studies on Russian-speaking immigrants in Israel. *Social Psychiatry and Psychiatric Epidemiology*, 44(3): 179–187.

Nossar, I., Johnstone, R. and Quinlan, M. (2004). Regulating supply-chains to address the occupational health and safety problems associated with precarious employment: the case of home-based clothing workers in Australia, *Australian Journal of Labour Law*, 17(2): 1–24.

OECD (Organisation for Economic Co-operation and Development) (2007). *The Future of International Migration to OECD Countries*, http://www.iadb.org/intal/intalcdi/PE/2009/03706.pdf.

Passel, J. (2007). *Unauthorized Migrants in the United States: Estimates, Methods, and Characteristics*, Working Paper (7), OECD, www.oecd.org/els/workingpapers.

Purse, K. and Guthrie, R. (2008). Workers' compensation policy in Australia: new challenges for a new government, *Journal of Applied Law and Policy*, 99–110.

Quinlan, M. and Mayhew, C. (2001). *Evidence Versus Ideology: Lifting the Blindfold on OHS in Precarious Employment*, Working Paper, UNSW, Sydney.

Quinlan, M., Bohle, P. and Lamm, F. (2010). *Managing Occupational Health and Safety: A Multidisciplinary Approach*, 3rd edn. Sydney: Macmillan.

Ross, C. and Rasmussen, E. (2009). Chronicle: June–September 2009, *New Zealand Journal of Employment Relations*, 34(3): 92–101.

Sargeant, M. and Tucker, E. (2009). Layers of vulnerability in OHS for migrant workers: case studies from Canada and the UK, *Policy and Practice in Health and Safety*, 7(2): 51–73.

Schenker, M. (2008). Work-related injuries among immigrants: a growing global health disparity, *Occupational and Environmental Medicine*, 65(11): 717–718.

Sénat (2006). Report of the Commission on Inquiry (1) on Illegal Immigration, created by a Resolution Passed by The Senate on October 27, 2005. Report Submitted to the President of the Senate April 6, 2006. Official Journal, 7 April 2006, http://www.senat.fr/rap/r05-300-1/r05-300-11.pdf.

Siddiqui, K. (2006). *Immigrant Women in Contingent Work in Toronto: Dealing and Coping with Health Related Problems in the Workplace*, Canadian Association for the Study of Adult Education (CASAE), National Conference Online Proceedings.

Spangenbergen, S., Baarts, C., Dyreborg, J., Jensen, L., Kines, P. and Mikkelsen, K.L. (2003). Factors contributing to the differences in work-related injury rates between Danish and Swedish construction workers, *Safety Science*, 41: 517–530.

Statistics New Zealand (2008). *Claims for Work-related Injuries by Ethnic Group and Sex*, http://www.stats.govt.nz/browse_for_stats/health/injuries/injurystatistics_hotp07.aspx.

Statistics New Zealand (2010). *Demographic Trends 2009*, http://www.stats.govt.nz/Publications/PopulationStatistics/demographic-trends-2009.aspx.

Tabtabai, H.M. (2002). Analyzing construction site accidents in Kuwait, *Kuwait Journal of Science and Engineering*, 29(2): 3–15.

Teicher, J., Shah, C. and Griffin, G. (2002). Australian immigration: the triumph of economics over prejudice?, *International Journal of Manpower*, 23(3): 209–236.

Timmins, J. (2008). *Why are There so Many Short Jobs in LEED? An Analysis of Job Tenure Using LEED*. Wellington: Statistics New Zealand and Department of Labour.

Tinghög, P., Hemmingsson, T. and Lundberg, I. (2007). To what extent may the association between immigrant status and mental illness be explained by socioeconomic factors? *Social Psychiatry and Psychiatric Epidemiology*, 42: 990–996.

Toh, S. and Quinlan, M. (2009). Safeguarding the global contingent workforce? Guestworkers in Australia, *International Journal of Manpower*, 30(5): 453–471.

Tucker, D. (2002). *Precarious' Non-standard Employment – A Review of the Literature*. Wellington: Department of Labour.

UNITE (2009). *International Students in the Workplace*, http://www.unite.org.au/2009/06/26/international-students-in-the-workplace/, accessed 23 April 2010.

United Nations (2002). *International Migration Report 2002*. Department of Economic and Social Affairs, Population Division, http://www.un.org/esa/population/publications/ittmig2002/2002ITTMIGTEXT22-11.pdf.

United Nations (2006). *State of the World Population, 2006*. United Nations Population Fund, http://www.unfpa.org/swp/2006/pdf/en_sowp06.pdf.

WHO (World Health Organization) (2007). *Employment Conditions and Health Inequalities Final Report to the WHO Commission on Social Determinatants of Health (CSDH)* http://www.who.int/socialdeterminants/resources/articles/emconet_who_report.pdf.

7

Occupational Health and Safety in Organisations: Applying Amartya Sen's Capability Approach and Organisational Climate

Andrea Bernardi[1]

Introduction

This chapter, after a brief statistical analysis of occupational safety trends within Italy specifically and Europe in general, summarises different research perspectives on occupational well-being and safety. There is no doubt from the statistics that higher incidences of accidents and fatal accidents occur among non-standard workers than among standard workers. Occupational health and safety (OHS) is a key organisational priority to reduce risk and promote employees well-being.

As well as applying Amartya Sen's Capability Approach to OHS behaviours, this chapter's contribution lies in the way it introduces and discusses the role of *organisational climate* as an important mediator linking workers' contractual status (standard/non-standard, permanent/atypical[2]) with their attitudes and

---

1   Andrea Bernardi is Assistant Professor in Organisation Studies at the University of Nottingham, in service at the Chinese campus of Ningbo. He is currently Finnish Government (CIMO) Visiting Scholar at the University of Helsinki.
2   According to Eurofound: Atypical work refers to employment relationships not conforming to the standard or 'typical' model of full-time, regular, open-ended employment with a single employer over a long time span. 'Typical' work in contrast is defined as a socially secure,

behaviour in relation to safety. As such, this chapter proposes a new theoretical
methodology to deal with OHS issues, and further suggests cross-border co-
operation among social sciences in this field.

The motivation for carrying out this research lies in the official statistics on
labour safety, although these in themselves present considerable difficulties.
Any comparison between European countries becomes immediately
methodologically difficult, especially when dealing with all 27 member states.
At best, standard indexes and harmonised figures therefore have to be used
as exemplified in Figure 7.1 (fatal accidents every 100 thousand workers).

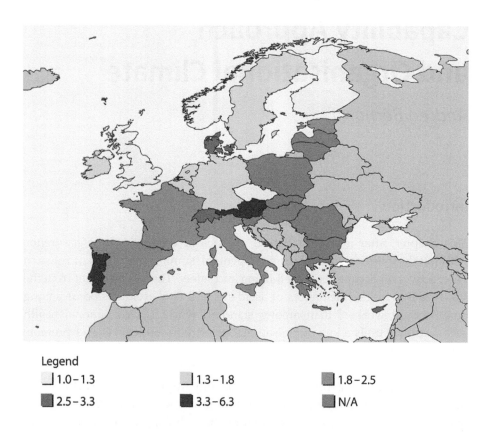

Legend

   1.0–1.3   1.3–1.8   1.8–2.5

   2.5–3.3   3.3–6.3   N/A

Figure 7.1   **Fatal accidents at work in Europe, standard impact on 100,000
workers, 2007**

Source: Eurostat (2010).

full-time job of unlimited duration, with standard working hours guaranteeing a regular
income and, via social security systems geared towards wage earners, securing pension
payments and protection against ill-health and unemployment.

As can be seen, countries are grouped into bands, identified by different shading. The safest of these countries records only 1 fatal accident per 100 thousand workers, compared with 6.3 per 100 thousand workers in the least safe place. It is notable that among the main economies, the UK and Germany outperform Italy in terms of their OHS records.

The background to this can partially be explained by the fact that, during recent years, Italy has experienced several tragic industrial accidents which have attracted the attention of the press, public opinion and policy makers alike. As a direct consequence of this poor trend, however, in 2008 the Italian Parliament reformed their health and safety law combining the many existing laws into a single act[3] and strengthened the penalties for non-observance or negligence of its stipulations to include prison sentences for employers or persons in charge of safety.

Predictably, however, this is not a simple case of Italy lagging behind the UK and Germany, as the statistics point to a much more nuanced and complicated picture. A map illustrating non-fatal accidents, for example, actually suggests that worse safety conditions exist in the UK and Germany than in Italy. Several other peculiarities can also be discerned: for instance in Italy and the UK the agricultural sector is more likely to experience accidents than that of construction, while in France precisely the opposite is true (Figure 7.2).

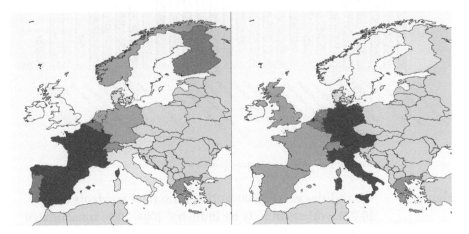

Figure 7.2   Accidents at work in Europe, agriculture and building, at least three days leave, standard impact on 100,000 workers, 2007, construction (left), agriculture (right)

Source: Eurostat (2010).

---

3   The so-called 'Testo Unico sulla salute e sicurezza sul lavoro' [Unified law on occupational health and safety].

A compiled index of disabilities and fatal accidents occurring at work in Italy, organised by industry (Figure 7.3) reveals, unsurprisingly, that banking, finance and education are the safest industries. Equally unsurprising is finding that the most 'dangerous' industries are named as being those associated with agriculture, wood and iron manufacturing. Other features are less predictable, however. The chemical, petrol, textiles and leather industries perform better than public administration (which is in fact deteriorating). Such findings strongly suggest that technology is not the only variable needed to explain risk. Safety culture (Gherardi and Nicolini, 2000, 2002), risk management and labour organisation are clearly very important as well.

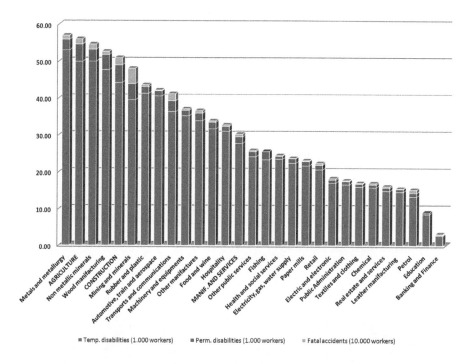

Figure 7.3   Disabilities every 1,000 workers and fatal accidents every 10,000 workers in Italy by industry, 2004–2006, consolidated averages

Source: INAIL (2010).

The relatively bad performance of public administration as illustrated in Figure 7.3 could in part be attributable to the police and armed forces being in themselves relatively dangerous jobs. Nevertheless, such linkages between safety and contractual flexibility often display consistency. For example, in Italy, the state is the largest employer of atypical workers thereby going against common assumptions.

It is against this context, mapping the variable performances of European states in OHS issues, that this chapter has the following objectives:

1.   To review the literature on risk and safety and to analyse the role of organisational climate in affecting safety.

2.   To discuss the feasibility of introducing the capability approach to organisation studies.

Safety, Risk, Well-being and Organisations

Although the general rate of occupational accidents has decreased in Italy during the last 30 years, there seems nevertheless to have been a noteworthy recent increase among atypical workers and foreign workers (typically Eastern Europeans or North Africans) in the same context. In 2008 Italy experienced about 1.140 fatal accidents and 874.866 accidents. In total this comprised one accident at work for every 23 people, but significantly also one accident at work for every 16 non-nationals.

This trend of greater risks for non-nationals is also borne out in other European locations. In Austria for example, 37 per cent of migrant workers surveyed felt affected by poor health conditions at work, compared with only 16 per cent of Austrian workers. Furthermore, some 30 per cent of migrant workers felt particularly affected by the risk of accident and injury in their workplace, compared with only 13 per cent of Austrian nationals. In Spain the statistics build a similar picture: in 2005 8.4 out of every 100,000 migrant workers died in labour accidents, a proportion in excess of that experienced by the Spanish labour force, who were said to have an accident mortality rate of 6.3 per cent (Eurofound, 2007). These findings support the contention that, not just in Italy, jobs with less contractual security are also those which also bring with them lower levels of social protection, higher risks and poorer safety standards.[4]

---

4   There is a growing debate in Italy on labour market deregulation. It seems that after 10 years
     of labour market reforms the outcome of increased job flexibility is, disappointingly, decreased

Risk, safety and well-being are complex phenomena that must be tackled at a systemic level, taking into account individual, organisational and institutional factors (Douglas, 1966; Tversky and Kahneman, 1974; Reason, 1990; Giddens, 1991; Beck, 1992; Weick and Sutcliffe, 2001, Weick, 1992; Weick and Roberts, 1993; Perrow, 1994; Gherardi, 2004; Gephart et al., 2009; James and Walters 1997; Guiol and Muñoz, 2009). Figure 7.4 illustrates this point, showing how micro-level behaviour is affected by a plurality of influences. The authors mentioned above and schematically presented in Figure 7.5 represent the most important sample of those who have addressed the risk issue academically. A large number of economic and psychological studies on the subject show how individuals calculate risk more or less rationally, both objectively and subjectively. This literature is supplemented by other research findings that stress the way that societies and governments (even in a Marxist perspective) calculate what they deem to be acceptable levels of risk. Additionally, literature within the fields of sociology and ergonomics has done much to emphasise the way technology affects modernity and has done much to illustrate how risk has become an intrinsic characteristic of modern societies.

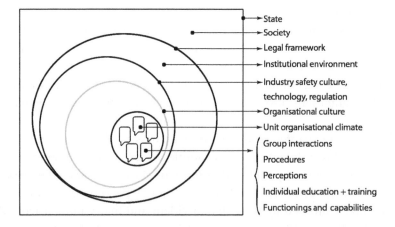

Figure 7.4   Levels of risk analysis

---

productivity and increased job insecurity. This is in line with findings by Kleinknecht, who showed that higher levels of employment flexibility such as policies dictated should be increasingly practised in Italy and other parts of the European Union did not increase productivity (Kleinknecht, 2008), although it may have increased employment (Kok, 2004). Although the issue of productivity is not tackled in this chapter, nevertheless it presents itself as an interesting field for further research, particularly if it were to be studied in a multidisciplinary perspective, integrating labour law, labour economics and organisation studies.

There is a long tradition of studies on risk and safety among social scientists.[5] In particular, much can be gleaned from the different standpoints and methodologies offered by organisation studies, which as a discipline pays much attention to the way perspectives have evolved over decades, simultaneously with broader influential changes in society, technology and economy.

Finally within organisation studies and industrial medicine, research has focused upon a more detailed and nuanced elucidation of the interrelationship between safety culture, climate[6] or workers' participation both as individual and cumulative factors contributive in helping to lower risk. A further issue, which has yet not received as much attention, would be to consider the difference between risk and uncertainty at work according to different possible perspectives such as those of Keynes, Knight or de Finetti.

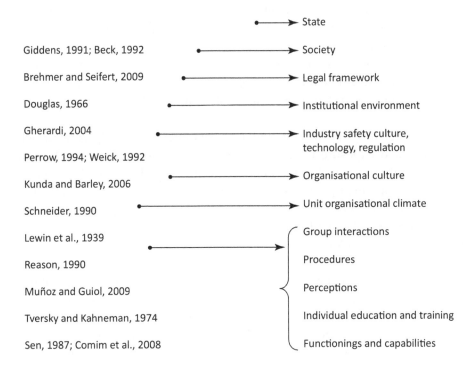

	State
Giddens, 1991; Beck, 1992	Society
Brehmer and Seifert, 2009	Legal framework
Douglas, 1966	Institutional environment
Gherardi, 2004	Industry safety culture, technology, regulation
Perrow, 1994; Weick, 1992	
Kunda and Barley, 2006	Organisational culture
Schneider, 1990	Unit organisational climate
Lewin et al., 1939	Group interactions
Reason, 1990	Procedures
Muñoz and Guiol, 2009	Perceptions
Tversky and Kahneman, 1974	Individual education and training
Sen, 1987; Comim et al., 2008	Functionings and capabilities

Figure 7.5   Levels of risk analysis, literature

---

5   A very good review is offered in the special issue on 'Organizations and Risk' of *Organization Studies*, 30/2009 issues 02 and 03.

6   Organisational climate and organisational culture are very close constructs. See for instance Denison (1996); Moran and Volkwein (1992); Kunda (1992).

With specific regard to an exploration of the connections between economic democracy (profit sharing, participation, co-operation) and occupational well-being the works of Guiol and Muñoz are particularly interesting. Their studies consider a sample of firms of different business sector and size in France and show that the organisations with the best record for safety and well-being are those where systems of workers' participation have been most actively implemented (Guiol and Muñoz, 2007, 2009). With regard to the Finnish context, a similar study has been conducted on the relationship between worker's well-being and participation (Bernardi and Köppä, 2011).

Supplementary to the available literature described in Figure 7.5 and above, this chapter explores an additional facet – the special aspect of western labour markets concerned with flexibility and atypical contractual arrangements (Amuedo-Dorantes, 2002, Barrett and Sargeant 2008) in a post-Fordism context. It would seem that any discussion of this 'non-standard' segment of the market challenges the suitability of some of the above-discussed model theoretical frameworks (risk society, post-modern society, and so on). Indeed, these frameworks alone cannot explain why in the same industry, and in the same organisation, a worker with a worse contractual status is more likely to be in jeopardy, having either more chance of being affected by occupational diseases, or increased chance of being involved in a fatal accident at work.

I consider that one way of exploring this interrelationship between job insecurity and exposure to risk at work would be to to apply the human development and capability approach formulated by Sen. This seems particularly pertinent given its intrinsic interest in freedoms and rights and its ability to discern between real and formal abilities and capabilities,[7] taking into account formal and informal institutions (De Muro and Tridico, 2008) and cultural constraints (Alkire, 2002).

This chapter postulates that, together with freedoms, rights and capabilities the role of organisational climate (Woodman and King, 1978; Waters, Batlis and Roach, 1974; Litwin and Stringer, 1968; Argyris, 1958) and culture (Schein, 2004; Kroeber and Kluckhohn, 1952; Hofstede, 1980) is highly important in affecting individual safety behaviours and performances. Furthermore,

---

7   'A functioning is an achievement, whereas a capability is the ability to achieve. Functionings are, in a sense, more directly related to living conditions, since they are different aspects of living conditions. Capabilities, in contrast, are notions of freedom, in the positive sense: what real opportunities you have regarding the life you may lead' (Sen, 1987). We can say that functioning means the act of function, capability instead being the ability plus the real condition and the freedom to use our own ability.

the way individuals and groups perceive risk can be variously influenced by organisational climate, by group leaders, by interactions, and by structures and cultures within organisations. As the climate influences the attitudes of workers and managers towards risks and helps to determine the conditions of well-being at work (Lewin et al., 1939; Schneider, 1990; Kunda and Barley, 2006), it seems logical to combine the capability approach and the organisational climate as theoretical tools to further examine certain trends and behaviours in the relationship between atypical workers and OHS.

INDIVIDUAL BEHAVIOUR, GROUPS AND SAFETY

Danger is evaluated by individuals not rationally but through filters of perception (Clarke, 1999). The difference between the real (or objective) risk and the perceived (thus subjective) risk is significant because the danger increases if individuals underestimate the real risk. The discrepancy between subjective and objective risk is taken into account in the theory of safety and in the theory of cognitive dissonance. In all cases, the organisational climate plays a role at the individual and group level in identifying and assessing risk.

Organisations can reduce the dissonance by acting on individuals: borrowing neo-institutional terminology, it is possible to influence safety behaviours with normative, cognitive and regulatory actions. The employee – a professional or a manual labourer (white or blue collar) – should be oriented by the organisation and other institutions in its behaviours or attitudes by communicating and explaining what is required to do (regulative), what is appropriate to do (normative), or what is right to do (cognitive). Attempts to change perceptions often encounter strong resistance, since these are the result of processes of self-learning and reinforcement.

The arguments, so far, have highlighted how perceptions influence the subjective cognition of danger and hence individual behaviour. From a systemic perspective it is also necessary to analyse the consequences that the individual perception of risk has on the behaviour of others. In particular, it is important to take into consideration the risk perceptions of executives and entrepreneurs, which are reflected in both the organisational climate and in the labour organisation. Furthermore, the socialising of experiences and perceptions increases both the quality and quantity of group assumptions. Group cohesion makes the socialisation even stronger, amplifying the effects. Safety culture is also built on training risk perceptions and on sharing cognitive elements (Roth et al., 2006; Payne and Mansfield, 1978).

ORGANISATIONAL CLIMATE AND SAFETY

Climate analysis and capabilities' development can be considered tools for OHS prevention: initially this chapter will consider the importance of climate, taking as axiomatic that organisational culture is the broader environment where climate develops.

There is a large literature on organisational climate (Lewin et al., 1939; Schneider, 1975, 1990) and several studies on safety climate in particular (Nasurdin et al., 2006; Johnstone and Johnston, 2005; Vaananen et al., 2004; Neal et al., 2000; Miceli and Near, 1985; Zohar, 1980). There are no major studies, however, on the relationship between safety, climate (in a broad, general, sense) and organisational well-being. In this section I will try to explain how the general climate and well-being can influence safety conditions and the level of objective risk.

The reality is a complicated one. Climatic elements can even promote, for instance, a no-blame approach (most easily exemplified via the airline industry). Some organisational cultures, in contrast (for example those developed around productivity stress or cocky and macho behaviours) may instead encourage the spread of assumptions without explicit managerial direction, which is particularly dangerous when linked to safety.

A useful means of highlighting the power of these different organisational climates would be to consider policies towards whistle-blowing, beyond the protection provided by the law for workers reporting illegal offences. In this context, it is important that internal mechanisms should permit employees to communicate sensitive information to top management or authorities in confidence. Organisations need to develop policies and tools to facilitate whistle-blowing, and above all, they have to foster a climate that encourages those behaviours and identifies them as safe and morally right. Judicial protection alone may not provide sufficient incentive.

The relationship between climate and safety therefore seems sensible, even self-evidential, and has already been studied in the literature. An organisation's success or failure can thus depend on its organisational climate. What is not explained, however, is how job insecurity varies amongst different categories of worker. How is it possible that a given job in a given factory is statistically more dangerous for non-standard and alien workers than for their so-called 'standard' counterparts? Some possible reasons readily present themselves (the dynamics of the underground economy, the propensity to assign harder tasks for weaker workers, and so on), but this phenomenon still lacks scientific analysis.

Figure 7.6   Contractual arrangement, climate, capabilities and behaviour

In Figure 7.6 I try to explain how the contractual arrangement influences behaviour and, in turn, safety performance: naturally contractual arrangements confer different status within organisational climate. The organisational climate is a mediator between individuals and the collective cognitive phenomena. It can amplify or limit the individual perceptions of risk. The climate can allow colleagues with full contractual rights to ask their atypical co-workers to be allocated the most risky, unsafe, unpleasant or stressful tasks. The climate can help the individual to define subjective risk and it can influence the group appraisal of objective risk.

To further elucidate this analysis the capability approach can be usefully applied. Given that the phenomenon described in this chapter is one mainly based on differential access to rights, since an employment contract is mostly an issue of rights and duties, it is my contention that the capability approach can supply a useful tool to dissect and understand the complex interrelationship between rights, well-being and safety.

The Capability Approach and Organisations

The Capability Approach (CA) was introduced by Amartya Sen in 1988, ten years before he received the Nobel Prize. Since then, the approach has been widely used among scholars of many disciplines, but mainly amongst those studying national or regional level phenomena. The main idea of this school stresses the need for both researchers and policy makers to look at capabilities, rather than merely consider economic data or formal legal systems (Fukuda-Parr, 2003; Sen, 1994). Equality and development should be pursued, Sen has argued, through capabilities that encapsulate notions of freedom and real opportunities regarding the desired life. Capabilities as defined by Sen are enabled by rights and functionings (in our case education, safety, health, and so on). The well-being of citizens and the development of nations rely on capabilities and real equality of opportunity and not on GDP per capita, which has sometimes been the principal measure of assets, or equality of resources, or primary goods as suggested by Dwarkin (2000) or Rawls (1972).

Currently, the capability approach is used by researchers with different educational backgrounds involving many fields of study, including economics, anthropology, philosophy, political science, psychology, education science, health studies, welfare and public policy. There are also studies on labour, welfare and happiness, with a micro – or macro – economic emphasis. There have been no applications to organisational studies, however. Traditional applications (as illustrated in Figure 7.7) have seen policy makers and researchers concentrating upon human development indicators, rather than on growth or economic development.

In a liberal and pluralistic view of individual ambitions and well-being, scholars utilising the CA believe that the state should grant citizens freedoms and opportunities to achieve certain essential 'rights' or functionings (health, education, safety, for instance). Given a personal set of functionings, human beings should then be able to pursue their own selected goals for well-being, thanks to their own capabilities. A given set of functionings can be defined as the creation of an environment that allows positive pluralistic opportunities for citizens to both be and behave. It provides a context in which there is freedom and there is real (not merely formal) equality of opportunity. Furthermore, once citizens are placed in such an environment they are given the possibility to acquire some capabilities and to use them autonomously in their own lives. Participation could well be considered as a functioning referring to workers' participation as well as the more traditional interpretation focussing on political participation.

A study of human development differs from other examinations of liberal frameworks of equality (see for instance those examined by Rawls or Dwarkin) because it does not focus on equality in terms of the rule of law or on access to primary goods or resources. Human development instead concentrates on the equal ability of citizens to pursue well-being in the context of all the cultural or social constraints on human development. It is worth noting that researchers of this school frequently also focus on economic development, but they believe that economic development is a consequence of human development, not its cause.

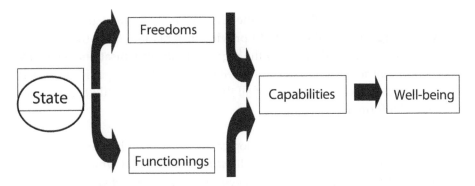

Figure 7.7   Capability approach and human development at a regional level

So far, the areas where the CA has been mostly developed are the analysis of human development at national or regional level (Sen, 1985a; Comim et al., 2008); the analysis of well-being and local development (Alkire, 2002); the study of the conditions of the poor in developing countries; the development itself (Klasen, 2000; Qizilbash, 2002); the measurement of poverty and welfare in advanced economies; the study of the difficulties of disabled people; the study of gender discriminations (Sen 1985b; Robeyns 2003; Costantini and Monni, 2008; Nussbaum, 2000) and the analysis of public policies (Schokkaert and Van Ootegem, 1990).

To the extent that organisational studies deals with the individual and collective welfare of workers, the development of their potential contribution, the understanding of the exchange of contributions and incentives, cultural diversity, the psychological components of organisational behaviour and with fairness, justice and change, the CA seems to offer an original opportunity for researchers. Perhaps surprisingly however, although this framework has been widely used, it has not been applied within organisational studies – yet its usefulness is immediately apparent. Rather than consider OHS, matters such as formal obligations, legal formalities or the presence of safety tools (hard hats and extinguishers for instance), it is perhaps more useful instead to focus on capabilities (the real abilities of workers to protect themselves) and on their freedom to request safe environments and proper procedures. This represents the measure of the potency of workers to affect or assume change within their working environments. Understanding the capabilities of atypical workers in this way, by locating them within their various organisational climates, therefore provides a tangible means of understanding how contractual insecurity turns into risk and helps explain why foreign workers are in greater danger where they lack education, language skills and rights.

In this chapter I explain how the CA can be combined together with analysis of organisational climate to provide insights into OHS trends at the organisational level. Shifting from the regional to the organisational level, the most important institution is no longer the state, but the organisation itself, given the importance and the role of all the other institutions (ILO, 2004), both formal and informal.

Figure 7.8 illustrates the methodological framework with reference to OHS and one specific capability which I call *safety capability* and which I define as *the worker's attitude to self-protection through the understanding of safety procedures, the proper assessment of the objective risk and the freedom to ask the organisation to respect the law and to implement safe work processes*[8] *fitting the environmental and technological context.*[9]

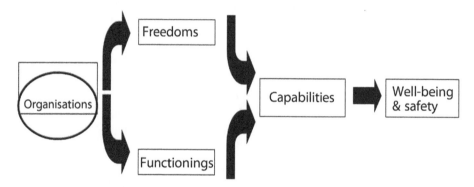

Figure 7.8   Capability approach and organisational development at the organisational level

Some preliminary studies (Bernardi 2009, 2010) have been conducted with this methodology. The empirical findings were interesting. In the workplace it seems that workers' capabilities are activated by particular functionings, namely autonomy, trade union rights, occupational well-being, organisational equity, labour rights and workers' safety awareness. As in Sen's original application, functionings need a general context of freedom in order to flourish.

To assess workers' human development (meaning the development of their functioning and capabilities), however, one needs to place them in the context of organisational development. This re-orientation recognises the importance of organisational development as the primary means of fostering both individual

---

8   Drury (1983).
9   Collinson (1999).

and collective well-being at work. Human development, in contrast, tends to be a more useful lens via which to analyse the economic and social development of a nation or region.

CAPABILITY APPROACH AND SAFETY

Sen introduces the idea that the satiation of basic needs is a means to ensure positive rights or to improve the ability of individuals to exercise their rights of freedom in different areas, ranging from the social to the political and economic. Sen tries to analyse and measure these individual achievements and values by focusing his research on what people are theoretically able (or, to use his term, capable) to do because of the context in which they exist, rather than focusing on the tangible economic opportunities offered to them through disposable income, consumption or spending. This analytical framework therefore measures not only earnings, property and consumption but individual self-esteem, the way an individual is regarded by the community and their well-being in the workplace (for the purposes of this chapter, organisational climate and OHS). In short, this model gives more emphasis to the well-being of individuals and to their satisfaction of feeling fully realised as human beings. These intangible conditions are harder to measure than national product, per capita income, or a nation's endowment of infrastructure. According to Sen, the capabilities of individuals to achieve what they aspire to match with freedom: the freedom to do what you want in a context of 'equality of opportunities'.

The capabilities' framework is based on two concepts: freedom and valuable beings and doings. Sen managed to summarise both terms into a single expression, *functionings*. This encapsulates what every person is able to obtain and to achieve during his lifetime, in Sen's terminology their 'doings' and 'beings'. But how can we achieve these *states of being*? At this point, Sen develops a path based on individual capabilities. According to him, the capabilities of a person depend on a variety of factors, including personal and social assets (that is, what the social conditions of individuals are and how society handles it). Every person, according to Sen, has a set of basic and general *capabilities*, which is one of the several possible combinations of functionings that he is able to achieve. The basic capabilities refer to the freedom to do whatever is necessary to escape from a state of poverty. This model has become crucial for the analysis of poverty, and more generally, to analyse well-being (quality of life) (for example, Nussbaum and Sen, 1993). 'General capabilities' are described as growing in a pleasant and healthy environment and refer to physical and mental health, education and knowledge, social relations and interactions, physical and moral well-being (Sen, 1983). The basic idea is that the abilities of individuals are linked to their actual freedom to be whatever they want and to achieve what they aspire to: that is 'what are the real opportunities you have to live as you want' (Sen, 1987). Freedoms are closely related to functionings which are what you absolutely need to carry out your own capabilities (Figure 7.7).

In this view, the capability approach can be used with regard to the development of individuals that are part of an organisation (see Figure 7.8). In particular, we look at the conditions that an organisation can provide to foster safety capability as defined above. Organisational freedoms refer to trade union rights, the respect of employment rights and freedom of association among workers. These freedoms underpin the functionings, relating to health and safety, that have already been identified earlier in this chapter: general organisational climate, safety compliance attitudes, well-being at the workplace, autonomy, participation, proper training, equity and the general respect of rules.

It is my contention, based on the existing and above mentioned literature on health, safety and risk at work, that this combination of functionings is the root of safety capability: namely a complex tacit knowledge acquired by the worker that allows him to understand the importance of safety standards, to demand respect for rules, to limit the divergence between objective and subjective risk evaluation and independently, if necessary, to take own measures to ensure his individual, group and organisational safety.

Possible Applications

This chapter aims to put forward a new tool for OHS analysis. To do so, I have proposed a new means of measurement, one that takes into account both the climate of organisational units and the capabilities of workers. The capabilities framework enables us to understand that human beings are fully able to exercise their rights, to express their personality, to achieve personal satisfaction only if they can rely on an endowment of skills, suitable physical and moral conditions (Herzberg, 1959), or knowledge. It is ineffective to know your rights if you are not able to make a full use of them. To give an example at national level, Sen would argue that nothing is achieved by allowing under-privileged black citizens in the USA formal political rights unless they feel enabled and motivated to vote. Similarly, the presence of a university in a town is of no value to women if the local culture prevents them from studying there. In the same way, the full benefit of having purchasing power is undermined by poor education if this leads to the consumption of junk food and a consequently lower life expectancy.

Following this line of argument, it is not enough for a worker to simply be aware of a safe procedure, especially if he is part of an organisation that fosters risky behaviours, either formally or informally. Awareness of risk may not lead to the adoption of safe procedures in the face of a challenging climate and the negative attitudes of colleagues, managers or groups. A positive circumstance would be one where the employee enjoyed a condition of freedom and well-being. In this context, organisational well-being is a necessary condition in order for the worker to be able to protect himself from risks. Freedom, which generally speaking suggests a condition of equity and the respect of rules, creates a situation whereby workers feel at liberty to call for safe tasks and procedures. Freedom is also the ability to make full use of a proper level of autonomy where the procedures are objectively hazardous or where it is necessary to intervene in order to avoid an accident. Finally, freedom implies that a worker may denounce violations of rules and proper procedure and illegal conditions without having to fear serious personal consequences.

Within a context of well-being, in a lawful environment where there is respect for safety rules, it is possible to reduce the cognitive dissonance between subjective and objective risks. Organisations should promote awareness and risk assessments that are reasonably objective (Neal et al., 2000). On the other hand, some organisational cultures may instead promote risky assumptions concerning processes, rules, procedures and safety-related behaviours.

Short-term and atypical workers, foreign citizens or illegal workers usually have little freedom, social security, education, psychological confidence, autonomy or bargaining power. That is why such workers have to fight against false assumptions, if they are to refuse to undertake excessively dangerous tasks or challenge the perception of risk within the organisational unit: factory, office, shop, small firm or complex organisation. Furthermore, the social interactions and organisational behaviour of employees, who are not fully free, either in terms of employment contract or in terms of evaluating skills, entail risk. The social construction of reality (Berger and Luckmann, 1966) among citizens who are not free or workers who are not skilled is risky.

Education, safety awareness, participation and the active use of civil and trade union rights give to any employee the capacity to take advantage of the available opportunities. It is the comparative lack of access to these that creates a situation of greater risk among foreign workers and non-standard workers. Further empirical studies could usefully study the relationship between safety attitudes (a capability), the organisational climate and the labour employment status (intended and measured both as functionings). Respondents would manifest their level of agreement with propositions on a Likert Scale. Sociodemographic information and health confidential data, anonymously coupled with each questionnaire, could be collected. The functionings could be measured from the questionnaire and from data on health conditions and safety history obtained from the employer and from national authorities.

The hypothesis that the safety capability of workers (dependent variable) depends on functionings (predictors, independent variables) could then be tested using a linear regression. At that point it would be possible to say whether the safety climate, the quality of work, the general respect for rules and the job stability and other possible factors are useful indicators to ensure that safety standards are understood and respected by workers with a proper attitude towards risk.

Conclusions

Going back to the original research question posed in this chapter, my purpose was to demonstrate that in OHS the overall organisational climate influences safety behaviours. Organisational studies can be very useful in dealing with safety at work, not least as it is clear that labour organisation and safety climate do matter; as evidenced in Figure 7.3. Using a complex definition of safety prevention skills and a broader definition of well-being, it is clear that not only the safety climate but the entire general climate within an organisation influences OHS-related behaviours.

Moreover, the aim of this piece was to introduce the capability approach to organisational studies researchers. In my view, this study has revealed no incompatibilities between this approach and the general theoretical framework of organisational studies. Indeed, it is hoped that this work will show how Amartya Sen's framework can be applied in the field of organisational studies by addressing not only issues of well-being and safety but also by using it throughout the array of existing research interests and methodologies. Finally, by combining these two approaches, this chapter should be seen as contributing to debates on economic democracy, not least with regard to the relationship that can be clearly mapped between workers' rights and participation and their occupational health.

References

Alkire S. 2002. *Valuing Freedoms: Sen's Capability Approach and Poverty Reduction*, Oxford: Oxford University Press.

Amuedo-Dorantes C. 2002. 'Work safety in the context of temporary employment: the Spanish experience', *Industrial and Labor Relations Review*, 55, 262–285.

Argyris C. 1958. 'Some problems in conceptualizing organizational climate: a case study of a bank', *Administrative Science Quarterly*, 501–520.

Barrett B. and Sargeant M. 2008. 'Health and safety issues in new forms of employment and work organization', *International Journal of Comparative Labour Law and Industrial Relations*, 24, 243–261.

Beck U. 1992. *Risk Society: Towards a New Modernity*, Thousand Oaks, CA: Sage.

Berger P.L. and Luckmann T. 1966. *The Social Construction of Reality*, Garden City, NY: Doubleday and Co.

Bernardi A. 2009. *Job safety and well-being in organizations. The climate, capabilities and functionings as tools for analysis and prevention*, doctoral dissertation in Italian, University of Milan, Bicocca.

Bernardi A. 2010. Studying occupational health and safety using the capability approach at organisational level. *Proceedings of Health and Safety and Vulnerable Workers in a Changing World of Work*, June 2010, London: Middlesex University.

Bernardi A. and Köppä T. 2011. 'Co-operatives as better working places. The Finnish case in a comparative organisational climate analysis', *The International Journal of Co-operative Management*, special issue on Finland, 5(2).

Brehmer W. and Seifert H. 2009. 'Sind atypische Beschäftigungsverhältnisse prekär? Eine empirische Analyse sozialer Risiken', *Zeitschrift für Arbeitsmarktforschung*, 4, 501–531.

Clarke S. 1999. 'Perceptions of organizational safety: implications for the development of safety culture', *Journal of Organizational Behavior*, 20, 185–198.

Collinson D.L. 1999. 'Surviving the rigs: safety and surveillance on North Sea oil installations', *Organization Studies*, 20(4), 579–600.

Comim F., Qizilbash M. and Alkire S. (eds) 2008. *The Capability Approach*, Cambridge: Cambridge University Press.

Costantini V. and Monni S. 2008. 'Environment, human development and economic growth', *Ecological Economics*, 64(4), 867–880.

De Muro P. and Tridico P. 2008. 'The role of institutions for human development', XX EAEPE Conference, Roma Tre University.

Denison D.R. 1996. 'What is the difference between organizational culture and organizational climate? A native's point of view on a decade of paradigm wars', *The Academy of Management Review*, 21(3), 619–654.

Douglas M. 1966. *Purity and Danger*, London: Ark Paperbacks.

Drury G.C. 1983. 'Task analysis methods in industry', *Applied Ergonomics*, 14, 19–28.

Dwarkin R. 2000. *Sovereign Virtue: The Theory and Practice of Equality*, Cambridge, MA: Harvard University Press.

Eurofound 2007. *Employment and Working Conditions of Migrant Workers*, Dublin: Eurofound.

Fukuda-Parr S. 2003. 'The human development paradigm: operationalizing Sen's ideas on capabilities', *Feminist Economics*, 9(2/3), 301–317.

Gephart R.P. Jr, van Maanen J. and Oberlechner T. 2009. 'Organizations and risk in late modernity', *Organization Studies*, 30(02 and 03), 141–155.

Gherardi S. 2004. 'Translating knowledge while mending organizational safety culture', *Risk Management: An International Journal*, 6(2), 61–80.

Gherardi S. and Nicolini D. 2000. 'To transfer is to transform: the circulation of safety knowledge', *Organization*, 7(2), 329–348.

Gherardi S. and Nicolini D. 2002. 'Learning the trade: a culture of safety in practice', *Organization*, 9(2), 191–223.

Giddens A. 1991. *Modernity and Self-identity*, Cambridge: Polity Press.

Guiol P. and Muñoz J. 2007. 'Management, participation et santé des salariés: des médecins et des salariés parlent' [Management, participation and employees' health: dialogues of doctors and employees], *RECMA*, 304, 76–96.

Guiol P. and Muñoz J. 2009. *Management des entreprises et santé des salariés*, Rennes: Presse Universitaires de Rennes.

Herzberg F. 1959. *The Motivation to Work*, New York: John Wiley and Sons.

Hofstede G.H. 1980. *Culture's Consequences – International Differences in Work-Related Values*, London: Sage Publications.

ILO 2004. *A Promotional Framework for Occupational Safety and Health*, Report 93 IV (1), Geneva: ILO.

James P. and Walters D. 1997. 'Non-union rights of involvement: the case of health and safety at work', *Industrial Law Journal*, 26(1), 33–48.

Johnstone A. and Johnston L. 2005. 'The relationship between organizational climate, occupational type and workaholism', *New Zealand Journal of Psychology*, 34(3), 181–188.

Klasen S. 2000. 'Measuring poverty and deprivation in South Africa', *Review of Income and Wealth*, 46, 33–58.

Kleinknecht A. 2008. The impact of labour market deregulation on jobs and productivity: empirical evidence and a non-orthodox view. EAEPE Annual Conference, University of Roma Tre, 6–8 November, Rome.

Kok W, 2004. *Facing the Challenge. The Lisbon Strategy for Employment and Growth.* Report from the High Level Group, chaired by Wim Kok. Luxembourg: Office for Official Publications of the European Communities.

Kroeber A. and Kluckhohn C. 1952. *Culture*, New York: Meridian Books.

Kunda G. 1992. *Engineering Culture. Control and Commitment in a High-Tech Corporation*, Philadelphia, PA: Temple University Press.

Kunda G. and Barley S.R. 2006. *Gurus, Hired Guns, and Warm Bodies: Itinerant Experts in a Knowledge Economy*, Princeton, NJ: Princeton University Press.

Lewin K., Lippitt R. and White R. 1939. 'Patterns of aggressive behavior in experimentally created social climates', *Journal of Social Psychology*, 10, 271–299.

Litwin G. and Stringer R. 1968. *Motivation and Organizational Climate*, Cambridge, MA: Harvard University Press.

Miceli M.P. and Near J.P. 1985. 'Characteristics of organizational climate and perceived wrongdoing associated with whistle-blowing decisions', *Personnel Psychology*, 38, 525–544.

Moran E.T. and Volkwein J.F. 1992. 'The cultural approach to the formation of organizational climate', *Human Relations*, 45(1), 19–47.

Nasurdin A.M., Ramayah T. and Beng Y.C. 2006. 'Organizational structure and organizational climate as predictors of job stress: evidence from Malaysia', *International Journal of Commerce and Management*, 16(2), 116–129.

Neal A., Griffin M.A. and Hart P.M. 2000. 'The impact of organizational climate on safety climate and individual behaviour', *Safety Science*, 34, 99–109.

Nussbaum M.C. and Sen A. (eds) 1993. *The Quality of Life*, Helsinki: Helsinki United Nations University, Wider, Helsinki.

Nussbaum M.C. 2000. *Women and Human Development: The Capabilities Approach*, Cambridge: Cambridge University Press.

Payne R. and Mansfield R. 1978. 'Correlates of individual perceptions of organizational climate', *Journal of Occupational Psychology*, 51, 209–218.

Perrow C. 1994. 'Accidents in high risk systems', *Technology Studies*, 1(1), 1–20.

Qizilbash M. 2002. 'A note on the measurement of poverty and vulnerability in the South African context', *Journal of International Development* (14), 757–772.

Rawls, J. 1972. *A Theory of Justice*, Oxford: Oxford University Press.

Reason J. 1990. *Human Error*, Cambridge: Cambridge University Press.

Robeyns I. 2003. 'Sen's capability approach and gender inequality: selecting relevant capabilities', *Feminist Economics*, 9(2–3), 61–92.

Roth E.M., Multer J. and Raslear T. 2006. 'Shared situation awareness as a contributor to high reliability performance in railroad operations', *Organization Studies*, 27(7), 967–987.

Schein E. 2004. *Organizational Culture and Leadership*, New York: Wiley Publishers.

Schneider B. 1975. 'Organizational climate: an essay', *Personnel Psychology*, 28, 447–479.

Schneider B. 1990. *Organizational Climate and Culture*, San Francisco: Jossey-Bass.

Schokkaert E. and van Ootegem L. 1990. 'Sen's concept of the living standard applied to the Belgian unemployed', *Recherches Economiques de Louvain*, 56 (3–4), 429–450.

Sen A.K. 1983. 'Development: which way now?', *The Economic Journal*, 93, 745–762.

Sen A.K. 1985a. 'A sociological approach to the measurement of poverty: a reply to prof. Peter Townsend', *Oxford Economic Papers*, 37(4), 669–676.

Sen A.K. 1985b. *Commodities and Capabilities*, Amsterdam: North Holland.

Sen A.K. 1987. *The Standard of Living*, Cambridge: Cambridge University Press.

Sen A.K. 1994. Growth economics: what and why? In: Pasinetti L. and Solow R.M. (eds), *Economic Growth and the Structure of Long-Term Development*, p. 560. London: Macmillan.

Tversky A. and Kahneman D. 1974. 'Judgement under uncertainty: heuristics and biases: biases in judgments reveal some heuristics of thinking under uncertainty', *Science*, 185, 1124–1131.

Vaananen A., Kalimo R., Toppinen-Tanner S., Mutanen P., Peiro J.M., Kivimaki M. and Vahtera J. 2004. 'Role clarity, fairness, and organizational climate as predictors of sickness absence', *Scandinavian Journal of Public Health*, 32, 426–424.

Waters L.K., Batlis N. and Roach D. 1974. 'Organizational climate dimensions and job-related attitudes', *Personnel Psychology*, 27, 465–476.

Weick K.E. 1992. 'The collapse of sense making in organizations: The Mann Gulch disaster', *Administrative Science Quarterly*, 38(4), 628–652.

Weick K.E. and Roberts K. 1993. 'Collective mind in organizations: heedful interrelating on flight decks', *Administrative Science Quarterly*, 38(3), 35–381.

Weick K.E. and Sutcliffe K. 2001. *Managing the Unexpected*, San Francisco: Jossey-Bass.

Woodman R.W. and King D.C. 1978. 'Organizational climate: science or folklore?', *The Academy of Management Review*, 3(4), 816–826.

Zohar D. 1980. 'Safety climate in industrial organizations: theoretical and applied implications', *Journal of Applied Psychology*, 12, 96–102.

8

The Health of Vulnerable Workers in Italy

Carlo Lucarelli and Barbara Boschetto[1]

Introduction

Increased focus of European policies on safety at work has led the EU to introduce legislative measures aimed at improving health protection in the workplace. Community strategy on health and safety at work 2002–2006 translated the entire regulatory structure developed in previous years into a framework law designed to implement in full the efforts made in this field through a significant improvement of conditions in the workplace (European Commission 2002). The strategy was based on adapting to the transformations in progress both in work and society. Various innovative features characterised this new European strategy compared to the mechanisms in place up to that time:

- promoting a global approach to well-being in the workplace that took into account ongoing changes in employment and the emergence of new risks (such as those of a psychosocial nature);

- consolidating a culture of risk prevention through various available strategic instruments (legislation, best practices, social dialogue, economic incentives);

---

1   Carlo Lucarelli, statistician and researcher in Istat (National Institute of Statistics) since 1997, is involved in methodological topics regarding the Labour Force Survey. Barbara Boschetto, graduated in social sciences, has worked at Istat (the Italian National Institute of Statistics) since 2002, at Labour Force Survey.

- facilitating the establishment of partnerships between operators in the fields of health and work safety;

- adopting an economic perspective towards the evaluation of costs arising from persistently high levels of poor safety in the workplace.

For this purpose, in selecting the issues to be investigated in detail through subject-specific modules in the labour force survey questionnaire in every Member State of the EU, Eurostat decided that for 2007 an ad hoc module on occupational accidents and work-related diseases should be included. This would make it possible to add to information from administrative sources such as the European Statistics on Accidents at Work (ESAW) and the European Occupational Diseases Statistics (EODS) alongside data from a reliable source such as the Labour Force Survey (LFS) in order to evaluate the effects of the strategy in force in the preceding five-year period as well as the baseline scenario in relation to the new 2007–2012[2] strategy on which the European Union was about to embark.

Consequently, in the second quarter of 2007 the LFS questionnaire included a supplementary section on *Health and safety in the workplace* (European Commission 2006). This module enabled them to collect information on aspects such as accidents at work, health problems caused or aggravated by occupational activity and the exposure of workers to health risk factors.[3]

Data from administrative sources indicate that in recent years accidents at work are slowly but gradually decreasing (INAIL 2008). Conversely, the number of workers suffering from health problems appears extremely high, as in particular does the number of those who for a variety of reasons perceive their workplace as unsafe. LFS sheds light on these latent, distressing and common below the surface aspects of the labour market, albeit through an occasional questionnaire.

---

2   Refer to European Commission (2007). For the first time, the strategy introduces the quantification of expectancy and sets the target of reducing accidents through the adoption of various instruments by 25 per cent.

3   In 1999 an ad hoc module was included in the then Quarterly Labour Force Survey. The results obtained from the module were unreliable and cannot be correlated with the current module due to differences in definitions and the questions asked.

Precarious Work and Health and Safety

Precarious work conditions are common in our working culture. The first half of the twentieth century was strongly marked by a struggle of the workforce to gain job security and control (Lewchuk et al. 2003), which finally resulted in huge improvements in working conditions. But the sustained recession of the 1980s and early 1990s, with its substantial privatisation and the development of new technologies, has led to a shift towards the recreation of a 'flexible workforce' by recruitment with temporary contracts or the outsourcing of many functions. Outsourcing, as well as subcontracting and the use of private employment agencies, increases the prevalence of non-standard forms of employment (Blum and Balke 2006).

Many researches indicate that changes to work organisation associated with outsourcing adversely affect occupational safety and health (OSH) for outsourced workers as well as for those who remain at a company (Mayhew and Quinlan 1999). Temporary workers are more often exposed to adverse conditions in their physical work environment, such as noise, painful and tiring positions and repetitive movements. They have also less control over working times, often work in less skilled jobs and have less insight into their work environment, mainly due to a lack of training (Benach et al. 2000, European Foundation for the Improvement of Living and Working Conditions 2001a, European Agency for Health and Safety 2007a). People working for temporary job agencies are often more vulnerable, as the scope of OSH responsibility between the employer, the temporary job agency and the temporary workers is often not clearly defined (European Foundation for the Improvement of Living and Working Conditions 2001a). Research carried out in Germany (Haigh and Mekel 2004) reveals that permanent workers have access to more training, have greater control over their work process and find more reward in their jobs while non-permanent workers face higher job insecurity, worse job conditions, higher job demands and more occupational accidents. A study conducted by Seitsamo and Leino (2005), among 907 adults 18–29 years old who had been in work during the last 12 months concludes that for the young, atypical work is not necessarily a threat to well-being and health. Fixed-term jobs and many work contracts have always been associated with the early stages of careers and it is possible that older workers are more likely to describe the ill effects of atypical work.

The relationship between work conditions, stress and illness can be explained by means of several stress models. Referring to the job demands–control model

(Karasek 1979), work strain combines two dimensions: job demands and job control – when control is low and demands are high, a job can be characterised as high straining or high stressing and increases the risk of work-related illness or injury. The model could be extended by other dimensions such as job insecurity, which was assumed to have an influence on the development of mental and physical health problems as well. Indeed, research proved that job insecurity increases psychological distress and somatic complaints (Strazdins et al. 2004). However, as the demands–control model is based on organisational environments and structures found mainly in permanent jobs (Cooper 2002), its applicability in explaining job strain in non-standard and precarious work is limited.

The vitamin model can also be employed to explain the impact of precarious work on mental health (Warr 1987). There are nine variables of the environment which are hypothesised to influence mental health: opportunity for control, opportunity for skill use, externally generated goals, variety, environmental clarity, availability of money, physical security, opportunity for interpersonal contact and valued social position. According to the specific employment situations, several of these variables can be insufficiently represented or not be represented at all and have an impact on mental health. Such consequences can be cognitive problems, anxiety or depression, as well as nervousness, fear, job dissatisfaction and lack of sociability and friendship relationships. These factors have been found to be strongly associated with precarious work (Benach et al. 2002). The implications for illness and injury connected with precarious work are varied. A study examining the effects of employment strain on health revealed that stress-related tension and exhaustion appear to be more severe for precarious workers than for workers in permanent jobs. Health is generally reported to be poorer in working conditions with high employment strain (Lewchuk et al. 2003) and data from France and Spain show much higher levels of occupational accidents for temporary workers than for permanent workers (Benach et al. 2002). Recent OECD research (2008) has also assessed to what extent employment patterns or working conditions may cause or aggravate mental illness. Switching from standard to non-standard employment, measured by the type of contract or working hours, has an adverse effect on mental health.

On the other hand, a few studies report no different implications at all for the health of precariously employed workers in comparison to permanent workers (Bardasi and Francesconi 2003). There is no evidence showing that temporary or part-time employment had negative long-term effects on mental health among

British men and women during the 1990s. Worse health outcomes were only found for some kinds of jobs such as in lean production or self-employment when compared with other forms of employment (European Foundation for the Improvement of Living and Working Conditions 2001a, b). In the UK study on call centres (Sprigg et al. 2003), employees with non-permanent contracts reported even better well-being than permanent employees. Fixed-term or temporary workers were less anxious, less depressed and more satisfied with their job. According to results from EWCS 1995 and 2000 (Paoli 1997, Paoli and Merllié 2001) among employed workers, the type of employment contract they have affects stress levels and detailed stress-related indices. Identifying four contract types – permanent contract, fixed term contract, temporary contract and apprenticeship – the studies showed that workers with permanent contracts displayed the highest stress levels both in 1995 and 2000. Some detailed well-being indices were also less favourable for this group in the 2000 survey, including irritability, sleeping problems and anxiety. The higher levels of stress, depression and anxiety among workers with permanent contracts compared to those with temporary contracts was also seen in Eurostat's data (Eurostat 2003). Eurofound, using the fourth European Working Condition Survey (EWCS) data, has outlined a tentative categorisation of 'very' atypical forms of work (European Foundation for the Improvement of Living and Working Conditions 2010). This includes three main categories of workers:

1.   workers who have no employment contract;

2.   workers who report working a very small number of hours (less than 10 hours a week);

3.   workers who hold a temporary employment contract of a duration of six months or less.

People in very atypical employment relationships are less likely to report work-related health problems than other workers. Interestingly, more conventional non-standard workers – holding a temporary employment contract for more than six months – report the highest levels of work-related health impact (37 per cent). The comparatively lower proportion of very atypical workers reporting negative health outcomes (31 per cent) may be explained by the fact that these employment contracts entail short tenure in a particular post or job, which reduces exposure and perceived health risks. However, despite the comparatively higher exposure of very atypical workers to the above ergonomic risk factors, these workers tend to report lower levels of physical and psychological health problems than workers in standard employment and, to some extent, other non-standard workers. Besides, an Italian survey carried out on a sample of 800 workers in different economic sectors showed that atypical workers tended to underestimate work-related risks (Battaglini 2006). In fact, as regards psychosocial risks, 57.8 per cent of atypical workers versus 41.4 per cent of standard workers tended to consider that they are very rarely or never exposed to these risks. Consequently, a negative impact on risk awareness and on how workers manage occupational risks is observed.

The status of temporary workers in companies creates difficulties in developing proper prevention and intervention strategies to lower health and injury risks (National Institute for Occupational Safety and Health 2002). National laws and guidance on worker involvement and participation concerning OSH policies do not always include the special case of temporary work arrangements (Quinlan et al. 2001). Documents that deal with temporary workers exist only in some Member States. For example, the *Management of health and safety at work regulations* in the UK (Health and Safety Executive 1999) obliges employers to provide temporary workers, before they start their work, with the necessary information to carry out their work safely. This information is related to occupational qualifications or skills which are needed in a given job, and health surveillance that is required to be provided to these employees.

Much attention has been given to the issue of the health consequences of job insecurity. The main theoretical bases to explain the negative health effects of job insecurity are for most researchers stress theories (Lazarus and Folkman 1984). The phenomenon of stress has often been linked to mental and physical illness. For instance, correlations to coronary heart diseases (Belkic et al. 2004), musculoskeletal diseases (Bongers et al. 1993) or depression (Tennant 2001) were found. Concerning job insecurity, researchers often focused on its effects on mental health, whereas the effects of job insecurity on physical health were considerably less often investigated.

Furthermore, some studies analyse the influence of job insecurity on work attitudes which are also related to workers' well-being. In this regard, mostly cross-sectional studies prevail, but more and more longitudinal studies are also being carried out (Hellgren and Sverke 2003).

Many studies usually indicate the relationship between job insecurity and poorer mental health. In this kind of study, mental health was usually measured with the general health questionnaire (GHQ) (Goldberg 1979) through a scale developed for the purpose of detecting non-psychotic mental health symptoms (such as sleeping problems, anxiety and depression) in the population. In another study (Sverke et al. 2002) carried out from 1980–1999, 37 surveys concerning this issue were included; this analysis demonstrated that the higher the job insecurity, the poorer the mental health. Other indicators of mental well-being in a few studies were used, for example burnout (Lim 1996), job-induced tension (Dekker and Schaufeli 1995) and depression (Ferrie et al. 2001). The impact of job insecurity on mental health is more frequently reported in men, and sometimes it seems to be irrelevant for women (De Witte 1999).

The relationship between job insecurity and physical health has been analysed in the above mentioned study by Sverke et al. which included 19 studies with a total number of 9704 respondents. The average correlation between the two variables was r = - 0.16, which means that the higher the job insecurity, the poorer the physical health. High job insecurity is connected with worse self-reported health, more frequent somatic ailments (for example headaches and spinal aches) and the appearance of long-lasting illnesses.

Discrepancies in the outcomes of these studies result from the fact that the effects of job insecurity depend on a number of additional factors. The most important variables are gender, occupational status, personal variables, social support and job insecurity measurement methods. There is evidence that social support is also an important moderator, both in the workplace and at home. The greater the support, the less likely job insecurity will have a negative effect on health (Lim 1996). Even if there is evidence that precarious work and job insecurity, or at least certain aspects of them, have a negative effect on workers' health and safety, more research is needed to identify specific risk factors. Research in this field often faces significant difficulties in measuring the negative effects or strains, because negative health effects due to precarious work do not occur immediately. Furthermore, temporary contracts often do not last long enough to provide the possibility of measuring negative health effects for researchers. Thus, there is a need to develop appropriate research methods in this field.

Finally there is a need to undertake more longitudinal studies, as so far there is not much research of that kind. The majority of the studies in this area are cross-sectional, which can only indicate the connections between job insecurity or precarious work and other constructs, but they are not able to prove causal connections.

Vulnerable Workers and the LFS Ad Hoc Module

From the labour force survey Istat derives its official estimates of the number of employed persons and job-seekers, as well as information about the main labour supply aggregates, such as occupation, economic activity area, hours worked, contract types and duration and training (ISTAT 2007).

Since being introduced at the beginning of the 1950s, the survey has played a primary role in the statistical documentation and analysis of the employment situation in Italy and has proven to be an indispensable instrument of knowledge for public decision-makers, the media and citizens alike.

The sample has two stages of selection. The primary units are the municipalities stratified into about 1,240 groups at the province level. The stratification strategy is based on the demographic size of the municipality. The sample scheme provides for one primary unit for each stratum. The secondary units are the households and they are selected from the municipality population register. The dimension of the sample is nearly 77,000 households, representing 175,000 individuals who are resident in Italy, even if they are temporarily abroad. Households usually living abroad and permanent members of communities (religious institutes, military barracks, and so on) are not included. The LFS sample is designed to guarantee annual estimates of principal indicators of labour market at province level (NUTS III), quarterly estimates at the regional level (NUTS II) and monthly estimates at the national level. Moreover the current sample survey is continuous insofar as information is collected during every week of the year and no longer during a single week per quarter. Each household is interviewed for two consecutive quarters, followed by a pause for the next two quarters, after which the household is again interviewed for another two quarters. In total, the household remains in the sample for a period of 15 months. A mixed mode techniques is adopted to conduct interviews. This data collection strategy, is a combination of different Computer-assisted Interviewing (CAI) techniques. More exactly, the CAPI (Computer-assisted Personal Interviewing) technique is used for the first interview, while the CATI (Computer Assisted Telephone Interviewing) technique is used for the interviews following the first. To conduct the interviews with CAI technique, a professional interviewer network has been created.

The survey target consists of persons aged 15 years and more, both employed and unemployed with previous working experience. The survey has been updated over the years to take into account continual transformations in the labour market on the one hand, and the growing information requirements of users regarding the social and economic reality of our nation, on the other (ISTAT 2006). The most recent change was undertaken at the beginning of 2004 in line with European Union regulations. A significant feature of the survey is the establishment of new criteria for identifying employed and unemployed individuals, as well as a far-reaching reorganisation of the data collection and production process.

The Labour Force Survey makes it possible to collect detailed information on the numerous types of employment relationships. In this sense it is necessary to define what is actually meant by vulnerable workers. On the Italian employment scene, such workers may be identified as those who hold less stable job positions or are provided with fewer guarantees of employment continuity. Based on this assumption, vulnerable workers may be considered as those employed under fixed-term contracts, however other types of employment relationship certainly exist that conceal high levels of precariousness, such as collaboration contracts. In this analysis, temporary freelancers, who are normally classified under the category of non-salaried labour, are included among the various forms of fixed-term employment due to the particular nature of their contracts which is generally exploited to recruit salaried staff at lower costs (Accornero 2006).

Further, it cannot be ruled out that what is ostensibly classed as self-employment may also mask a salary-based relationship between worker and employer which is not declared as such for tax-saving reasons or expediency, although the LFS does not allow a clear-cut distinction to be made between such relationships and self-employment proper. It is however possible to identify a category of self-employed people that may be considered vulnerable due to the characteristics of the activity they perform, namely self-employed workers who provide their services to a single client. These self-employed people, who do not belong to a professional register or employ other workers, are basically distributed throughout all sectors of the economy, particularly agriculture and commerce, and are vulnerable in that their business connections are limited to a single interlocutor.[4]

It is possible, therefore, to distinguish between the different forms of contract under which fixed-term workers are hired and to include among these temporary freelancers workers and 'vulnerable' autonomous workers as

---

4   This body of workers is conventionally referred to as the 'VAT contingent'.

mentioned previously. For the purpose of the proposed study, these workers were grouped into the following homogeneous categories:

- fixed-term employment contracts under a National Collective Labour Agreement (CCNL);

- training contracts (apprenticeships, on the job training and so on);

- labour leasing or temporary agency work;

- other forms of fixed-term employment;

- temporary freelance contracts (coordinated or occasional);

- vulnerable autonomous workers.

LFS data for the second quarter of 2007 indicate the number of people in employment as 23,298,000, 17,155,000 of whom are wage and salary workers. Workers under a temporary freelance contract and vulnerable autonomous workers amount to 510,000 and 750,000 respectively, hence the target population of this study amounts to 18,415,000.

Table 8.1   People in employment by typology of contract

Typology of contract	People (000s)	Percentage
Permanent contract workers	14850	80.6
Fixed-term employment contracts under CCNL	1484	8.1
Training contracts	500	2.7
Labour leasing or temporary-agency work	64	0.3
Other forms of fixed-term employment	257	1.4
Temporary freelance contracts	510	2.8
Vulnerable autonomous workers	750	4.1
Total	18415	100

All permanent contract workers were also taken into account for comparative and reference purposes, while autonomous workers were excluded.

As regards wage and salary work, the vast majority of contracts are permanent. Conversely, most fixed-term contracts are based on collective agreements and the LFS indicates that temporary agency work is extremely low (0.3 per cent of employed people taken into consideration).

The ad hoc module on accidents at work and work-related health problems is divided into three sections:

- accidents resulting in injuries at work or in the course of work occurred during the past 12 months (accidents during the journey from home to work or from work to home are not included);

- illnesses, disabilities or other physical or mental problems caused or made worse by work suffered by the person during the past 12 months;

- exposure at work to selected factors that can adversely affect physical or mental health.

The analysis includes the following risk factors:

- chemicals, dusts, fumes, smoke or gases;

- noise or vibration;

- difficult work postures, work movements or handling of heavy loads;

- risk of accidents;

- time pressure or overload of work;

- harassment, bullying or discrimination;

- violence or threat of violence.

The presence of particular exposure to other factors not included in the previous list is also questioned. People in employment involved in the mentioned aspects regarding health and safety at work are shown in Table 8.2:[5]

Table 8.2   People in employment by typology of health issue

Typology of health issue	People (000s)
Victims of accidents at work	514
Affected by health problems	1316
Exposed to risk factors:	8179
• chemicals, dusts, fumes, smoke or gases	3024
• noise or vibration	2818
• difficult work postures, work movements and so on	3742
• risk of accidents	3930
• time pressure or overload of work	2628
• harassment, bullying or discrimination	958
• violence or threat of violence	311
• other factors not mentioned above	308

According to LFS data, again for the second quarter of 2007 and in relation to the employed people taken into consideration, over 8 million declared the presence of at least one aspect of poor safety, as described above.

The Health of Vulnerable Workers

The aim of this study is to investigate whether vulnerable workers are subjected to poorer work health and safety conditions than their counterparts in better safeguarded and protected job positions. The wide spectrum of information available suggested data might be most appropriately analysed using synthetic

---

5   The ad hoc module has been submitted to a wider population than that considered in this document. In particular accidents at work refers to employed or unemployed people with a work experience that ended less than one year before the date of the interview, work-related health problems involves employed people or unemployed people with work experience while exposure to risk factor regards only employed people.

data tools. In this case a logistic model (Fabbris 1997) was used in which the variable dependent is represented by job position reclassified as follows:

- vulnerable workers comprising those with fixed-term National Agreement contracts, training contracts, temporary agency work, other forms of fixed-term wage and salary employment, vulnerable autonomous workers;

- protected workers, namely those permanent employed.

An alternative model was also developed in which the independent variable does not include those defined as vulnerable autonomous workers in the category of vulnerable workers. This model will make it possible to determine whether the inclusion of vulnerable autonomous workers (whose professional profile differs from that of wage and salary workers) in the category of vulnerable workers tout court leads to a change in their attitude as regards the pattern of work health and safety-related variables.

The explanatory variables used in the model can be combined into three groups:

- Demographic background:
  - Sex (Male, Female)
  - Age (15–24, 25–34, 35–44, 45–54, 55–64, 65 and older)
  - Geographic area (North, Centre, South)
  - Educational level (Low, Intermediate, High).

- Features of work activity:
  - Economic activity (agriculture, energy, manufacturing, construction, commerce, hotel, transport, financial intermediation, company services, public administration, education, health, other services)
  - Working time (Full-time, Part-time)
  - Evening and night work, work during unsocial hours (Very often, Often, Sometimes, Rarely, Never)
  - Saturday work (Often, Sometimes, Never)
  - Sunday work (Often, Sometimes, Never)
  - Shift work (Yes, No).

- Health and safety at work:
  - Accidents at work in the last year (Yes, No)
  - Work-related health problems in the last year (Yes, No)
  - Exposure to chemicals, dusts, fumes, smoke or gases (Yes, No)
  - Exposure to noise or vibration (Yes, No)
  - Exposure to difficult work postures, work movements or handling of heavy loads (Yes, No)
  - Exposure to risk of accident (Yes, No)
  - Exposure to time pressure or overload of work (Yes, No)
  - Exposure to bullying, harassment or discrimination (Yes, No)
  - Exposure to violence or threat of violence (Yes, No).

An analysis of the odds ratios (Table 8.3) primarily indicates that very high significance levels are associated with all categories except for exposure to excessive noise or vibrations in the case of the model that excludes vulnerable autonomous workers. This is due to the large sample size of the survey and points to a high degree of reliability of the estimates.

The two models show strong analogies between all observed characteristics. As regards demographic background, it can be noted that vulnerable workers are mostly young females working prevalently in the south of the country who have high academic qualifications. This latter aspect is principally due to the fact that on completing their education young people enter employment mainly through fixed-term or temporary freelance contracts.

Various aspects of the conditions in which vulnerable workers operate differ somewhat to conventional beliefs and an overall picture emerges that tends to dispel certain misconceptions surrounding workers in less secure positions. In Italy, those in the more precarious jobs work less during the so-called unsocial hours (after 8 p.m.) and do less shift work than their permanent counterparts. Conversely, they occupy more part-time jobs and work more at weekends. Placement of vulnerable workers is oriented towards two sectors: one more physical function-based, principally in the agricultural, hotel and catering sector, the other more intellect-based, in the field of education and company services in which temporary freelancers are most prevalent.

As regards health and safety in the workplace, several distinctions emerge between the two models particularly in terms of exposure to psychological health risk factors. In effect, in the model that includes autonomous workers in the category of vulnerable workers, exposure to threats and physical violence

Table 8.3   Outcomes of logistic model – odds ratios

Variables	Items	P (vulnerable workers)	
		With vulnerable autonomous workers	Without vulnerable autonomous workers
Sample dimension		48571	46312
Independent variable: Typology of workers	Vulnerable vs protected		
Sex	Male vs female	0.852	0.775
Geographic area	North vs south	0.768	0.672
	Centre vs south	0.945	0.880
Age	25–34 vs 15–24	0.319	0.262
	35–44 vs 15–24	0.190	0.129
	45–54 vs 15–24	0.144	0.079
	55–64 vs 15–24	0.163	0.069
	65 e oltre vs 15–24	0.848	0.331
Educational level	High vs low	1.349	1.565
	Intermediate vs low	0.879	0.895
Economic activity	Agriculture and fishing vs other services	7.202	7.171
	Energy vs other services	0.468	0.612
	Industry vs other services	0.605	0.649
	Construction vs other services	0.773	0.695
	Wholesale and retail vs other services	0.926	0.610
	Hotels and restaurants vs other services	1.185	1.198
	Transports and communications vs other services	0.822	0.810
	Financial sector vs other services	0.548	0.458
	Real estate vs other services	1.046	1.122
	Public admin vs other services	0.574	0.799
	Education vs other services	1.340	1.935
	Health vs other services	0.590	0.694
Working time	Part-time vs full-time	1.716	2.101
Evening and night work/ Work during unsocial hours	Frequently vs never	0.787	0.825
	Often vs never	1.050	0.979
	Sometimes vs never	0.937	0.810
	Rarely vs never	1.235	0.975

Table 8.3   Outcomes of logistic model – odds ratios *concluded*

Variables	Items	P (vulnerable workers)	
		With vulnerable autonomous workers	Without vulnerable autonomous workers
Saturday work	Often vs never	1.221	1.015
	Sometimes vs never	1.168	1.076
Sunday work	Often vs never	1.550	1.354
	Sometimes vs never	1.140	1.125
Shift work	Yes vs no	0.645	0.968
Accidents at work	Yes vs no	1.118	1.152
Work-related health problems	Yes vs no	0.960	0.948
Exposure to chemicals, dusts, fumes, smoke or gases	Yes vs no	0.960	0.956
Exposure to noise or vibration	Yes vs no	0.941	not signif.
Exposure to difficult work postures, work movements or handling of heavy loads	Yes vs no	1.055	1.027
Exposure to risk of accident	Yes vs no	0.982	0.926
Exposure to time pressure or overload of work	Yes vs no	0.868	0.836
Exposure to harassment or discrimination	Yes vs no	0.940	1.133
Exposure to violence or threat of violence	Yes vs no	1.158	0.829

assumes significant proportions and extends to the entire group of vulnerable workers whereas this is not the case when the autonomous group is not taken into consideration. In the model that excludes autonomous workers, evidence clearly emerges of exposure to bullying, harassment and discrimination, whereas these phenomena retrogress when the group of autonomous workers considered is included in the model. In this regard, it is clear that the group of vulnerable autonomous workers is subjected to a more extreme work environment with more evident elements of conflict. In fact, the model that includes autonomous workers indicates higher odds ratio values in sectors (for example wholesale and construction) where the physical component of the work is greater. Exposure to bullying and discrimination is instead apparent among vulnerable workers when the group of autonomous workers is excluded. In this case, such phenomena are more closely connected with sectors of the knowledge-based services such as education, public administration and health, in which latent harassment is more common. As regards the other variables related to health in the workplace, the two models basically indicate analogous patterns. Vulnerable workers are more prone to accidents than their counterparts with greater contractual security but declare a lower incidence of work-related health problems. Further, vulnerable workers have a reduced perception of exposure to health risk factors except for the assumption of harmful postures or movements that impact negatively on their health and which can probably be attributed to higher negligence in applying correct ergonomic criteria in the case of workers in precarious and temporary employment.

Conclusions

To remain competitive in a situation of global competition, companies are becoming more and more flexible. Outsourcing or new forms of flexible employment such as part-time work, different kind of temporary works and 'vulnerable' autonomous work have emerged. These non-standard forms of employment are often related to job insecurity, as they mostly offer only low levels of income, low social protection, temporary employment and general low control over work life. Job insecurity and increased work-related stress due to precarious work negatively affect workers' health and safety. Additionally, workers in these types of contract are more vulnerable than permanent workers, as they usually carry out the most hazardous jobs, work in poorer conditions, and are the subject of less OSH training, which increases the risk of occupational accidents.

Precarious and insecure work is not believed to be an inevitable consequence of reorganisations which involve personnel reduction. An important element of prevention is organisational communication. The management could pay attention to informing employees in good time about the planned changes, even if this information might be painful. The validity of such a policy has been supported by a study (Dekker and Schaufeli 1995) which shows that job insecurity is more detrimental to a worker's health than certainty, even about job loss. It is important for management to communicate with employees not only before any planned changes but also afterwards. In this situation, it is important to convince remaining employees that their jobs are still secure A more elementary policy to prevent employees from excessive job precariousness is to make them familiar with the idea of 'the boundless career', to train them on how to take ownership of their career path (Canaff and Wright 2004) and also how to remain flexible and open to change. For people who already experience high job insecurity, it is very important to provide them with social support, both in the workplace and at home. As mentioned above, support reduces the negative effects that job precariousness has on health. The institutional form of such support is counselling employees who feel high job insecurity (Bongers et al. 1993).

The results of our experience point to the fact that precarious employment contracts do not always coincide with poorer safety conditions in the workplace (Boschetto and Lucarelli 2008). Vulnerable workers, however, emerge as sustaining more frequent injuries than their more protected counterparts and being more exposed to psychological pressure in that those who exert such pressure are generally able to exploit the insecurity and instability of their job position (European Agency for Health and Safety at Work 2007b, European Foundation for the Improvement of Living and Working Conditions 2008). The model also highlights an overall reduced perception of health risk factors by vulnerable workers which probably derives from their different attitude towards the issues of health and safety in the workplace, in that they are more concerned with the instability of their job rather than the potential hazards of their working environment. The fact that vulnerable workers are also less affected by work-related health problems can be attributed to their young age and to the fact that these problems normally and prevalently affect older employees.

It would be interesting if such information were available today in order to evaluate the impact on safety in the workplace of the current deep economic crisis which, after expelling from the labour market principally the more vulnerable members of the labour force, now also seems to be affecting those with more secure job positions and whose workplace health and safety scenario may not be too dissimilar from that of their less privileged counterparts.

References

Accornero A., (2006), *San Precario lavora per noi* [Saint Precarious work for us], Rizzoli, Roma.
Bardasi E. and Francesconi M., (2003), *The Impact of Atypical Employment on Individual Well-being: Evidence from a Panel of British Workers*, Working Papers of the Institute for Social and Economic Research, Paper 2003–2, University of Essex, Colchester.

Battaglini E., (2006), *Percezione dei rischi e politiche di tutela nell'Impresa post-fordista, Sintesi del rapporto di ricerca* [Risk perception and protection policies in the post-Fordist enterprise summary of the research report], IRES Istituto di Ricerche Economiche e Sociali, Rome.

Belkic K.L., Landsbergis P., Schnall P.L. and Baker D., (2004), Is job strain a major source of cardiovascular disease risk?, *Scandinavian Journal of Work, Environment and Health*, 30(2), 85–128.

Benach J., Benavides F.G., Platt S., Diez-Roux A. and Muntaner C., (2000), The health damaging potential of new types of flexible employment: a challenge for public health researchers, *American Journal of Public Health*, 90(8), 1316–1317.

Benach J., Gimeno D. and Benavides F.G., (2002), *European Foundation for the Improvement of Living and Working Conditions, Types of Employment and Health in the European Union*, Office for Official Publications of the European Communities, Luxembourg.

Blum R. and Balke K., (2006), *Confronting the Inequalities of Precarious Work*, IMF Special Report, http://www.imfmetal.org/files/06060216314379/Precarious_work_2-2006_web.pdf.

Bongers P.M., deWinter C.R., Kompier M.A.J. and Hildebrandt M.D., (1993), Psychosocial factors at work and musculoskeletal disease, *Scandinavian Journal of Work, Environment and Health*, 19, 297–312.

Boschetto B. and Lucarelli C., (2008), *Sicuri di lavorare insicuri: nuove prospettive dall'indagine sulle forze di lavoro* [Certain to work in uncertainty: new prospects from the Italian LFS], AIEL, Brescia, http://www.aiel.it/bacheca/BRESCIA/papers/boschetto_lucarelli.pdf.

Canaff A.L. and Wright W., (2004), High anxiety: counseling the job-insecure client, *Journal of Employment Counseling*, 41, 2–10.

Cooper C.L., (2002), The changing psychological contract at work, *Occupational and Environmental Medicine*, 59, 355.

De Witte H., (1999), Job insecurity and psychological well-being: review of the literature and exploration of some unresolved issues, *European Journal of Work and Organizational Psychology*, 8, 155–177.

Dekker S.W. and Schaufeli W.B., (1995), The effects of job insecurity on psychological health and withdrawal: a longitudinal study, *Australian Psychologist*, 30, 57–63.

European Agency for Safety and Health at Work, (2007a), *OSH in Figures: Young Workers – Facts and Figures*, European Agency for Safety and Health at Work, Luxembourg.

European Agency for Safety and Health at Work, (2007b), *Expert Forecast on Emerging Psychosocial Risks Related to Occupational Safety and Health*, European Agency for Safety and Health at Work, Luxembourg.

European Commission, (2002), *Adattarsi alle trasformazioni del lavoro e della società: una nuova strategia comunitaria per la salute e la sicurezza 2002–2006* [Adapting to change in work and society: a new Community strategy on health and safety at work 2002–2006], Communication from the Commission to the Council and the European Parliament, Brussels.

European Commission, (2006), *Commission Regulation N.341/2006 Adopting the Specifications of the 2007 ad hoc Module on Accidents at Work and Work-related Health Problems Provided for by Council Regulation (EC) No 577/98 and Amending Commission Regulation (EC) No 384/2005*, Official Journal of the European Union, Brussels.

European Commission, (2007), *Migliorare la qualità e la produttività sul luogo di lavoro: strategia comunitaria 2007–2012 per la salute e la sicurezza sul luogo di lavoro* [Improving quality and productivity at work: Community strategy 2007–2012 on health and safety at work], Communication from the Commission to the Council and the European Parliament, Brussels.

European Foundation for the Improvement of Living and Working Conditions, (2001a), *Working Conditions in Atypical Work: Resumée*, Office for Official Publications of the European Communities, Luxembourg.

European Foundation for the Improvement of Living and Working Conditions, (2001b), *The Impact of New Forms of Work Organisation on Working Conditions and Health*, Background paper to the European Union Presidency Conference 'For a better quality of work', Office for Official Publications of the European Communities, Luxembourg.

European Foundation for the Improvement of Living and Working Conditions, (2008), *Flexibility and Security Over the Life Course*, European Foundation for the improvement of Living and Working Conditions, Dublin.

European Foundation for the Improvement of Living and Working Conditions, (2010), *Very Atypical Work: Exploratory Analysis of Fourth European Working Conditions Survey*, Background Paper, European Foundation for the Improvement of Living and Working Conditions, Dublin.

Eurostat, (2003), *Work and Health in the EU – A Statistical Portrait. Data 1994–2002.* Eurostat, Luxembourg.

Fabbris L., (1997), *Statistica multivariata – Analisi esplorativa dei dati* [Multivariate statistics – exploratory data analysis], McGraw Hill, Milano.

Ferrie J.E., Shipley M.J., Marmot M.G., Martikainen P., Stansfeld S. and Smith G.D., (2001), Job insecurity in white-collar workers: toward an explanation of associations with health, *Journal of Occupational Health Psychology*, 6, 26–42.

Goldberg D., (1979), *Manual of the General Health Questionnaire*, NFER Nelson, London.

Haigh F. and Mekel O., (2004), *Policy Health Impact Assessment for the European Union: Pilot Health Impact Assessment of the European Employment Strategy in Germany*, European Commission, Brussels.

Health and Safety Executive, (1999), *Management of Health and Safety at Work Regulations*, Health and Safety Executive, London.

Hellgren J. and Sverke M., (2003), Does job insecurity lead to impaired well-being or vice-versa? Estimation of cross-lagged effects using latent variable modeling', *Journal of Organizational Behavior*, 24, 215–236.

INAIL, (2008) *Rapporto annuale 2007* [Annual report 2007], INAIL, Rome.

ISTAT, (2006), *La rilevazione sulle forze di lavoro: contenuti, metodologie, orginazzazione* [Labour force survey: matters, methodology and organisation], Metodi e Norme, Roma.

ISTAT, (2007), *Indagine continua sulle Forze di Lavoro*, Media 2006, Roma.

Karasek R.A., (1979), Job demand, job decision latitude, andmental strain – implications for job redesign, *Administrative Science Quarterly*, 24, 285–308.

Lazarus R.S. and Folkman S., (1984), *Stress, Appraisal, and Coping*, Springer, New York.

Lewchuk W., de Wolff A., King A. and Polanyi M., (2003), From job strain to employment strain: health effects of precarious employment, *Just Labour*, 3, 23–35.

Lim V., (1996), Job insecurity and its outcomes: moderating effects of work-based and nonwork-based social support, *Human Relations*, 49, 171–194.

Mayhew C. and Quinlan M., (1999), The effects of outsourcing on occupational health and safety: a comparative study of factory-based workers and outworkers in the Australian clothing industry, *International Journal of Health Services*, 29(1), 83–107.

National Institute for Occupational Safety and Health, (2002), *The Changing Organisation of Work and the Safety and Health of Working People – Knowledge Gaps and Research Directions*, National Institute for Occupational Safety and Health, Cincinnati, http://www.cdc.gov/niosh/docs/2002-116/pdfs/2002-116.pdf.

OECD (Organisation for Economic Co-operation and Development), (2008), *Are all Jobs Good for Your Health? The Impact of Work Status and Working Conditions on Mental Health*, OECD Employment Outlook 2008, Paris.

Paoli P., (1997), *Second European Working Conditions Survey, European Foundation for the Improvement of Living and Working Conditions*, Office for Official Publications of the European Communities, Luxembourg.

Paoli P. and Merllié D., (2001), *Third European Working Conditions Survey 2000, European Foundation for the Improvement of Living and Working Conditions*, Office for Official Publications of the European Communities, Luxembourg.

Quinlan M., Mayhew C. and Bohle P., (2001), The global expansion of precarious employment, work disorganization, and consequences for occupational health: placing the debate in a comparative historical context, *International Journal of Health Services*, 31(3), 507–536.

Seitsamo J. and Leino T., (2005), Type of employment, qualities of work and well-being among Finnish young adults, Finnish Institute of Occupational Health. *Proceedings of the International Symposium on Youth and Work Culture, Espoo.*

Sprigg C.A., Smith P.R. and Jackson P.R., (2003), *Psychosocial Risk Factors in Call Centres: An Evaluation of Work Design and Well-being*, Research Report 169, Health and Safety Executive, London.

Strazdins L., D'Souza R.M., Lim L.L., Broom D.H. and Rodgers B., (2004), Job strain, job insecurity and health – rethinking the relationship, *Journal of Occupational Health Psychology*, 9(4), 296–305.

Sverke M., Hellgren J. and Näswall K., (2002), No security: a meta-analysis and review of job insecurity and its consequences, *Journal of Occupational Health Psychology*, 7, 242–264.

Tennant C., (2001), Work-related stress and depressive disorders, *Journal of Psychosomatic Research*, 51(5), 697–704.

Warr P.B., (1987), *Work, Unemployment and Mental Health*, Clarendon Press, Oxford.

9

Employees Without Protections: The Misclassification of Vulnerable Workers in New York

J. Ryan Lamare[1]

Introduction

The issue of worker misclassification has increasingly garnered considerable interest within the United States. This issue has become one of paramount importance to not only employers and employees, but also to regulatory bodies such as state and federal government agencies. In an effort to more comprehensively understand the extent to which worker misclassification is occurring, and the consequences of this practices to companies, workers and taxpayers, several studies have been conducted in recent years. These studies have taken place most often at either the state or national level, and predominantly use audit data as their empirical foundation. Researchers have conducted studies of misclassification in Massachusetts (Carré et al. 2004), Maine (Carré et al. 2005), Michigan (Cooley 2008), Florida (de Silva et al. 2000), Ohio (Cordray 2009), Connecticut (Alpert 1992), Illinois (Kelsay et al. 2006), Minnesota (Nobles 2007), and other states over the past few years. The results of these studies have led to significant change to states' labour and employment laws, and have highlighted an issue of growing concern to government officials. The issue of misclassification has been considered at the highest levels of public policy in the United States, with Congress debating a

1   Lecturer in Human Resource Management, Manchester Business School, University of Manchester; e-mail: ryan.lamare@mbs.ac.uk. The author would like to acknowledge Linda Donahue and Fred Kotler, who contributed to the policy report on which this chapter is based. Portions of this chapter are taken, with permission, from *The Cost of Worker Misclassification in New York State* (2007) by Linda Donahue, James Ryan Lamare, and Fred B. Kotler (a full citation is found in the references section).

bill that would toughen penalties on employers who violate the laws related to employee classification, and President Obama allocating $25 million of the 2011 fiscal budget to investigate employer misclassification (Schoeff 2010).

The aim of this chapter is to profile and document the extent of worker misclassification in New York, relying on audit data provided over a four-year period, from 2002 to 2005, and focusing on the costs of this practice to three groups: employers, employees and taxpayers. Misclassification affects each of these groups in a number of different ways. Employees are harmed by lost benefits and rights, particularly in terms of workers' compensation allowances if they are injured during the course of their employment. Employers are affected as companies that are engaging in misclassification are able to undercut the established market pay rates for labour, thereby lowering their production costs and gaining a competitive advantage over firms obeying the law. This creates an incentive for employers to misclassify in order to remain competitive. Finally, the public interest is harmed in that it loses a substantial amount of payroll and other taxes that would be collected if the company's workers were correctly classified as employees.

In profiling the extent of worker misclassification in New York, special consideration is given to two factors: the construction industry and vulnerable workers. Firms operating in the construction industry will be arguably more likely to engage in misclassification than firms operating in other industries, given that both anecdotal evidence from New York and empirical data from other states suggest that misclassification is particularly widespread amongst construction firms. There is also a significant association between misclassification and vulnerable workers; to a large degree, misclassification occurs in situations where workers do not know their legal rights. Often, these workers are considered vulnerable, and in many cases are migrant workers who are unaware of the protections that are available through U.S. labour and employment law. Thus, it can be argued that misclassification affects vulnerable workers most substantially in New York, particularly within the construction industry.

Definition of Misclassification

Misclassification occurs when an employer, at hiring, improperly classifies a worker as an independent contractor rather than an employee (U.S. Government Accountability Office 2009). The distinction between 'employee' and 'independent contractor' relates to the right of control; however, the ability to test this distinction is quite complicated and to a large degree depends on the particular law under which the company operates. Employers have the right to direct the means, methods and outcomes of their employees' work. Independent contractors, properly classified, are not employees but are in business for themselves.[2] They are hired to accomplish a task or tasks determined by the employer but retain the right to control how they will accomplish it. In a number of situations, employers can legitimately hire independent contractors, offering firms the benefit of flexibility in production and the use of temporary workers, while simultaneously allowing workers to maintain a sense of control (other benefits to workers are quite pragmatic, such as taxation flexibility for independent contractors).

Further, not all misclassification is deliberate. Responsible employers may misclassify workers because they are unclear or confused about how to apply complex, inconsistent and varying standards. Well-intentioned employers may have difficulty determining whether a worker is an employee or can properly be classified as an independent contractor.[3] However, other employers intentionally misclassify workers, assuming the risk of incurring penalties, as a strategy to significantly cut labour costs, limit their liability and gain an unfair competitive advantage.

The Impact of Worker Misclassification

Misclassification often severely impacts three groups: (1) workers, (2) employers in those industries where the practice is prevalent, and (3) government and taxpayers. It is worth considering the effects of misclassification on each of the three groups.

WORKERS

Almost uniformly, misclassification is harmful to workers who are improperly denoted as independent contractors rather than employees. This is true for a

---

2   For a thorough discussion of federal IRS standards, see *IRS Publication 15-A, Employer's Supplemental Tax Guide*, hereinafter IRS 15-A, available online at www.irs.gov. For NYS DOL standards, see *Covered and Excluded Employment under the UI Law* at www.labor.state.ny.us/ui.

3   For a review of various tests applied by courts and federal and state agencies, see Employment Arrangements: Improved Outreach Could Help Ensure Proper Worker Classification, Report to the Ranking Member, Committee on Health, Education, Labor, and Pensions, U.S. Senate, United States Government Accounting Office, July 2006.

number of reasons. For one, misclassification denies many workers protections and benefits to which they are entitled. For another, worker misclassification disrupts labour markets by enabling unscrupulous employers to ignore labour standards. Each of these two issues deserves separate discussion.

In an employer–employee relationship in the United States, the employer must withhold income taxes, withhold and pay Social Security and Medicare taxes, pay unemployment tax on wages paid, provide workers' compensation insurance, pay minimum wage and overtime wages, and include employees in employee benefit plans.[4] Employers are not generally obligated to make these payments to, or on behalf of, independent contractors. Workers classified as employees receive unemployment and workers' compensation benefits and are typically protected by a broad spectrum of federal and state legislation affecting wages, health and safety, the right to organize, family and medical leave and pension security.[5] Independent contractors, however, are generally excluded from the coverage of protective legislation.

Misclassified workers – as putative independent contractors – are directly and immediately burdened in several ways. They generally do not file for unemployment insurance benefits even though they may be eligible and do not receive appropriate levels of workers' compensation insurance (de Silva et al. 2000). If they are unemployed or injured on the job, the economic consequences can be devastating. Additionally, they are solely responsible for withholding and reporting taxes at the substantially higher self-employed tax rate. Their employers might provide them with the required IRS Form 1099-MISC showing gross wages paid (Schedule C – self-employment) or simply pay cash 'under the table' – without regard to tax laws, statutory wage standards and 'below the radar screen' of state regulators. Further, it is often the case that these workers do not benefit from Social Security, and are not party to employer-provided health care or retirement plans. These workers may also be required, as a condition of employment, to purchase their own workers' compensation and liability insurance coverage, and to sign waivers releasing

---

4   IRS 15-A at 6; U.S. Government Accountability Office (2006), at 25.
5   Misclassification can impact workers' rights and protections pursuant to these federal and state statutes: U.S. Department of Labor (Fair Labor Standards Act, Family and Medical Leave Act, OSHA); Internal Revenue Service (FICA, Federal Unemployment Tax Act, Self-Employment Contributions Act); U.S. Department of Health and Human Services (Medicare); Pension Benefit Guarantee Corporation (ERISA); Equal Employment Opportunities Commission (Title VII of the Civil Rights Act, Americans with Disabilities Act, Age Discrimination in Employment Act); National Labor Relations Board; Social Security Administration; NYS Department of Labor (unemployment insurance); Workers Compensation Board; NYS Department of Taxation and Finance (U.S. Government Accountability Office 2006, at 8).

employers from liability and other obligations inherent in a typical employer–employee relationship (Carré et al. 2004: 8–9). If they wish to avail of typical employee protections, misclassified workers must first realize that they are misclassified, understand what that means, and then successfully challenge their misclassification through administrative or court action to confirm their eligibility for and receive the aforementioned statutory protections – an impractical remedy for many because of the time, expense and risk involved (U.S. Government Accountability Office 2006).

Although it is the case that some workers choose independent contractor status, many others are obligated to accept this classification. In the former case, facilitated by recent changes in the workplace, in technology and communications, many higher-paid, high-skilled workers choose to be independent contractors, contracting for particular projects for particular employers, often because independent contractor status carries desirable tax advantages, such as the range of available deductions, increased flexibility over time and greater control over work (de Silva et al. 2000).

In the latter case, many workers simply do not have a choice as to their employment status. Without the same levels of skill, education and training associated with higher-paid workers, without the benefit of collective bargaining and with little or no individual bargaining power, these workers are often compelled by employers to accept independent contractor status, at low pay with no health, pension, or retirement benefits and without the protection of laws covering 'employees' such as wage and hour standards.[6] These workers cannot afford to make contributions into retirement accounts and generally will not file for and collect unemployment insurance when needed.

Undocumented workers, whose status makes them even less likely to challenge the employer's designation, are among the most vulnerable. These workers are often immigrants, who know very little by way of U.S. labour and employment law, and often are ignorant to their own rights on the job. For example, employers may choose not to inform these workers about their rights to overtime pay or workers' compensation. Given this lack of education regarding their entitlements, immigrant workers are more likely to be misclassified than are other workers (U.S. Government Accountability Office 2009).

---

6   de Silva et al. (2000), in their study for the US DOL, found that the majority of independent contractors, without making a distinction between those properly classified and those misclassified, have no health insurance or retirement benefits and earn middle to low-level wages.

Worker misclassification is of particular interest within the construction industry. In this industry, workers are often paid in cash only, which leads to issues related to taxation. Evidence suggests that the misclassification of employees as independent contractors is especially prevalent amongst construction firms (U.S. Government Accountability Office 2009). For instance, one study investigated over 600 businesses, most of which were construction firms, and found violations of labour standards in over half the companies. Upon further investigation, it was found that tens of thousands of employees were improperly classified as independent contractors, leading to unpaid wages of around $12 million (U.S. Government Accountability Office 2009).

Misclassification affects the health and safety of workers to a great degree. One of the primary motivations behind employers' choices to misclassify their employees is the cost of workers' compensation payments if an employee is injured while on the job (California Department of Labor 2010). According to a recent study, millions of dollars in workers' compensation penalties are lost due to misclassification in the construction industry alone (U.S. Government Accountability Office 2009). In light of this, the Employee Misclassification Workers' Compensation Coverage Model Act was proposed in 2009 in order to 'establish clear definitions of an employee and an independent contractor for the purposes of workers' compensation benefits.'[7]

EMPLOYERS

Misclassification is also of considerable consequence to employers, particularly in that its usage tends to destabilize the business climate, creating an unlevel playing field and causing law-abiding businesses to face unfair competition. Responsible employers who properly classify their workers as employees have higher costs and are underbid by competitors who intentionally misclassify their workers. The immediate advantages of misclassifying a worker are, for many employers, worth the more remote risk of being caught and penalized. To the extent that there is insufficient monitoring, oversight and regulation by policymakers and affected state and federal agencies, misclassification will continue to destabilize the business climate in certain industries.[8]

---

7   See the National Conference of Insurance Legislators Workers' Compensation Insurance Committee working draft (2009), p. 1.
8   The arguments regarding misclassification's consequences to employers have been affirmed by several governmental resources, including the Michigan Department of Labor, the Kansas Department of Labor and several other governmental bodies, all of which support the arguments promulgated here regarding the effects of misclassification on employers.

It is important to consider the costs of these taxes to firms that do not misclassify in order to more comprehensively understand the benefits gleaned by misclassifying employers. For instance, Social Security and Medicare taxes – paid by employers who properly classify their workers as employees – amount to 7.65 percent of wages paid. Unemployment taxes paid to the federal government are at 0.8 percent of the first $7,000 of remuneration.[9] Combined federal and state unemployment insurance taxes are higher.[10] Finally, steadily rising medical costs and workers' compensation premiums represent a significant cost factor in certain, more injury-prone industries such as construction.

Evidence indicates that responsible employers tend to carry an additional undue burden: to the extent that misclassifying employers are not paying into insurance funds, responsible employers make up the difference in higher premiums.[11] This clearly leads to significant cost increases for law-abiding firms. Again, it is worth noting that in highly competitive industries like construction, any marginal increase in cost will often force firms into a state of non-competitiveness. It is also worth considering that factors related to workplace health and safety are of paramount importance to employers who misclassify. Avoiding workers' compensation payments is the leading reason that employers intentionally misclassify workers, a larger factor than non-payment of unemployment insurance contributions. A study of several states' insurance funds conducted for the U.S. Department of Labor concluded that employers will take the risks associated with misclassification to gain a competitive advantage by not paying workers' compensation premiums – risks they would not likely take for unemployment insurance cost savings alone, as indicated by the following:

The number one reason why employers use independent contractors and/ or misclassify employees is the savings in not paying workers' compensation premiums and not being subject to workplace injury and disability-related

---

9   Commerce Clearing House, Business Owner's Toolkit at www.toolkit.cch.com.

10 In New York State, the unemployment insurance tax rate is based on an employer's experience with the system and its account balance. See NYS Unemployment Insurance Law Article 18 §581et. seq.

11 Another problem for the business community concerns mistaken, but not intentional, misclassification due to inconsistent standards and the inconsistent or conflicting application of standards among various federal and state agencies. For example, under §530 of IRS regulations, an employer may appropriately classify individuals as independent contractors while the states might hold them to be employees. See http://www.unclefed.com/Tax-News/1996/Nr96-44.html. Employees' wages may be taxable for state purposes and would not be taxable for FICA, FUTA, or Federal withholding. Also see de Silva et al. (2000) and U.S. Government Accountability Office (2006).

disputes (de Silva et al. 2000: iii).[12] Direct and immediate cost savings are an obvious incentive but so are potential cost savings from limiting or eliminating employer liability. In an employer–employee relationship, employers are liable for the torts committed by their employees within the scope of their employment. Employers are not liable for the torts of independent contractors. According to one advisor, 'the tax savings [from hiring independent contractors] pale in comparison to the elimination of tort liability'.[13]

As noted, studies conducted by the U.S. General Accounting Office and for the U.S. Department of Labor underscore that the construction industry stands out both as the industry with the highest percentage of independent contractors (22 percent) but also as the industry with the 'highest incidence of misclassification'.[14] It is worth detailing precisely why this finding should come as no surprise, by more explicitly highlighting the elements that make construction a particularly prone area for misclassification. Construction is an expanding but fiercely competitive contract industry, characterized by slim profit margins, high injury and compensation rates, comprised largely of numerous small to medium-sized companies whose numbers and size may make them more likely to operate beyond the view of state regulators. It is labour intensive, its jobs are temporary, and many jobs, particularly in unlicensed trades, can be broken down into piece work. It is a lucrative employment source for immigrant, often undocumented, workers and unscrupulous employers use their workers' alleged independent contractor status to circumvent employer obligations under federal immigration laws. Further, the construction workforce is mobile – making it difficult for regulators to track down particular employers. All the elements are present throughout the industry, but misclassification and 'under the table' practices operate with particular impunity in the large and expanding residential and commercial sectors (de Silva et al. 2000; U.S. Government Accountability Office 2006).[15]

---

12 States providing data: California, New Jersey, Maryland, Florida, New Jersey, Washington, Indiana, Minnesota, Ohio, Wisconsin, Colorado, Connecticut, Nebraska, New Mexico, Oregon, Pennsylvania and Texas.

13 A later comment in the same study: 'In high risk industries, workers' compensation was the single most dominant reason for misclassification. Many employers believe the risk of being caught is acceptable if it means the survival of their business' de Silva et al. (2000: 92).

14 Commerce Clearing House, *Business Owner's Toolkit*, at www.toolkit.cch.com.

15 Other industries with disproportionately high numbers of independent contractors – and high rates of misclassification – include trucking, home health care, and retail services.

GOVERNMENT AND TAXPAYERS

The costs of worker misclassification extend well beyond workers and employers in those industries where it is most widely practiced. Misclassification costs government at all levels by way of substantial, uncollected revenues, resources that are needed for vital government programs and services and for the maintenance of a productive workforce and economy. The Internal Revenue Service last estimated misclassification's cost to the nation in 1984. Their estimate in 2006 dollars for tax loss in Social Security tax, unemployment insurance tax, and income tax is $2.72 billion (U.S. Government Accountability Office 2006, 2009).[16] Given the substantial growth in the nation's economy, population and workforce since 1984, as well as recent shifts toward contingent and casual labour, it is reasonable to assume that the true figure today would be much higher. Further, the implications for overall lost state revenues are also severe. One recent estimate of the total tax loss due to misclassification in California is as high as $7 billion.[17] A 2004 study in Massachusetts estimates losses of $12.6 to $35 million to that state's unemployment insurance system, a loss of $91 million in state income tax revenue, and $91 million in unpaid workers' compensation premiums (Carré et al. 2004).

Misclassification's impact on workers' compensation systems is beyond the scope of this chapter but deserves further attention. An analysis involving five other states showed that misclassification penalized workers' compensation insurers through the 'retroactive use' of the system when independent contractors file claims as employees for injuries received on the job:

> The insurers have to pay benefits for workers they never received premiums for. Some workers, who have been independent contractors and therefore exempted from workers' compensation for many years, become employees and get covered under workers' compensation without having paid premiums for all of the previous years (de Silva et al. 2000).

This evidence indicates that, just as responsible employers bear the costs of unfair competition in higher insurance premiums and lost business opportunities, so each state's taxpayers are short-changed in resources lost to

---

16 U.S. Government Accountability Office (2009) indicates that the U.S. government is in the process of updating this information.

17 Jerome Horton, California State Assembly Member, 51st Assembly District, recorded interview within '1099 Misclassification: It's Time to Play by the Rules,' video stream currently available at http://www.mosaicprint.com/client_preview/1099/index.html#.

government and have to make up the difference. Significant revenue shortfalls also translate into broad social costs (less money available for communities, for school districts, hospitals, law enforcement, and the various other vital services of state, county and municipal governments). To the extent that employer-based plans do not provide for health care or retirement, additional costs are borne by government-run or sponsored programs.

Profiling Misclassification in New York

Given the considerable consequences of employee misclassification as independent contractors to employees, employers and the public, this chapter seeks to address the extent to which misclassification is occurring in New York and its economic costs, with a particular emphasis given to vulnerable workers within the construction industry. Before sharing the results of the study, it is important to discuss the methodology used in collecting and analyzing the data.

DEFINING THE DATA

The data for this study come from audits provided by the New York State Department of Labor, Unemployment Insurance Division.[18] Audit data are commonly used as measurements for aggregated, macro-level analyses of misclassification, and are recommended by government organizations as the appropriate tool for attempting to identify firms and employees who are in violation (see de Silva et al. 2000). The aggregated and objective data are also useful in that they provide a tangible means of capturing a population notoriously difficult to study. Many workers who are misclassified are vulnerable, migrant workers; these individuals are quite transient and sit at the fringes of the employment sphere, and are often reticent when it comes to speaking about their employment status (U.S. Government Accountability Office 2009). Because of this inaccessibility, in many cases it is extremely difficult to know even the most basic information about these individuals, such as the population of migrant workers who should be targeted for study. Therefore, one way of working around the issue of accessibility is to rely on empirical data, collected through objective audits.

---

18 In the audit data, some firms are identified as having 'alleged independent contractors', which can be considered misclassified employees. However, these workers may not necessarily all be misclassified. It has been generally acceptable to use a form of 'independent contractor' allegations to measure misclassification.

The NYS DOL runs two types of audits on employers statewide: general and specific. General audits are conducted on employers who are not suspected violators of state laws.[19] On the other hand, the 'specific' group consists of employers who, for one reason or another, are suspected to be violators of state laws. They are targeted based on multiple factors, including prior violations and other variables that increase their likelihood of non-compliance. This group is not drawn at random in any way; a firm's inclusion in this audit group is subjective.

The data give both general and specific employer information over a four-year period, from 2002 to 2005. This period was chosen because it can be used to show recent trends in the data. Rather than simply including a snapshot of worker misclassification, the study seeks to analyze patterns, both in the types of audits performed and in the scope of non-compliance. In the analysis, the general and specific data are analyzed separately, but also combined into a third category that constitutes all audits. These aggregate data give a broader picture, which can be used to approximate what is happening across all those industries included in NYS DOL audits.

Prevalence of Misclassification in New York

EMPLOYER MISCLASSIFICATION PREVALENCE

Based on Department of Labor audits, misclassification of employees as independent contractors is clearly prevalent in New York State. The data show that over the four-year period, 10 percent of all audited firms misclassified employees as independent contractors (9.3 percent of generally audited firms and 24.8 percent of specifically targeted firms, on average). The trends in the percent share of misclassifying firms are interesting. The share of specifically targeted firms misclassifying actually dropped 8.5 percent over the four-year period (from 30 percent to 21.5 percent), though the percentage figures for this group remained significantly higher than those firms selected under the 'general audit' category. Generally audited firms fluctuated slightly in their

---

19 It is important to note that these audits are not statistically random; that is, the DOL uses a complex method to determine which industries should be more heavily scrutinized in general. Industries are selected, among other reasons, on a cyclical basis: it is not the case that all employers are drawn arbitrarily in the 'general' sample. For this reason, all statewide extrapolations have been performed using data for only audited industries (a full list of these industries is available on request). However, it is significant that each of the employers has no reason to be a likely violator and should thus not be considered a specifically targeted entity.

misclassification share, comprising between 7.9 and 10 percent of all audited firms. There was no obvious trend in the percentage of generally audited firms misclassifying across all industries.The construction industry, on the other hand, gives somewhat different results. Across all audits, the percent of misclassifying construction firms has increased from 11 percent to 16.6 percent, clearly representing an upward trend. Interestingly, there was also a significant upward trend in the share of misclassifying employers amongst generally selected firms, where no such trend was found for all audited industries. The average percent of audited construction firms misclassifying employees stood at 12.4 percent over the four years, a number higher than the figure for all audits.

The data found in the audits can be used to approximate the statewide severity of misclassification in New York. Table 9.1a gives an approximation of the number of employers amongst all audited industries in New York State with misclassified workers, while Table 9.1b provides the same information for the construction industry only. Over the four-year period, it is approximated that, on average, nearly 40,000 firms within audited industries misclassified at least one worker statewide each year. The numbers appear to be on the rise, although the last two years remained relatively stable.

Amongst construction employers, an average of 5,880 employers misclassified at least one employee as an independent contractor in each of the four years. The trends in construction are different from those statewide; it appears that the number of employers engaging in misclassification rose fairly rapidly over the timeframe.

Table 9.1a   **Total number of employers in New York State with workers misclassified as independent contractors (audited industries)**

Year	Statewide approximation
2002	34,243
2003	37,608
2004	43,282
2005	43,206
Average	39,587

Table 9.1b   **Total number of employers in New York State with workers misclassified as independent contractors (construction industry)**

Year	Statewide approximation
2002	4,740
2003	5,230
2004	6,057
2005	7,493
Average	5,880

When considering at the share of construction firms amongst all misclassifying employers statewide, the results are somewhat interesting. From 2002–2004, construction's share of misclassifying employers remained stable at around 14 percent. However, for the year 2005, construction firms accounted for 17.2 percent of all misclassifying firms in New York State, a significant increase over the previous three years. It is not clear whether this leap is an anomaly or a sign of heavier trends in construction firm noncompliance.

PREVALENCE OF EMPLOYEE MISCLASSIFICATION

The previous section demonstrated the prevalence of misclassification by employers in New York State over a four-year period. The chapter turns now to the trends in misclassification of employees at those firms found to be noncompliant. The percent of employees misclassified at all noncompliant firms has remained relatively stable, though slightly increasing over the four-year period. Across all audited industries, about one in every ten employees was misclassified as an independent contractor. As expected, the level of misclassification was significantly higher for specifically selected firms (22.3 percent) than those generally audited (9.1 percent).

Within the construction industry alone, data indicate that, amongst generally audited firms, employees were more likely to be misclassified than employees at all audited industries, averaging 14.8 percent over the four-year period. Conversely, specific audits produced a far higher prevalence of employee misclassification in all audited industries than in construction alone, which had a rate of 14.5 percent. In all, due to the higher rate of employee misclassification in the general audits, construction had a higher overall misclassification prevalence amongst employees, with 14.8 percent of employees misclassified on average, as opposed to 10.3 percent in all audited industries. This would indicate that, when employers misclassify, they do so extensively in the construction industry, far more heavily than in all the audited industries.

Using the results of the audit data and statewide employment information, it is possible to approximate the number of employees misclassified over the four-year period in New York State. On average, about 705,000 workers were misclassified each year across all audited industries as independent contractors in New York during the four years studied, with yearly numbers ranging between about 680,000 and 734,000. These numbers appeared to be on the rise – the largest two figures were found in 2004 and 2005, with the largest number of misclassified employees occurring in the last year. It would appear that employee misclassification continued to worsen on a statewide level during the four-year period of interest.

Looking at the construction industry only, the results are slightly more ambiguous. An average of about 45,000 construction workers were misclassified as independent contractors each year over the four year period in New York State, with individual yearly misclassification rates ranging from about 37,000 to 52,000 construction employees. Contrary to the data found for all industries, the numbers did not appear to be on the rise; 2002 and 2003 recorded the highest approximations of statewide employee misclassification. Yet the 2005 figure may indicate that the statewide prevalence of employee misclassification was again on the rise.

Economic Costs of Misclassification in New York

While the misclassification of employees bears many significant burdens on all parties affected by the non-compliance, one measure of cost can be demonstrated economically. This cost of misclassification is shown in the form of taxable wages underreported, tax underreported and lost unemployment insurance. Misclassification directly hurts workers in terms of lost wages and benefits, amongst other costs, and it hurts employers in terms of penalties levied by the state if caught. Further, a critical component is the economic loss incurred by the state itself when an employer is noncompliant. The following section will discuss these economic losses at length.

TAXABLE WAGES UNDERREPORTED

The data show that the taxable wages underreported for each misclassified worker across all industries ranged from about $5,500 to $6,500 per employee. With one exception (2003), the underreported wages were uniformly higher at the specifically selected firms than at the generally audited companies. When looking at construction firms only, employers underreported more taxable wages in general audits than in specific audits, contrasting markedly with the results for all audits. Again, a notable exception is 2003, in which specific audit wage losses were higher. However, the substantially higher per-worker wage underreporting amongst generally audited construction firms substantially raised the overall figure within this industry, which ranged from about $6,600 to $8,600 per employee across the four years, a figure much higher than the overall audit results.

Using an approximation based on statewide employment information, one can make an educated guess as to how much money was lost on taxable wages underreported statewide across all audited industries. The results (in Table 9.2) show that the money lost on underreported wages in New York averaged over $4 billion across the four years, with the latest year of data (2005) having significantly higher losses than the previous three – the loss figure in 2005 alone was nearly $4.8 billion.

Table 9.2   **Total taxable wages underreported statewide for workers misclassified as independent contractors (audited industries)**

Year	Statewide approximation (US$)
2002	4.34 billion
2003	3.78 billion
2004	4.22 billion
2005	4.79 billion
Average	4.28 billion

Tax underreported

A major cost of misclassification to New York State comes in the form of lost tax revenue from underreported tax information. As with wages underreported, the highest levels of underreported taxes come in the specific audits, which showed an average of tax revenue loss of $279 per worker, compared with $216 for generally audited firms – the combined figure showed an average of $228 of tax underreported per worker. There also appears to be a slightly increasing trend in the amount of tax underreported across the audited employers; within each of the audit types, 2005 was the most costly in terms of taxes lost.

Similar to taxable wages underreported, the data show a significant difference in tax underreported for construction firms when compared to all audited industries. Generally selected firms underreported only slightly higher amounts of average tax across the four years when compared with specifically selected companies. Equally, there appeared to be a strong upward trend in the underreported tax of generally audited firms. The 2005 per-worker amount of $362 was 38 percent higher than both the 2002 amount ($262) and the amount found across all industries for 2005 ($262). In keeping with the trends set by taxable wages, construction firm underreporting was significantly higher across the board than that found for all industries – the data show per worker totals of $311 and $293 for general and specific audits, respectively, with a total combined average tax underreporting of $292 per worker, considerably higher than the $228 found in all audited industries.

While the per-worker dollar amounts may appear small (registering only in the hundreds), one must consider that there are hundreds of thousands of misclassified employees in New York State alone each year, which leads to severe losses in underreported tax revenue for the State of New York, which can be seen in Table 9.3. It can be approximated that, over the last four years, the State of New York has lost hundreds of millions of dollars in tax revenue due to misclassification of workers as independent contractors. In terms of trends, the statewide tax losses appear to be headed upward, with 2005 being the most costly to New York State.

Table 9.3   **Total tax underreported statewide for workers misclassified as independent contractors (audited industries)**

Year	Statewide approximation (US$)
2002	168.8 million
2003	133.1 million
2004	194.9 million
2005	205.9 million
Average	175.7 million

Unemployment insurance taxes underreported

The final measure of economic cost for this report comes from unemployment insurance taxes underreported by noncompliant employers. While there are several non-wage contributions that employers must make to the state for each of their employees, the most readily measurable in New York was unemployment insurance.

Table 9.4 shows the percentage of unemployment insurance taxes that were underreported due to misclassification by employers. Over the four-year period, 6.9 percent of unemployment insurance taxes were underreported as a direct result of misclassification. As with many of the findings, the data appear to be trending upward: 2005 again had the ignominy of claiming the highest underreporting amount of all the years.

Table 9.4   **Percentage of statewide unemployment insurance taxes underreported due to workers misclassified as independent contractors (audited industries)**

Year	Statewide approximation (%)
2002	7.6
2003	5.0
2004	7.3
2005	7.9
Average	6.9

Conclusion

When workers are misclassified as independent contractors, they are denied fundamental legal protections, responsible employers face unfair and potentially disabling competition and state government loses substantial revenue essential for the maintenance of vital public services. Misclassification is especially prevalent amongst vulnerable workers, who may not be aware of their legal entitlements. Many of these workers are migrants, and sit at the fringes of the labour force. This makes them easily exploitable, particularly as they do not often have recourse to collective voice (that is, unionization). The practice is commonly found in the construction industry, due to its competitive nature, where incentives to cut labour costs are extremely high.

Given these considerations, this chapter has attempted to document the prevalence and consequences of worker misclassification in New York. Knowing the key role played by the construction industry as a conduit for misclassification, special consideration has been given to these firms and employees, but this chapter has also looked at the broader, cross-industry statewide picture as well. Audit data from a four-year period (2002 to 2005) were used to more comprehensively document not only single-year occurrences of misclassification, but also trends in the data.

A key consideration of this study is the use of audit data as the methodological tool. This approach was predicated on studies performed by the Department of Labor (de Silva et al. 2000) and also scholarly research assessing misclassification within individual states, such as Massachusetts and Maine (Carré et al. 2004, 2005). Using audit data to study misclassification is beneficial in that it allows for researchers to understand aggregate, macro-level trends and numbers, and relies on objective data collected by the public sector. A significant problem in studying misclassification is that the individuals of interest (that is, misclassified workers) are often difficult to approach and are generally quite a transient group, thus making them quite inaccessible. This is particularly true of vulnerable migrant workers, who are often the misclassified party. Although audit data do not allow for more nuanced, individual-based methods of analysis (such as personal interviews, for instance), they offer researchers an opportunity to capture this population using verifiable records. However, in order to extrapolate beyond only the firms chosen for audits, a fundamental assumption must be made regarding the data, which is that one must be able to generalize the audit data to the population as a whole. The extrapolations found in this chapter are supported by previous studies (highlighted above), all of which used the same techniques and were accepted as legitimate and representative. Further, care has been taken not to include in the results any sectors that were not audited and thus cannot be brought into the larger state wide results.[20]

Assuming the audit data outcomes are acceptable for extrapolation, the results may be used as the basis for discussing potential protections against misclassification, which include providing both greater scrutiny of employers, and offering more accessible protections for workers. For instance, as a first step in addressing the problem, it may be appropriate for state agencies to presume employee status when determining whether a worker is an employee

---

20 The most critical group affected by this are those who work in the public sector – given that public sector firms were not audited, only private sector extrapolations were made.

or independent contractor. Legislation in other states (see Massachusetts for instance) seeks to clarify and streamline the determination process by presuming employee status so that independent contractor classification is recognized only if all three elements of a three-part test are met:

1.   the individual is free from control and direction in connection with the performance of the service, both under his contract for the performance of service and in fact;

2.   the service is performed outside the usual course of the business of the employer; and

3.   the individual is customarily engaged in an independently established trade, occupation, profession or business of the same nature as that involved in the service performed.[21]

Similarly, New Mexico presumes an employee–employer relationship for all workers in the construction industry.[22] New York took a significant step in this regard by enacting the New York State Construction Industry Fair Play Act in September 2010, which presumes employee status for construction workers, in direct response to the substantial misclassification occurrences in this industry (Malik 2010).

A second step in addressing the issue of worker misclassification would be to extend employee protections to independent contractors. This notion has been echoed by previous research of its type. For instance, recognizing that workforce changes that have left many workers, both properly classified and misclassified independent contractors, beyond the protections and benefits of more traditional employer–employee relations, a 2000 report for the U.S. DOL recommends a 'multi-agency dialogue' to study a series of questions regarding protections for independent contractors. These include queries related to unemployment insurance, workers' compensation, and minimum wage requirements for independent contractors, amongst other protections (de Silva et al. 2000).[23] If state labour laws were extended to all workers, whether employees or independent contractors, the classification of these workers would no longer be an issue. This notion has some support in other states;

---

21 M.G.L. Chapter 149, Section 148b (http://www.mass.gov/legis/laws/mgl/149-148b.htm).
22 See http://legis.state.nm.us/sessions/05%20Regular/bills/senate/SB0657CTS.pdf.
23 See also 'Lone Rangers: Are those in the free-agent economy just getting to the future ahead of everyone else?' *Common Wealth*, Winter 2005, available on line at www.hidden-tech.net/articles/CommonWealth-Summer-2005.htm.

Colorado, for example, requires that workers' compensation coverage be extended to all construction workers.[24]

A third step would be to provide more resources for enforcement of punishment, and to promote more information sharing among state agencies tasked with handling misclassification. State agencies need the tools to motivate employers or compel compliance with classification guidelines. As noted in the 2000 DOL report, 'State and federal agencies have insufficient staff to crack down on employers who misclassify workers' (de Silva et al. 2000: 43). Issuing stiff penalties for violating classification rules would likely encourage greater attention to those rules by employers. Also, permitting aggrieved workers private rights of action would further motivate compliance, and enhancing the data collection and audit capabilities of state agencies and requiring a collaborative approach to misclassification identification and enforcement would likely make a dramatic difference. New York took considerable steps in this direction when then-governor Eliot Spitzer enacted an executive order creating an inter-agency taskforce to address the problem in 2007 (Greenhouse 2007).

A final step to stemming misclassification may be to extend current outreach and education efforts to workers themselves. State agencies might consider providing all workers and employers with information about how 'employees' and 'independent contractors' are distinguishable (for example, workplace posters similar to minimum wage postings). While this information is available at the NYS DOL and Internal Revenue Service websites, misclassified workers may not question their status until after a situation (layoff, on-the-job illness or injury, etc.) has occurred.[25] This would be particularly useful for vulnerable migrant workers, who may not yet be informed of the distinguishing characteristics between employee and independent contractor status. New York may wish to take a similar approach to other states in terms of ensuring that workers feel able to report classification errors/abuses by affording them whistleblower-type protection. For example, the National Employment Law Project (NELP) references the San Francisco Minimum Wage Ordinance, which presumes that any adverse action taken against a complaining worker is retaliatory if it occurs within 90 days of a worker's complaint.

---

24 See htttp://www.leg.state.co.us/CLICS2004A/csl.nsf/fsbillcont3/7F2516C7B4E9B70087256D790 073B01D?Open&file=1090_enr.pdf.
25 See http://www.labor.ny.gov/ui/dande/ic.shtm.

All of these recommendations are driven by the results found not only in this study of New York, but also in the numerous misclassification studies that have occurred in recent years, and the various responses at policy levels to the problem. It has become clear that, in the United States at least, misclassification is a significant issue that crosses jurisdictions and state boundaries. Often those most harmed by the practice are workers with very little knowledge of their rights, who are unable to provide themselves with traditional means of employee voice. The construction industry is particularly affected by this practice. The results of this study indicate that, unless significant steps are taken to reduce worker misclassification in New York, the practice will likely continue to worsen, and the economic costs to the public will be substantial. Some steps have already occurred at the statewide to help solve the problem, such as creating an interagency task force to address misclassification and presuming employee status for construction workers. However, there is still much that can be done to offer vulnerable workers the protections that they need from employer misclassification.

References

Alpert, William T. 1992. *Estimated 1992 Costs in Connecticut of the Misclassification of Employees*. Department of Economics, University of Connecticut.

California Department of Labor. 2010. *Misclassification of workers as 'independent contractors' rebuffed by the California Court of Appeal*. Department of Industrial Relations, Division of Labor Standards Enforcement. http://www.dir.ca.gov/dlse/MisclassificationOfWorkers.htm.

Carré, Françoise, and Randall Wilson. 2004. *The Social and Economic Costs of Employee Misclassification in Construction*. Construction Policy Research Center, Labor and Worklife Program, Harvard Law School, Harvard School of Public Health.

Carré, Françoise, and Randall Wilson. 2005. *The Social and Economic Costs of Employee Misclassification in the Maine Construction Industry*. Construction Policy Research Center, Labor and Worklife Program, Harvard Law School, Harvard School of Public Health.

Cooley, Keith W. 2008. *Interagency Task Force on Employee Misclassification*. Report to Governor Jennifer M. Granholm, 1 July, unpublished.

Cordray, Richard. 2009. *Report of the Ohio Attorney General on the Economic Impact of Misclassified Workers for State and Local Governments in Ohio*. February, unpublished.

de Silva, Lalith, Adrian W. Millett, Dominic M. Rotondi, and William F. Sullivan. 2000. *Independent Contractors: Prevalence and Implications for Unemployment Insurance Programs*. Planmatics, Inc. Prepared for U.S. Department of Labor Employment and Training Administration. February, unpublished.

Donahue, Linda H., James Ryan Lamare, and Fred B. Kotler. 2007. *The Cost of Worker Misclassification in New York State*. Cornell University: ILR School.

Greenhouse, Steven. 2007. State takes aim at evaders of wage and tax laws. *New York Times*. September 8.

Internal Revenue Service. 2010. *Employer's Supplemental Tax Guide*. Publication 15-A. Cat. No. 21453T. Department of the Treasury, Washington, DC.

Kelsay, Michael P., James I. Sturgeon, and Kelly D. Pinkham. 2006. *The Economic Costs of Employee Misclassification in the State of Illinois*. December, unpublished.

Malik, Adam. 2010. New York enacts 'Construction Industry Fair Play Act' to address employee misclassification. *Wage and Hour Counsel*. September 9, http://www.wageandhourcounsel.com,2010/09/articles/independent-contractor-issues/new-york-enacts-construction-industry-fair-play-act-to-address-employee-misclassification.

National Conference of Insurance Legislators. 2009. *Proposed Employee Misclassification Workers' Compensation Coverage Model Act*. Working Draft.

National Employment Law Project, Immigration and Nonstandard Worker Project. 2005. *Combating Independent Contractor Misclassification in the State: Models for Legislative Reform*. December, unpublished.

Nobles, James. 2007. *Misclassification of Employees as Independent Contractors*. Office of the Legislative Auditor, State of Minnesota. November.

Personal communication. 2007. New York State Department of Labor Unemployment Insurance Division.

Schoeff, Mark, Jr. 2010. Labor agency cracks down on employee misclassification. *Workforce Management*. February 16, http://www.workforce.com/section/news/article/labor-agency-cracks-down-employee-misclassification.php.

U.S. Government Accountability Office. 2006. *Employment Arrangements: Improved Outreach Could Help Ensure Proper Worker Classification*. Report to the Ranking Member, Committee on Health, Education, Labor, and Pensions, U.S. Senate.

U.S. Government Accountability Office. 2009. *Employee Misclassification: Improved Coordination, Outreach, and Targeting Could Better Ensure Detection and Prevention*. GAO-09-717. August.

10

The Right to Occupational Health and Safety and its Legislation in China

Chang Kai[1]

Introduction

The right to occupational health and safety is a basic employment right. Its distinction from other rights is that it directly involves the workers' life and health. Hence the protection of workers occupational health and safety should be the most fundamental and urgent task. However, whilst recent labour legislation developments in China have begun to address health and safety issues, they do not go anywhere near far enough. Confronted with alarming occupational health and safety problems, building and improving the legal framework in this area is of the utmost urgency for the Chinese government.

Workers' Right to Life and Health

Occupational health and safety refers to the protection of workers' health and safety in the employment process through relevant means adopted in respect of legislation, technology, equipment and education.[2] This right refers not only to the prevention of accidents or sickness, but also to the promotion of physical and mental health by way of high standards of safety and hygiene at the workplace.[3]

---

1   Chang Kai is Professor in Renmin University, Ph.D. supervisor and Director of the Institute of Industrial Relations. He was Professor of Kyushu University from 2003–2004 and Visiting Professor of Tokyo University (2009).
2   China National Bureau of Technological Monitor, Terminology of Occupational Health and safety, issued on 5 October 1994, implemented on 1 June 1995.
3   ILO: Article 3, C155 Occupational Health and Safety Convention, 1981.

In China, the right to occupational health and safety refers to the right to labour protection in a narrow sense. The generally accepted definition of the right to labour protection indicates a comprehensive content of labour protection, including wages, working time, working conditions, working insurance and other laws and regulations concerning all of the workers' interests. Indeed, in this sense, labour law is in fact the labour protection law.[4] However, the labour protection law can also be narrowly defined as the laws and regulations concerning the relevant measures adopted to protect workers' health and safety,[5] which is commonly employed by the labour relations academia in China. The Labour Law of People's Republic of China (1994) adopted the definition of 'labour (occupational) health and safety protection' given by the ILO, to make it clearer and more specific than the notion of labour protection.

The right to occupational health and safety is in essence the right to life and health for workers. It is an important part of personal rights, of which the right to life and health is the primary and fundamental condition.[6] The right of life and health, as the premise of human existence, is the most basic personal interest. It therefore produces a great volume of litigation, at multiple levels.

The right to occupational health and safety is derived from the right of personality in the field of labour relations rights. The labour laws define and protect the right of occupational health and safety, thereby protecting the right of life and health of workers.

Offences against life and health usually occur in three ways: against the right to life by causing death; against the right of the body's physical integrity; and against the right of health.[7] Violations of life refer to fatal accidents in the mining industry, through fire or other work-related fatalities. Violations of the physical integrity refer to accidents causing disability, for example, mechanical or chemical accidents, such as mutilation or pneumoconiosis. Violations of the right to health refer to harms on health caused by high levels of mental stress, overwork, adverse working conditions and so on.

Since China started its market reforms in the 1980s, economic development has occurred at a great pace. However, the situation relating to occupational

---

4   Tanjing, Shi (1990: 44.
5   Shangkuan, Shi (1978: 344–345.
6   'Law Dictionary' Editing Committee (1984: 12).
7   Liang, H.X. (1996: 106–107).

health and safety is alarming and less than satisfactory. During the earlier period of the command economy, the Party-state paid direct attention to these rights of workers. The emphasis on occupational safety as well as health precautions was a priority for production at the workplace. Due to the dynamic nature of labour relations and interest divisions between labour and capital in the transition, the pursuit of profit maximisation has become the primary goal of enterprises, especially in the private sector. As a consequence, the right to health and safety has been largely neglected or weakened. The high incidence of industrial accidents has undermined the right to life and health. Since the 1990s, the rapid development of the economy has led to a significant deterioration in the standards of occupational health and safety.

The rate of industry fatalities across the whole nation is very high. Although the number of accidental deaths in enterprises experienced a slight decline to 15,146 in 1992, it increased dramatically and hit highs of 19,800 in 1993 and 20,300 in 1994.[8] In the second half of the 1990s there was a decrease, but the fatalities increased again to 17,315 in 2003. Since then, the figure has remained around15,000 per year.[9]

In relation to occupational disease, according to the Ministry of Public Health, by the end of 2009, there were more than 578,000 workers identified as suffering from pneumoconiosis, a number equal to all other countries' combined. However, it is estimated that the real number in China may be 10 times more than this official figure. The official statistics tends to focus on the stated-owned coal mining enterprises, with nothing about the incidence of those occurring at the local private enterprises, or the smaller enterprise below the village level.[10] In 2009 alone, there were 14,500 newly reported cases of pneumoconiosis, of which those in both the coal mining and jewel-crafting industry accounted for 92 percent. In that year, 2,343 workers died due to pneumoconiosis, triple the figure in coal mining or other industrial accidents. In 2007, the Ministry of Public Health also revealed that there were more than 16 million enterprises not providing workers with necessary health and safety protections, and more than 200 million workers suffering from different levels of occupational diseases.[11]

---

8   Wang, Y.S. (1995).
9   National Production Safety Bureau (2008).
10   *China Youth Daily* (2010).
11   Chen (2007).

The figure for disabilities caused by injuries at the workplace is also astonishing. For instance, in Shenzhen, 1998 saw 11,341 workers permanently disabled due to industrial injuries, with more than 90 per cent of them losing their fingers, palms or arms. In some areas, the amount of the lost fingers can be measured in baskets.[12]

The Situation of Laws of Chinese Occupational Health and Safety: Achievements and Problems

According to the ILO Convention 155, all three parties in the industrial relations system are obliged to fulfill their duties in guaranteeing workplace health and safety. China ratified the convention in 2007, and there are a set of laws regarding labour protection. In the 1950s and 1960s, China enacted a series of labour regulations, of which labour protection was an important component. The Criminal Law in 1979 specifically provides for the violation of regulations, dereliction of duty and other criminal acts that cause significant industrial accidents. In last two decades, China has enacted Trade Union Law, Mining Industry Safety Law, Labour Law, Production Safety Law, Occupational Disease Prevention Law, Noise Standards in Industrial Enterprise, a Sanitation Standard Designed for Industry, and some other important laws. So far, there are more than 100 national occupational health and safety standards and regulations in both substantial and procedural terms.

In the 1994 Labour Law, there was a special chapter for occupational health and safety. This law emphasises and clarifies employers' duties by requiring employers to have their health and safety responsibilities. Moreover, workers are allowed not to work if employers break the law or put them at risk, and are required to report and accuse employers who break the law (Article 52, 53, 54, 55, 56 of 1994 Labour Law). Meanwhile, the Production Safety Law provides for detailed rights for workers at the workplace.

Although the framework of health and safety legislation in China has been established, its effectiveness is subject to scepticism. In a nutshell, the salient occupational health and safety problems can be largely attributed to inadequate and ineffective legislation. First, the legal ideology does not take the protection of workers' health and safety as the basis and starting point of the legislation. For instance, the Production Safely Law sets the priority of 'guaranteeing the production safety' (Article 1, Article 6, Articles 44–52 of 2002 Production

---

12 Sun (1999).

Safety Law), which is in essence different from the nature of protective laws for workers. Secondly, despite the enactment of relevant laws and regulations, there is not a coherent legal system. Those major laws such as the Production Safety Law, Mining Industry Safety Law and Occupational Disease Prevention Law are divided in accordance with sectors that have not been well-integrated with each other. Thirdly, in relation to technical aspects of the legislation, some of the provisions are difficult to operationalise. Furthermore, the employer's liability as a result of violation of the law is slight. All the above have greatly weakened the effectiveness of the legislation. Fourthly, when it comes to enforcement, there is no unified administrative body to enforce and supervise the laws. It is commonplace in China that governments are accountable for enforcing the law. However, in reality, the authority is rather paradoxical. For instance, the Public Health Administration authorises occupational disease prevention and management, whilst the Safety Production Supervision Bureau is in charge of all inspection activities. And the Labour Bureau (renamed the Human Resource and Social Security Department) has no obligation in the issues of occupational health and safety. This confused arrangement leads to chaos in its enforcement and inspection.

Legal Framework of Occupational Health and Safety: Features and Requirements

> The legal remedy of the right to occupational health and safety adopts the principle of 'consequentialism'.[13]

Infringement of workers' rights to occupational health and safety is essentially an impingement on the right to life and health. In comparison with the civil law, the liability and remedy in labour law is based on the principle of *liability without fault*. That is to say, during the labour process, when employees' health and safety are violated due to unpredictable causes or accidents, or even the workers' own negligence or mistakes – but not necessarily the employer's fault – the employer has a liability for part of the compensation.

From the perspective of consequentialism, regardless of the particular causes, employers and the state always have liability when workers are injured at the workplace, unless they injure themselves intentionally. This indicates the supreme status of human rights in contemporary industrial society. And it is

---

13 Huang, Y.Q. (1994: 39).

also the foundation for regarding the right to occupational health and safety as a basic labour right.

> *The right to occupational health and safety is empowered by the protections of both public rights and private rights.*

The right to occupational health and safety is first and foremost a public right. By virtue of the national labour standard, the state provides for the statutory rights to occupational health and safety. For employers, they are compelled to fulfil the corresponding public duties regulated by the national labour standard. Additionally, the national labour standard offers the basic bedrock for the establishment of the employment contract. Standards stipulated in the employment contract cannot go below the national labour standard. Additionally, employer's occupational health and safety duties, even if not explicitly stated, are imposed by provisions of national labour standards and implied in every contract of employment.

The nature of private law in this right implies the contractual terms based on the agreement of both sides. However, by contrast with contracts in the civil law, the private rights in employment are confined by the public right and in these rights to occupational health and safety, workers are the right holders while employers are obligors. In addition, as Shi pointed out, in the labour law, on the one hand, workers are the right holders, claiming employers' duties of fulfillment of private rights; on the other hand, the state is the obliger, claiming employers' duties of the fulfillment of public rights.[14]

In this sense, workers have the right to claim a remedy for the breach of employment provisions related to occupational health and safety, and the state has the right to enforce or punish employers when employers infringe upon the labour standards.

It is suggested that the construction of the legal framework of occupational health and safety takes into account these features discussed above: firstly, the protection of workers' occupational health and safety is central to this framework and it is contingent on the tripartite parties in the employment relationship to ensure the standards are adhered to. Employers are the obligors in both the sense of private and public rights; while the state is also the obligor for workers to protect the rights of citizens, especially in the field of public laws. Hence, workers are the rights holders, and their rights to occupational

---

14 Shi, S.K. (1978: 345).

health and safety are the core of the framework. In this sense, it is erroneous to highlight economic development whilst overlooking workers' rights. Secondly, in China, the primary problem is weak implementation of the law, which calls for reflection on the part of the relevant government sectors. This has given rise to the criticism of the present system of the health and safety protection that it is based on punishing violations of standards, rather than as a positive means of preventing accidents in the first place. Therefore, rearranging and integrating the current administrative institutions so that they reinforce the labour bureau's main role in implementing and inspecting the laws is urgent. Thirdly, workers' status in the occupational health and safety system should be supported through trade unions. Chinese unions ought to be the positive activists in monitoring the legislation. Articles 23 and 24 of the 2001 Trade Union Law empower the union to protect workers' rights to occupational health and safety. Nevertheless, in reality, Chinese trade unions have largely failed in representing and protecting workers. In light of ILO Convention 155, a tripartite mechanism should be established by the government in health and safety institutions. This occupational health and safety tripartite mechanism should also be integrated into the wider and already established tripartite consultation system. Fourthly, employers' violations of health and safety standards should be stringently punished, thereby encouraging enterprises to fulfil their duties under the legislation.

Conclusion

The violation of workers' rights to occupational health and safety is a widespread issue across the world but in developing regions the problem is strikingly severe, and has been accentuated by the pressures of globalisation. It is de facto a result of capital accumulation at the early stages of marketisation in these areas, where workers' basic rights are undermined by the maximisation of capital expansion. In political and legal terms, it is also a result of governments' overlooking the supervision of occupational health and safety while concentrating on economic development. As a result, the legal framework of occupational health and safety in China has not been effectively established and implemented. The fast growth of Chinese economic development has been achieved at the expense of workers' health and safety conditions. There is an urgent need for China's law makers, government, employers and trade unions to take the necessary actions to improve the protection of workers' health and safety.

References

Chen, P.S. (2007) 'More than 200 million workers having occupational disease', *China Youth*, 10 May.

China Youth Daily (2010) 17 May, http://zqb.cyol.com/content/2006-05/17content_1385296.htm.

Huang, Y.Q. (1994) *Analysis on Labour Law*, Taiwan: National Chengchi University.

'Law Dictionary' Editing Committee (1984) *'Law Dictionary'*, Shanghai: Cishu Press.

Liang, H.X. (1996) *An Overview of the Civil Law*, Beijing: Law Press.

National Production Safety Bureau (2008) *China's Work Safety Yearbook*, Beijing: China Coal Industry Publishing House.

Shangkuan, Shi (1978) *The Original Theory of Labour Law*, Taiwan: Zheng DA Press.

Shi, S.K. (1978) *Original Theory of Labour Law*, 2nd Edition, Taiwan: Zhengda Press.

Sun, F.H. (1999) 'The worrying situation of workplace safety in Shenzhen migrant workers', *Workers' Daily*, 3 March.

Tanjing, Shi (1990) *Labour Law*, Beijing: Economic Science Press.

Wang, Y.S. (1995) 'Occupational health and safety is facing the severe challenges', *Workers' Daily*, 7 August, 1995.

11

Seeking Solutions to Precarious Working in the Growth of New Zealand Dairy Farming – A Research Agenda

Rupert Tipples[1]

Introduction

Today agriculture overall is New Zealand's largest export earner. In the year to 31 March 2009 dairy exports contributed 27 percent of total merchandise export value (MAF, 2009). New Zealand is the world's largest exporter of dairy produce. These exports were produced by 4.1 million cows in 11,618 herds (LIC, 2008–09). Dairy export value to 31 March 2009 was $NZ 11,323 million, which is projected to increase to $NZ 11,905 million in 2013 as a result of higher volumes and prices (MAF, 2009).

Worldwide most milk is consumed in the country of production. Only 5 percent of New Zealand milk is consumed in New Zealand, with the remainder exported as various milk products. Some 97 percent of New Zealand milk is processed by Fonterra, the farmers' dairy cooperative company. Fonterra is also New Zealand's largest company employing some 17,400 staff worldwide and it is the sixth-largest international dairy company (Fonterra, 2007).

1 Rupert Tipples is Senior Lecturer in Employment Relations, Agricultural Management and Property Studies, Faculty of Commerce, Lincoln University, New Zealand. He specialises in rural aspects of employment relations and rural labour markets, as well as local and industry history. This research was funded by Lincoln University Research Fund (Award INTE013).

The medium-term prospects for dairy production are considered to be good (MAF, 2010). The European Union has been able to export dairy products without export subsidies for the first time since its creation 50 years ago. However, future prospects, while looking good, are still quite uncertain if the production potential of a number of large countries (for example China, USA, Russia and those of Eastern Europe) is focused on milk production (Woodford, 2007; MAF, 2009). Sustaining milk production and productivity therefore has vital importance for the overall state of the New Zealand economy.

History and Employment in New Zealand Dairy Farming

Dairy farming has been a significant New Zealand economic activity since the introduction of refrigerated shipping in the 1880s. That permitted the export of butter and cheese, which subsequently became major exports. For many years dairy farming was primarily a family enterprise with little or no employed labour. That is still the dominant form of dairy farming in the North Island. Dairy farmers were opposed to organised labour, especially trade unions, because they interfered with the export of their primary produce. This came to a head when in 1913 farmers became temporary policemen, known as Massey's Cossacks, to ensure their produce could get through for shipping for export (McLean, 1990).

In the 1930s under the first Labour government agricultural employment was regulated through the first Agricultural Workers Act, 1936, but dairy farmers only agreed to accept the proposals when the government promised to keep them out of the Industrial Conciliation and Arbitration Act and guaranteed then better prices for their produce. However, farmers were not prepared to improve these conditions in subsequent years when better prices were not available (Tipples, 1987). The dominant culture of the industry has been opposed to employment save on the conditions set by the employing dairy farmers. Even the Farm Workers' Association, a farm workers' collective formed specifically to keep farm workers out of industrial unionism in the 1970s, was not fully supported by the farming community and eventually was largely killed off by dairy farmers refusing to grant any kind of membership clause to the Association when they were experiencing financial difficulties because farm workers were failing to join (Tipples, 1987; Angove, 1994).

Sustained opposition to representative farm worker organizations has left workers without representation in the most recent attempts to address the farm labour crisis, such as the setting up of *Human Capability in Agriculture and Horticulture* following the Human Resources in Agriculture and Horticulture Workshop held in Rotorua in 2002 (Tipples, 2004). The only organization promoting farming amongst the young has been the Federation of Young Farmers' Clubs, which runs a very successful televised 'Young Farmer of the Year' competition (Tipples and Wilson, 2007).

While not an employee organisation, the Agriculture Industry Training Organisation (Agriculture ITO), constituted under the Industry Training Act 1992 (Murray, 2006), has been required by the statute to have an employee representative on its board. The representative since 2006 has been a delegate of the Federation of Amalgamated Workers' Unions (AWU), nominated by the Combined Trade Unions (CTU). The representative was chosen because of geographical proximity to Wellington, but not cheap air flights. Consequently, continued monthly participation in the Agricultural Health and Safety Council with representatives of Federated Farmers, Federated Farmers' Wives, the Accident Compensation Corporation, the Department of Labour and the Police, has not been economic. Funding from union members' fees has been insufficient to make regular attendance possible (McLaughlan, 2010). Nevertheless, the same representative, as an Agriculture ITO board member, has been part of that organisation's promotion of agricultural training with a significant OSH component. For example, the first module of an introductory national certificate in agriculture is 'Staying Alive', with units in personal safety, vehicle safety and 'looking after yourself' (Agriculture ITO, no date). So while unionization of farming is practically non-existent, the Agriculture ITO does play a significant role in promoting employee interests through training and skills developments, which incorporate careers' possibilities and substantial OSH content. Also, between 2002 and 2008 the number of dairy trainees doubled from 3,750 to 7,857 (Agriculture ITO *Annual Reports,* 2002–2008).

The Occupational Structure of the Dairy Industry

Two sources of data are available, the five yearly *Census of Population and Dwellings*, and data from LEED. The census is limited to who is usually living in a particular location on a given March census night. Visitors who live in New Zealand for less than 12 months are excluded. LEED is a longitudinal database that has been developed by Statistics New Zealand. It is based on the integration of monthly data on employee earnings with data on employers and firms. The LEED dataset covers all individuals ('employees') who receive income from which tax is deducted at source.[2] The key basis of the LEED quarterly measure is 'jobs'. A job is defined as a unique employer–employee pair in the reference quarter. Unlike the census LEED data provide an ongoing measure of employment as the data is continuously being collected. However, there are also major limitations to the data. For example there is no information on ethnicity or country of birth (Callister and Tipples, 2010).

DAIRY EMPLOYMENT IN CENSUS DATA 1991–2006

In the 2006 Census of Population 24,795 people were found to be working with a main occupation as dairy farming (Statistics New Zealand, 2007). The number of people employed as dairy farmers/dairy farm workers (occupation classification 61211) had fallen from 29,976 in 1996 to 26,328 in 2001 to 24,795 in 2006 (Wilson and Tipples, 2008). The numbers of self-employed dairy farmers has been declining and the number of paid employees has been increasing. Table 11.1 shows the percentages for each category in recent census years. People are classified according to whether they are working for themselves or for other people – it is recorded for the main job only (Wilson and Tipples, 2008). Of note is that the 'large increase in employees is not matched by significantly increasing numbers of employers' (Wilson and Tipples, 2008). Further, the data reported may understate the proportion of employees, when those resident for less than 12 months are excluded from the Census. There has also been a profound ageing of the dairy farming population, with the relative share of the population aged less than 35–39 decreasing and that aged more than 45 increasing. Over the 15-year period from the 1991 census, the biggest change has been an increase in the 15–19 year age group (from 4 percent in 1991 to 7.9 percent in 2006) and a decrease in the 25–29 year and 30–34 year age groups (from 13.5 percent and 16.9 percent to 9.4 percent and 12 percent respectively) (Wilson and Tipples, 2008 pp. 8–11).

The traditional dependence on a high proportion of young workers for basic farm work like milking has proved increasingly problematic (Wilson and Tipples, 2008). Not only are they difficult to recruit and retain, but they are going to be increasingly difficult to source, especially in districts where the ageing of the population is most marked. The expansion of the industry has largely taken place in the South Island, particularly Canterbury, not a traditional dairy farming area, and Southland. Typically these are large herd developments, often based on corporate capital, irrigated land and employed

---

2   LEED data include social assistance payments such as paid parental leave, student allowances, benefits, pensions and ACC payments.

labour. At present Canterbury's workforce is relatively young, nearly two-thirds are employees, compared to just over one-third of the New Zealand dairy workforce as a whole. Ageing of the traditional dairy workforce in the North Island implies a productivity risk, while with recruitment and retention already a problem the attrition in younger age groups suggests a capacity risk (Strack et al., 2008). To retain the dairy industry's comparative advantage in production developing new potential sources of recruits will be crucial in years to come. As Strack et al. (2008) conclude, adopting 'a demographic risk management approach now – before their competitiors do and before it is too late to effectively respond to the changes that lie ahead' is critical to the industry and the New Zealand economy as a whole. As attracting sufficient talented people looks somewhat unlikely from the local population alone, the 2009 Dairy Strategy includes a provision to 'Influence government on legislation relating to immigrant workers' (DairyNZ, 2009, p. 21).

Table 11.1   Dairy farming population proportions (%) by status in employment (Censuses of Population 1991, 1996, 2001, 2006)

Status (% of status group)	1991	1996	2001	2006
Paid employee	18	21	24	37
Employer	25	26	32	29
Self-employed and without employees	52	41	38	27
Unpaid family worker	4	10	5	6
Not stated	1	2	1	1
Total	100	100	100	100

HOURS OF WORK

The other striking Census data relate to the long hours of work, one of the factors thought to make dairy farm work unattractive. Long hours are nothing new in dairy farming. Doig (1940) reported dairy farmers as working very long hours in 1937–1938, with 65 percent working 65–84 hours per week in busy times, or an average of 70.0 hours per week, while permanent hired employees averaged 65. In his sample there was an average of half a permanent employee per farm. McMeekan, one of the fathers of modern New Zealand dairy farming recollected from his youth: 'milking was the main chore, and its drudgery left such an indelible mark upon youth that many of the best were permanently lost to agriculture' (quoted by Paine, 2010).

At that time mechanisation of milking was already making an impact and only the smallest herds (<20 cows) were still milked by hand. When McMeekan was writing in 1960 he considered milking had been revolutionised by mechanisation, 'making it one of the more pleasant jobs on farm', but that was long before the huge growth in herd size and the extended milking times of the new millennium.

With the most recent (2006) increase in the proportion of employees, there has only been a slight diminution in the hours worked. The proportion working over 70 hours per week had been increasing over the previous three censuses (1991, 1996 and 2001) to reach 32 percent in 2001, but had fallen to 27 percent by 2006 (Wilson and Tipples, 2008, pp. 18–20) compared to the industrial norm of 40 hours per week (Figure 11.1) (Blackwood, 2007).

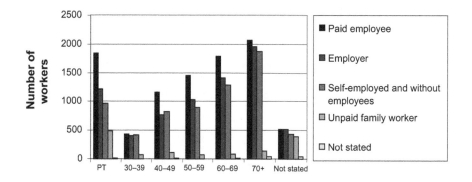

Figure 11.1   Hours worked in main job (by status in employment, 2006)

The ongoing recruitment and retention problems facing the industry are not described well by the census data available, particularly because they exclude those who are not part of the usually resident population, that is those who have lived in New Zealand for less than 12 months. Since the 2006 Census of Population this group has expanded quite dramatically, as shown in Table 11.2 (Callister and Tipples, 2010).

Table 11.2   Numbers of temporary work permits issued for dairy farm work

Nationality	2003/04	2004/05	2005/06	2006/07	2007/08	2008/09
Philippines	16	40	74	278	806	898
South Africa	75	114	100	89	139	166
Fiji	1	3	18	22	75	130

Nationality	2003/04	2004/05	2005/06	2006/07	2007/08	2008/09
Brazil	3	7	41	45	105	128
Chile	7	21	15	24	45	100
Uruguay	12	25	23	31	47	42
Argentina	20	12	13	21	31	26
Great Britain	126	111	97	74	111	96
India	16	21	28	42	70	72
Sri Lanka	7	20	21	21	30	43
Nepal	7	7	2	8	13	33
Ireland	39	26	28	24	16	26
Germany	8	9	10	14	27	20
Others	179	234	171	187	226	177
Total permits	516	650	641	880	1741	1957

Source: Callister and Tipples (2010).

Figure 11.2   Migrants in the news

These statistics are reinforced by case studies, student experiences and media comment (for example Figure 11.2; Enterprise North Canterbury, 2009; Rawlinson, 2010). However, this expansion in the supply of dairy farm labour would seem to be dependent on increasingly 'precarious' migrant employees (Tucker, 2002), who provide short-term solutions for dairy farmers but do not seriously address the long-term demographic risks.

DAIRY EMPLOYMENT IN LEED DATA

The following figures are drawn from the LEED dataset. The data presented focus on growth in employee numbers (Figure 11.3) (Callister and Tipples, 2010). The growth in these data between 2001 and 2006 is in contrast with the census which shows a decline. It seems likely that the introduction of migrants in response to the staff shortage is responsible for this growth. Figure 11.3 also shows some relatively strong seasonality in employment. For dairying the peak each year is in the fourth quarter. The second quarter, effectively winter, is always the low point in employment. This phenomenon may be explained by the practice of 'Gypsy Day', which happens on 1 June each year. It is the time when share tenancies come to an end and new ones begin, and similarly for employment contracts. New staff are then supposed to be ready for calving in the third quarter, and full production in the fourth (Tipples and Lucock, 2004).

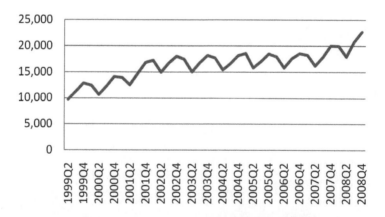

Figure 11.3   Number of dairy farming workers, 1999–2008
Source: LEED data.

DAIRY STAFF TURNOVER

While the Census only measures employment at one time, and where the subject was five years previously, the LEED data is able to show the pattern of staff turnover on dairy enterprises (Figure 11.4). The worker turnover rate is calculated using the counts of accessions and separations, which are defined using a reference date concept. Figure 11.4 shows that turnover rates always peak in the third quarter for dairying, which is the spring quarter, the time of calving and peak workloads. They are noticeably higher than for 'all employees'. Figure 11.4 also shows that the overall turnover rates are trending down, which may also be attributed to the introduction of migrants and the visa conditions that relate to their employment[3] (Callister and Tipples, 2010).

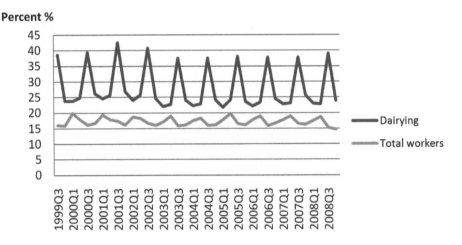

Percent %

Figure 11.4   Worker turnover rate, 1999–2008
Source: LEED data.

---

3   The Department of Labour use the Intermediate Skill Shortage List (ISSL) only in relation to temporary work policy. If migrants come to work in New Zealand based on meeting the ISSL requirements, there is no direct link to residence. Four occupations are related to dairy farming – assistant farm or herd managers and full farm or herd managers, requiring a mix of 2–3 years experience and National Certificates equivalent to New Zealand's Level 2 or Level 4. Immediate Skill Shortage List: Effective 26 November 2009. http://www.immigration.govt.nz/ templates/custom/SearchskillshortagesPopup.aspx?NRMODE=Published&NRNODEGUID= %7b17CCA408-8572-4E07-80EB-26FAC203D4F7%7d&NRORIGINALURL=%2fmigrant%2fstr eam%2fwork%2fskilledmigrant%2fLinkAdministration%2fToolboxLinks%2fessentialskills%2 ehtm%3flevel%3d1&NRCACHEHINT=Guest&level=1.

Figure 11.5 shows that dairy farm employees have seen their quarterly earnings grow over time. However, earnings are still well short of quarterly earnings across the whole economy. When the long hours worked by dairy workers are taken into consideration, they are very low at an average level. However, once advancing up the dairy career structure rates do improve quite quickly, as do the hours of work. Nevertheless, only 39.4 percent of farmers record staff hours, leaving considerable scope for paying an hourly rate of pay below the minimum hourly rate of pay set for a normal 40-hour week (Minimum Wages Act 1983). They claim average hours range from $14.67 for Farm Assistants to $26.69 for Operations Managers (Federated Farmers of New Zealand and Rabobank, 2010). The statutory minimum rate is $12.75 or $510 for a 40 hour week.

Besides potentially illegally low hourly rate wages, only just over three-quarters of farmers had written contracts with their employees. To have a written contract has been a requirement since the Employment Relations Act 2000.

Three-quarters of farm workers were provided with accommodation. Some pay rent (15 percent), some are taxed on the notional value of the accommodation (63 percent), and for 19 percent it is part of their total remuneration package (Federated Farmers of New Zealand and Rabobank, 2010). Anecdotal opinion is that the standard of farm worker accommodation has improved over the last 20 years, but where that is motel-type units it does not work well if small children are part of the family and parents can only get disturbed sleep (Rawlinson, 2010).

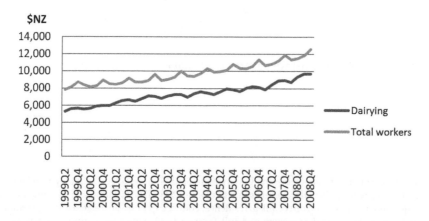

Figure 11.5   Mean quarterly earnings, 1999–2008

Note: Employees' rewards: in terms of earnings the following LEED data represent quarterly earnings, are inclusive of tax and include payments reported as lump sums to Inland Revenue.

Source: LEED data.

Accidents in Dairy Farming

The poor safety record of dairy farming continues to be a concern. The major source of accident data is New Zealand's Accident Compensation Corporation (ACC), which collects levies from employers to fund the costs of accidents throughout the community on a 'no fault' basis. Essentially the data only relate to accidents giving rise to a claim, but after the initial claim there may be ongoing expenditure on treatments and other expenses. ACC use 31 different agricultural premium classes for levying employers for accepted claims, one of which is for dairy farming claims – Class 1300. The claims data for the six year period 1 July 2004 to 30 June 2010 for all claims (medical and entitlements from accidents for example loss of income, homecare, transport and lump sums of compensation) for the whole of farming and dairy farming are summarised in Table 11.3. They related to an estimated inter-censal dairy farming population of 34,275 or 48.6 percent of the farming population. Dairy farming cost ACC and dairy farmers nearly $NZ 24.2 million in 2009–10. Overall dairy farming costs ACC a lot for these accidents, but then dairy farmers are charged levies to pay for them, which increases farmers' costs. Thus an improved OSH record for lower claims and entitlements would benefit employees directly (less injuries and time off),

Table 11.3   Accepted ACC agricultural claims 1 July 2004–30 June 2010

Year – claims details	Dairy farming	Total agriculture	Dairy/total %
2004–5			
New entitlements/claims	1,533	4,276	35.9
Cost ($NZ) of active claims	18,857,475	52,023,100	36.2
2005–6			
New entitlements/claims	1,505	4,127	36.5
Cost ($NZ) of active claims	20,462,212	55,297,316	37.0
2006–7			
New entitlements/claims	1,478	3,940	37.5
Cost ($NZ) of active claims	22,058,310	58,248,885	37.9
2007–8			
New entitlements/claims	1,372	3,625	37.8
Cost ($NZ) of active claims	23,413,674	59,129,737	39.6
2008–9			
New entitlements/claims	1,440	3,570	40.3
Cost ($NZ) of active claims	24,827,031	62,108,507	40.0
2009–10			
New entitlements/claims	1,278	3,503	36.5
Cost ($NZ) of active claims	24, 232,179	58, 945,627	41.1

and employers both directly in losing less employee time through accidents and indirectly in lower levels of ACC levies. There might also be savings from reduced accidents in other sectors unrelated to dairy farming, where causes could be attributed to dairy farm work, for example general road accidents attributed to excess fatigue from working long hours milking cows, but this point needs further investigation.

Why has dairy farming formed a greater share of ACC's agricultural expenditure when it has been experiencing a training boom, which promotes safe and healthy practices, while ACC have been making claims tougher? With the growing proportion of employees in dairying and a contracting one in other sectors, it might be suggested that claims are easier for employees than other more self-employed farmers, resulting in higher expenditure for dairying. Further, the situation is complicated by claims which continue over several years.

The Precariousness of Dairy Farming Based Upon Migrants

The presence of a migrant element in the dairy farm labour force suggests an increased degree of precariousness in dairy farm employment. The degree of precariousness of the supplementary migrant workforce may be evaluated by comparison with Tucker's Indicators of Precariousness and others' research (Tucker, 2002; Hannif and Lamm, 2005). Unrepresentative opinions of employers and employees indicate that the degree of precariousness may be a lot less than it was thought to be, and less than in teleworking, for which there is no shortage of willing employees (Hannif and Lamm, 2005). No data appear to have been collected on ACC claims among temporary migrant workers, which might indicate precariousness.

The nature of dairy farming places constraints on employers, with its dependence on cows which have to be milked at regular intervals, and the perishability of milk. If there are labour problems and production ceases, even temporarily, dairy employers stand to lose their product milk, their income and maybe affect their longer term production adversely. Thus the effect of employees absenting themselves is a major threat and gives employees some countervailing power to the omnipotence of the employer. A dairy farmer cannot afford to be without employees, no matter how inappropriate their behaviour sometimes.

Ways to Overcome Staffing Problems while Maintaining Productivity

The dairy farm staffing problems described above have now been apparent since the late 1990s, in greater or lesser degree, depending on the region of New Zealand considered (Tipples et al. 1999; Morriss et al., 2001; Tipples et al., 2004; Wilson and Tipples, 2008). Tipples et al. (2004) considered all influences on future supply and demand factors for dairy farm labour, whether demographic, technical, economic or competitive. One idea which became apparent at that time was the practice of 'Once-a-Day' (OAD) milking rather than the more usual practice of 'Twice-a-Day' (TAD) milking (Tipples et al., 2004, pp. 83–84). This appeared to have more potential than the more expensive automatic milking systems, which could also reduce the drudgery of milking TAD. Then a serendipitous convergence of circumstances and resources led to an initial OAD milking project being well publicised and the Livestock Improvement Corporation initiating and financing a more detailed social study of OAD's effects (Verwoerd and Tipples, 2007).

In our second study we found the farmers studied changed 'because they were looking for a better way to farm', which included 'better health for their animals, more sustainable use of the land, more production for less input, and above all, a better and more satisfying life for themselves and their families on the land' (Verwoerd and Tipples, 2007, p. 54). Thus from the farmers point of view OAD enhanced the social sustainability of dairy farming. For farm employees, the response from the small number in the study was positive. The change, which was unexpected, was the reduction in the use of employees in favour of family. Managing staff was stressful and only family helpers entailed less formal staff management procedures. Whether OAD milking will have the same appeal to corporate dairy farming, which is increasing, is unclear. Rakaia Island Dairies' experiences as a family business operating at a corporate scale suggests that it has great potential for large dairy farming businesses, but it does not appear to be favoured by Fonterra as its widespread adoption potentially reduces national milk yields.

A radical approach, increasing the use of farm labour to reduce fatigue and improve efficiency, has been advanced (Kyte, 2008). This freed up the sharemilker's time for training staff; introducing new farming systems; and putting family first. The study concluded:

> *To introduce more labour into the system you must be able to capture increased productivity so, yourself or someone else on the team must be skilled in the area of staff management. Time must be put into training and the implementation of new and existing systems/science/technology … Increasing the number of staff on dairy farms, compared to current industry standards, is an approach that runs contrary to current thinking as well as demographic and economic trends. However, if the industry did this the reduced hours and improved conditions means the pool of people available to the industry would become larger as it became more competitive with other industries. It would lead to more people making the Dairy industry their career of choice. (Kyte, 2008, pp. 11–12).*

Thus a solution to tackle dairy farming's staff retention and productivity issues is possible, but what light does research from other fields shed on these issues?

The Research Context – A Review of Relevant Literature

The linkages betweeeen workplace health and safety and the performance of firms and their productivity have been highlighted, especially the risks associated with working longer hours, issues of job quality with a rise in work strain from work intensification and the damaging effects this has on the overall levels of job satisfaction (Wilkins, 2005; Massey et al., 2006). These factors are also associated with loss of personal discretion in daily work tasks (Green, 2004). Loss of job involvement has also been associated with increased emotional exhaustion and diminished personal acomplishment, or job burnout, leading to negative effects on employees' Organizational Citizenship Behaviour (OCB). Thus employers need to use stress intervention mechanisms to prevent employees from withdrawing from positive work behaviours (Chieu and Tsai, 2006). Prevention of emotional exhaustion by reducing levels of workload has been suggested. Further, improving workers' health and motivation through task redesign and improving staff retention through paying attention to staff career expectations may also be useful (Houkes et al., 2003).

These international findings are also supplemented by local research directly addressing problems of labour turnover and staff retention. Boxall et al. (2003) found no one factor explained intentions to leave. The strongest attractor and retainer of staff was interesting work. In addition, there was a growing concern with work–life balance and maintaining good relationships with co-workers and supervisors. Boxall et al. advised firms with retention problems to measure their employee attitudes towards the organization of work and employment policies and practice with a view to their improvement. Overall this area might be described as one of lack of 'organizational effectiveness' in the dairy industry. This might be explored through studying virtuous organizations via Positive Organizational Scholarship (POS) and contrasting them with normal ones and unvirtuous ones (Cameron, 2005). Michie and Sheehan (2003) have highlighted the dangers of 'unvirtuous behaviour'. The possibilities of labour market deregulation and 'flexibility', such as short-term and temporary contracts, lack of employer commitment to job security and low levels of training, for them were negatively correlated with innovation, whereas virtuous practices, such as 'high commitment organisations' or 'transformed' workplaces correlated positively with innovation, a feature much sought after for a more productive dairy industry. Dairy farming would seem to have some room to improve its performance in these areas.

The attraction and retention of talented people continue to be key priorities of the dairy industry (DairyNZ, 2009). They are to be underpinned by developing a quality work environment, which will also help to ensure continued improvements in dairy farming productivity. That is envisaged to retain the New Zealand industry's place as one of the world's lowest-cost dairy producers (DairyNZ, 2009). The aim of developing research in this area is to try and explore whether dairy farming could avoid many of the problems described above by adopting siginificant system changes, which would involve working shorter hours. The long-term culture of dairy farming has included expectations of long hours, which contribute to the employment problems confronting the industry at present. To develop new systems with shorter hours of work and more choice and discretionary time available to management and staff may help to improve standards of occupational health and safety; develop the resilience of dairy farming and make dairy farming and dairy farming communities more socially sustainable as well as enhancing their public reputation. These are vital strategies for the long-term health of the New Zealand economy and many rural areas.

Research Programme

Initial review of the literature suggests a number of farmer initiatives have already occurred in this field. The substantive research project proposed brings together an interdisciplinary team. To improve the employment aspects of dairy farming systems the perspectives of each discipline can add to the value of the project (Launis and Pihlaja, 2007). Monodisciplinary science can be a barrier to system improvements. The research suggested here is in line with what industry states it wants and needs (DairyNZ, 2009). Several steps are suggested in a broad research agenda:

1. Investigation of time at work, overwork and fatigue in dairy farming and how that might be related to the very high level of farm workplace accidents – these are potential barriers to the attraction and retention of 'good' employees in dairy farming, who are open to innovation and enhancing industry productivity.

2. Precariousness and job stability in the current dairy farming labour force – investigating dependence on a migrant labour force and the degree of precariousness highlighted by the Tucker (2002) framework.

3. Does migration legislation and administration make migrants' situations more or less precarious?

4. Because the dairy industry is concerned about its future sustainability, increasing the efficient use of its resources and reducing reliance on non-renewable resources, it should start considering its workforces' time as one of its vital non-renewable resources, properly budgeted out on 'opportunity cost' principles (see De Bruin-Judge, 2007; Kyte, 2008). OAD milking certainly impacts that. That might also help explain why statutory compliance is such a concern to dairy farmers and many other small and medium enterprises.

5. Dairy farms could be considered as 'greedy organizations', which 'make total claims on their members' and 'attempt to encompass the whole personality'. They are described as greedy because they demand 'exclusive and undivided loyalty' and try to 'reduce the claims' of their members. 'Their demands on the person are omnivorous' (Coser, 1974). The implications of 'greedy' status for work–life balance for family and employees could then be considered.

To this end it is suggested that a combined research and policy based approach is needed. A precedent for the type of research envisaged has already been set with the research underpinning the development of the New Zealand Recognised Seasonal Employer (RSE) policy for the horticultural and viticultural industries (Hill et al., 2007; Tipples and Whatman, 2009). This approach was founded on a Finnish 'change laboratory' learning process and work research techniques such as Developmental Work Research (DWR) and Cultural Historical Activity Theory (CHAT) (Engstrom, 1987, 1999, 2000, 2001). These were underpinned by what has been called in New Zealand, the 'pure business' model, a radical new inside-out approach to policy development (Whatman et al., 2005). It essentially involves achieving an understanding of all the activites and parties involved in policy making and in enterprises in their historical context. Then from the disaggregated parts, with a clear view of what is to be achieved, bringing those parts back together in a more logical and supported way.

Engstrom (2001) outlines five principles under activity theory, based on the fundamental unit of analysis, the *activity system*, set in its system context. It is collective, aimed towards an object, and mediated by rules or cultural norms. *Multivoicedness* expresses that the activity system always comprises a mixture of individual and collective points of view, interests and traditions. The activity system can only be properly understood in terms of its *historical evolution*. Further, *contradictions* are the starting point for development, not problems, but structural tensions between the parts of the system. The chance for *expansive transformation* (learning) is always there, leading to new objects and purposes in a shared and deliberate way. Such transformation comes from a cycle of expansive learning as used on the New Zealand apple industry (Hill et al., 2007). This cycle involved six stages:

1. *Questioning*. Criticising aspects of accepted practice and exisiting knowledge.

2. *Analysing the situation*. In discussion, by thinking or in practice. Two types of analysis are used:
   - *historical*: seeks to explain the situation by tracing its origins and evolution using similar techniques to those used in anthropology (for example ethnography): and
   - *actual–empirical*: seeks to explain the current problematic situation by constructing a picture of its inner relationships.

3.   *Modelling the newly found explanatory relationship*. Constructing an explicit, simplified model of the new idea that explains, and offers a solution to, the situation.

4.   *Examining the model*. Operating, running and experimenting on the model in order to fully grasp its dynamics, potentials and limitations.

5.   *Implementing the new model*. Making the model concrete, by means of practical applications (for example pilots).

6.   *Reflecting on the process and consolidating the practice*. Evaluating the new model and the process, and consolidating the new practices into a new stable form of activity (Hill, 2007, p. 363).

The expansive learning cycle is shown diagrammtically in Figure 11.6.

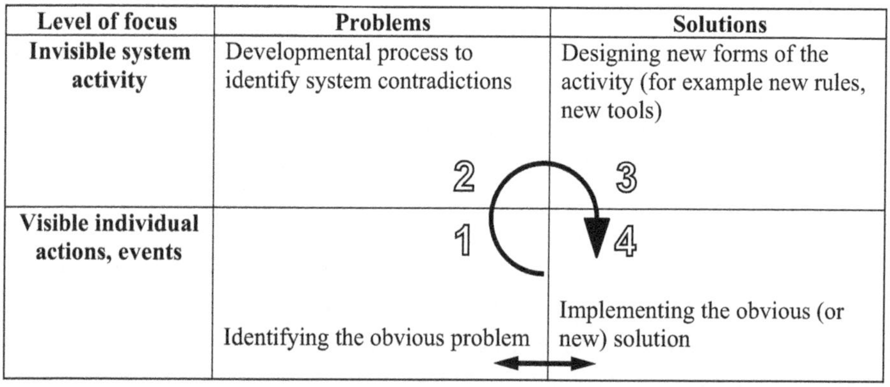

Level of focus	Problems	Solutions
Invisible system activity	Developmental process to identify system contradictions	Designing new forms of the activity (for example new rules, new tools)
Visible individual actions, events	Identifying the obvious problem	Implementing the obvious (or new) solution

Figure 11.6   Managing change using an expansive learning cycle
Source: Hill et al. (2007, p. 364).

In typical learning situations at work in New Zealand people connect the 'obvious' problem (Quadrant 1, Figure 11.6) with the 'obvious' solution (Quadrant 4, Figure 11.6). That is the typical pragmatic Kiwi way of addressing a problem. The DWR process is a more robust form of problem identification that finds not only the obvious or visible actions or events, but can also bring out the less visible ones that may be the actual causes of the problems. From this more comprehensive understanding, participants can design new forms of the activity, which can then be implemented to give new solutions. These may not be so obvious (ibid.).

Cultural–historical activity theory (CHAT) can be used as a developmental tool in complex conditions. It is an 'interventonist theory of learning, innovation and change' (Hill et al., 2007, p. 364). In it the whole activity system is analysed. For a dairy farming research project it might lead to participants looking at the following questions:

1. What do they agree should be the object or collective purpose of the system for example for the farmer, income, return on investment, lifestyle; for dairy employees, interesting work, income, rural life?

2. Who is the subject of this system (for example dairy farmers, sharemilkers, contractors, dairy workers, consultants)?

3. What tools are used in this system (for example TAD milking, OAD milking, artifical insemination (AI)?

4. What are the rules, both the official ones (for example tax laws, Fonterra's specifications, health and safety, environmental), and the ones that do not always get talked about (for example expectations of long hours because 'that's the way we've always done things in dairying')?

5. What is the division of labour? Who does what, on farm and off?

6. Who is actually the community of practice of this system (for example dairy farming community, Agriculture Industry Training Organisation, rural community, farm consultants, Fonterra, DairyNZ)? Where do government agencies fit in the model (for example Department of Labour, Inland Revenue Department, Ministry of Social Development)? (Hill et al., 2007; Hill, 2010).

7. What are the outcomes from the activity (for example increased productivity, attraction and retention of talented people, a safer and healthier industry, long-term sustainability of the industry)?

Project Progress

DairyNZ's Proposed Investment Priorities 2009–2015 included a category 'People: There is increasing difficulty in finding suitable labour for employment on dairy farms'. The substantive project would fit into that category. They also allocate some 8 percent of their annual levy investment to human capability issues. In late 2010 DairyNZ asked to incorporate this proposal into a major multi-institution research programme on farmer wellness and wellbeing over the period 2010–2018, to be led by the New Zealand Institute for Rural Health. The researcher's dream of 2007, after a project on 'Once-a-Day' milking, may be about to become reality.

References

Agriculture ITO (no date) *Skills and Learning for Careers in Dairying – A Guide to National Qualifications in the Dairy Industry*. Wellington: Agriculture ITO.

Agriculture ITO (2002–2008) *Annual Reports*. Wellington: Agriculture ITO.

Angove, N. (1994) 'The New Zealand Farm Workers Association: its rise and fall 1974–1987' in Pat Walsh (ed.) *Trade Unions, Work and Society – the Centenary of the Arbitration System*. Palmerston North: The Dunmore Press Ltd, pp. 155–175.

Blackwood, L. (2007). *Employment Agreements: Bargaining, Trends and Employment Law Update*. Wellington: Industrial Relations Centre, Victoria University.

Boxall, P., Macky, K. and Rasmussen, E. (2003) 'Labour turnover and retention in New Zealand: the causes and consequences of leaving and staying with employers', *Asia Pacific Journal of Human Resources*, 41, 2, 195–214.

Callister, P. and Tipples, R. (2010) *Essential workers in the dairy industry*. Working Paper 10/08, Institute of Policy Studies, Victoria University of Wellington. June.

Cameron, K. (2005) 'Organizational effectiveness: its demise and re-emergence through positive organizational scholarship', in K.G. Smith and M.A. Hitt (eds) *Great Minds in Management. The Process of Theory Development*. Oxford: Oxford University Press, pp. 304–330.

Chieu, S.-F. and Tsai, M.-C. (2006) 'Relationships among burnout, job involvement, and organizational citizenship behavior', *The Journal of Psychology*, 140, 6, 517–530.

Coser, L.A. (1974) *Greedy Institutions: Patterns of Individual Commitment*. New York: Free Press. Quoted in T. Bartram, R. Burchielli and R. Thanacoody (2007) 'Work–family balance or greedy organizations', AIRAANZ conference, University of Auckland. February.

DairyNZ (2009) *Strategy for New Zealand Dairy Farming 2009/2020*. Downloaded 27 April 2009 from http://www.dairynz.co.nz.

De Bruin-Judge, R. (2007) 'Invisible work of partners in compliance for small-business operators', in M. Waring and C. Fouché (eds) *Managing Mayhem – Work–life Balance in New Zealand*. Wellington: Dunmore, pp. 235–253.

Doig, W.T. (1940) *A Survey of Standards of Life of Dairy Farmers*. Bulletin No. 75, Social Science Research Bureau, Department of Scientific Research. Wellington: Government Printer.

Engstrom, Y. (1987) *Learning by Expanding: An Activity–Theoretical Approach to Developmental Research*. Helsinki: Orienta-Konsultit.

Engstrom, Y. (1999) 'Expansive visualization of work: an activity–theoretical perspective', *Computer Supported Cooperative Work*, 8, 63–93.

Engstrom, Y. (2000) 'Activity theory as a framework for analyzing and redesigning work', *Ergonomics*, 43, 7, 960–974.

Engstrom, Y. (2001) 'Expansive learning at work: toward an activity–theoretical reconceptualization', *Journal of Education and Work*, 14, 1, 133–156.

Enterprise North Canterbury (2009) *Amuri Dairy Employers Group Research, Findings and Recommendatins 2009*. May. 23 pp.

Federated Farmers of New Zealand and Rabobank (2010) *Farm Employee Remuneration Report 2010*. Wellington.

Fonterra (2007) *Fonterra Leading the Way*. Downloaded 19 October 2007 from http://www.fonterra.com/wps/wcm/connect/fonterracom/fonterra.com/our+business.

Green, F. (2004) 'Work intensification, discretion, and the decline in well-being at work', *Eastern Economic Journal*, 30, 4, 615–625.

Hannif, Z. and Lamm, F. (2005) 'When non-standard work becomes precarious: insights from the new Zealand Call Centre Industry', *Management Review*, 16, 3, 325–353.

Hill, R., Capper, P., Wilson, K., Whatman, R. and Wong, K. (2007) 'Workplace learning in the New Zealand apple industry network: a new co-design method for government "practice making"', *Journal of Workplace Learning*, 19, 6, 359–376.

Hill, R. (2010) Personal communication by email, 29 January.

Houkes, I., Janssen, P., De Jonge, J. and Bakker, A.B. (2003) 'Specific determinants of intrinsic work motivation, emotional exhaustion and turnover intentions: A multisample longitudinal study', *Journal of Occupational and Organizational Psychology*, 76, 427–450.

Johnston, F. (2007) *Why We Need to Reduce Fatigue Risk. Shiftwork Services*, May. Downloaded 29 April 2010 from http://www.shiftwork.co.nz/files/32291237 514111WhyWeNeedtoReduceFatigueRisk.pdf.

Kyte, R. (2008) 'A different approach to staffing in the dairy industry', *South Island Dairy Event (SIDE)*, Discussion paper downloaded 26 November 2008 from http://side.org.nz/index.php?BackStructure=4&Layout=print&MainLayout=print.

Launis, K. and Pihlaja, J. (2007) 'Changes in production concepts emphasize problems in work-related well-being', *Safety Science*, 45, 603–619.

LIC (2008–09) *LIC Dairy Statistics 2008–09*. Newstead, Hamilton: Livestock Improvement Corporation Ltd.

MAF (2009) *Situation and Outlook for New Zealand Agriculture and Forestry (July 2009)*. Wellington: MAF Policy.

MAF (2010) *Situation and Outlook for New Zealand Agriculture and Forestry (June 2010)*. Wellington: MAF Policy.

Massey, C., Lamm, F. and Perry, M. (2006) *Understanding the link between Workplace Health and Safety and Firm Performance and Productivity*. Report prepared for the Department of Labour. NZ Centre for Small and Medium Enterprise Research, Massey University.

McLaughlan, W. (2010) Personal communication by telephone, 3 May.

McLean, G. (1990) *Masters or Servants? A Short History of the New Zealand Merchant Service Guild*. Wellington: N.Z. Merchant Service Guild.

McMeekan, C.P. (1960) *Grass to Milk*. Wellington: The New Zealand Dairy Exporter.

Michie, J. and Sheehan, M. (2003) 'Labour market deregulation, "flexibility" and innovation', *Cambridge Journal of Economics*, 27, 123–143.

Minimum Wages Act (1983) Wellington: Government Printer.

Morriss, S., Tipples, R., Townshend, W., Mackay, B. and Eastwood, C. (2001) *Skill and Labour Requirement in the Primary Sector – 'People Make the Difference'*. Report prepared for the Ministry of Agriculture and Forestry, Massey and Lincoln Universities.

Murray, N. (2006) 'Knowledge and skill "down on the farm": Skill formation in New Zealand's agricultural sector', *New Zealand Journal of Employment Relations*, 31, 1, 2–16.

Paine, M. (2010) 'Building a better workplace', *Inside Dairy*, March, 2.

Rawlinson, P. (2010) Personal communication by email 15 and 29 March.

Statistics New Zealand (2007) *Census of Population and Dwellings 2006*. Additional tables provided for *The Human Face of Once-a-Day Milking* study by Statistics New Zealand.

Strack, R., Baier, J. and Fahlander, A. (2008) 'Managing demographic risk', *Harvard Business Review*, February, 119–128.

Tipples, R. (1987) 'Labour relations in New Zealand agriculture', *Sociologia Ruralis*, XXVII, 1, 38–54.

Tipples, R. (2004) 'A solution to too few working down on the farm – The Human Capability in Agriculture and Horticulture Initiative. Proceedings of the Eleventh Labour, Employment and Work in New Zealand 2004 Conference, Victoria University of Wellington, 22–23 November, pp. 41–48.

Tipples, R., Hoogeveen, M. and Gould, E. (1999) Psychological contracts in dairy farming. In R. Tipples and H. Shrewsbury *Global Trends and Local Issues*, 7th Annual International Employment Relations Association Conference, Lincoln University, 13–16 July, at the Copthorne Hotel, Durham Street, Christchurch, pp. 545–556.

Tipples, R. and Lucock, D. (2004) 'Migrations and dairy farming', *Primary Industry Management*, 7, 1, 33–35.

Tipples, R. and Verwoerd, N. (2005) Social impacts of once-a-day milking on dairy farms in New Zealand. *Teaching, Learning and Research in Institutions and Regions. Proceedings of the 5th Annual Pacific Employment Relations Association Conference*, Yeppoon, Queensland, Australia, 21–24 November 2005, pp. 291–302.

Tipples, R. and Whatman, R. (2009) 'Employment standards in world food production – the place of GLOBALGAP supply contracts and indirect legislation. Regulating for decent work: innovative regulation as a response to globalization', Conference of the International Labour Organisation, Geneva, 8–10 July 2009: Track 2: *New directions in the implementation and enforcement of 'non-core' norms*.

Tipples, R. and Wilson, J. (2007) 'Work–sport competition: the role of agricultural contests in New Zealand', *Rural Society*, 17, 1, 34–49.

Tipples, R., Wilson, J. and Edkins, R. (2004) *Future Dairy Farm Employment*. Report prepared for Dairy InSight Research Contract 10015/2003.

Tucker, D. (2002). *Precarious Non-standard Employment – a Review of the Literature*. Wellington: Labour Market Policy Group, Department of Labour.

Whatman, R., Wong, K., Hill, R., Capper, P. and Wilson, K. (2005) 'From policy to practice: the pure business project', *Proceedings of the 11th ANZSYS/Managing the Complex V conference*, Christchurch, New Zealand, 5–7 December.

Wilkins, R. (2005) 'Do longer working hours lead to more workplace injuries? Evidence from Australian industry-level panel data', *Australian Bulletin of Labour*, 31, 2, 155–170.

Wilson, J. and Tipples, R. (2008) *Employment Trends in Dairy Farming in New Zealand, 1991–2006*. Agriculture and Life Sciences Division Research Report no. 2, February. Canterbury, NZ; Lincoln University.

Woodford, K. (2007) 'Moving forward in dairy', an address to the Australia Dairy Business of the Year Conference, Melbourne, 18 May.

12

Occupational Health and Safety of Contingent Migrant Labour in the Kuwait Construction Industry

Cathy Robertson[1]

Introduction

Over half of all construction businesses in Kuwait are small firms employing fewer than 10 employees, in which most of the employees are contingent, migrant workers (Kartam et al. 2000). There are indications that the injury and illness rates amongst construction workers in Kuwait are abnormally high (Kartam and Bouz 1998). However, there are few studies on the OHS of migrant construction workers in Kuwait and most are from a singular perspective, such as medicine or engineering. What is urgently needed is a multidisciplinary approach in order to capture the multifaceted nature of Kuwaiti OHS policy and practice and to better understand why and how migrant workers are employed, the characteristics of the employment relationship and what steps can be taken to improve the situation (Quinlan, Mayhew and Bohle 2001; Sargeant and Tucker 2009; Toh and Quinlan 2009; Quinlan, Bohle and Lamm 2010). This chapter proposes the development of a case study which focuses on the experiences and perceptions of contingent migrant labour in the Kuwait construction industry.

---

1   Cathy Robertson is a Senior Research Fellow for the Centre for Occupational Health and Safety Research at the Auckland University of Technology.

Background

During the past two decades, profound changes have taken place within the labour market in Kuwait. The construction industry is characterised by both its dependence on foreign, 'disposable' workers, who now make up over 66 percent of the Kuwaiti population, and the predominance of small subcontracting firms, which constitutes 60 percent of the construction industry (Kartam and Bouz, 1998; Kartam et al. 2000). Although there are no entirely accurate statistics on the number of migrants employed as contract workers in the Kuwaiti construction industry, there is evidence that many of the foreign migrant workers are employed in small sub-subcontracting firms (Kartam et al. 2000).

Typically employers control both migrants' work and living conditions and frequently expect their workers to work in hazardous conditions for meagre wages (Kartam et al. 2000; Abdul-Aziz 2001). Higher rates of work-related injury and illness occur among migrant labour in Kuwait compared to Kuwaiti nationals and migrant workers often suffer from psychosocial problems (Kartam et al. 2000). Kartam et al. (2000) state that many of the injuries and fatalities among migrant construction workers in Kuwait are the result of poor communication, different labour cultures and traditions, different work habits, lack of education and training, origins in poor communities and willingness to work in hazardous conditions. Whilst the findings in Kuwaiti government reports undoubtedly underestimated, it does indicate that health and safety amongst contingent, migrant workers is a major problem.

During this time of political, social and legal reform in Kuwait during the past decade, there has been a major influx of migrant labour. These events, together with the recent economic downturn, have created high levels of political, social, economic and ethnic tension. It has also meant that advances towards improved OHS may be in jeopardy. However, what is not clear is whether, and the extent to which, these reforms have had an impact on the lives OHS of migrant workers in the Kuwaiti construction industry. Indeed, we know very little about the OHS experiences of migrant workers in Kuwait. What we do know is that OHS in Kuwait cannot be examined without taking into consideration the multiple factors affecting Kuwait employment relations and occupational health and safety.

The purpose of this proposed study is to enhance our understanding of OHS of migrant workers in Kuwait and contribute to the wider research on the OHS of migrant construction workers. Moreover, it is anticipated that the study will also help to develop robust research methods and principles that are capable of capturing meaningful data on vulnerable and 'invisible' workers who are typically inaccessible. It is intended that the findings and recommendations from the proposed study will positively influence managerial and OHS practices in Kuwait. The study will examine migrant labour growth in Kuwait and discuss the way in which the employment relationship and OHS is managed within the Kuwaiti regulatory framework. In order to clarify the context in which this study is proposed, it is first necessary to develop an overview of current trends in the international growth of migrant labour, secondly its effect on the construction industry and thirdly, from a Kuwaiti perspective, including employment relations issues and management systems within the Kuwaiti regulatory framework.

The International Growth of Vulnerable Migrant Labour

Since the mid-1970s labour markets of most industrialised countries have experienced significant change. Many organisations have decreased their numbers of permanent workers and increased the numbers of contracted migrant labour employed in temporary, part-time or casual contracts, creating jobs and selecting workers through intermediaries (Lewchuk et al. 2003). The reasons for these changes have been attributed to global competitiveness, privatisation of services, just-in-time production, the growth of flexible human resource management strategies and the economic downturn (Quinlan et al. 2001; Sargeant and Tucker 2009). The process of the creation of an estimated 200 million jobs filled by migrant workers has contributed towards the formation of a global industrial environment which has collectively eliminated the implicit agreements associated with standard employment relationships (Schenker 2008). International laws which regulate the relationship between worker and employer and are designed to support the standard employment relationship, such as the right to minimum labour standards, adequate compensation and the right to bargain, have become eroded (Lewchuk et al. 2003). In a growing number of countries there are concentrations of migrant workers in industries with a high dependence on foreign, 'disposable' workers, so-called 'perfect immigrants' – workers who are prepared to do the dirtiest and hardest work, whose home countries survive on the remittances of foreign workers (Hahamovitch 2003: 4). The working lives of these workers have become insecure. Many migrant workers face constant uncertainty about their future, the terms and conditions of their work, their access to basic household needs, access to compensation and their ability to provide for their families, a situation which is being increasingly compared by researchers to those which existed in the nineteenth and early twentieth century (Quinlan 2010; Sargeant and Tucker 2009).

Vulnerable Migrant Workers in the Construction Industry

There is growing evidence that migrant construction workers are particularly vunerable (Abdul-Aziz 2001; Lewchuk et al. 2003; Hahamovitch 2003; Sargeant and Tucker 2009; Quinlan et al. 2010). It is suggested that this exploitation of migrant construction workers whose employers control both their work and living conditions and who expect their workers to work in hazardous conditions for meagre wages (Kartam et al., 2000) has led to a situation similar to that in Upton Sinclair's novel *The Jungle*, which was based on the horrific conditions under which immigrants in the Chicago stockyards were forced to work 100 years ago (Schenker 2008: 717).

Subcontractors and sub-subcontractors in the construction industry are generally at the lower end of the organisational hierarchy in any construction project and their ability to exert influence on the decision-making process concerning health and safety standards is limited (Holmes et al. 1999). In addition, these firms operate within a multilayered contracting system in which construction workers are recruited through main contractors, subcontractors and labour intermediaries. Yun (2007) refers to this process as 'horizontal contracting out' (2010:2). This multilayered system in which the main construction company is hidden behind several layers of subcontractors, has, at the same time, given rise to layers of vulnerability in occupational health and safety and health for migrant workers as the process undermines the enforcement and implementation of labour regulations (Sargeant 2009; Yun 2007).

There is growing empirical evidence that the growth of migrant labour employed in construction sites and subjected to these new practices has a detrimental impact on injury and illness, reporting propensity, treatment and rehabilitation (Kartam and Bouz 1998; Valcarel 2004; Xia, Lu and Liang 2004; Nosar et al. 2004). It Is estimated that at least 60,000 fatalities occur at construction sites around the world every year. Migrant labour in the construction industry contributes significantly to this figure (Valcarel 2004; Nosar et al. 2004; Quinlan et al. 2010).

The number of fatal occupational accidents in global construction sites is not easy to quantify and the industry is notorious for failing to release accurate statistics. Quinlan et al. (2010) link this phenomenon to the dominant view of occupational injury. Firstly, occupational illness and injury has been historically attributed to individual worker behaviour, leading to the practice of blaming the victim, emphasising the characteristics and behaviour of workers as the root cause of injury or illness. Quinlan (1988), in his critical assessment of occupational health and safety research, argued that the dominance of industrial psychologists in conducting early occupational health and safety research has created a propensity to attribute accident causation to the individual worker, who reacts to a given set of environmental factors in a manner determined by their own personal characteristics. This 'blame the victim' mentality has extended itself into the analysis of migrant occupational health and safety.

Secondly, early studies of accident causation led to the growth of the study of ergonomics, which is primarily concerned with the relationship of the worker with the physical working environment and how worker attitudes and behaviour within this environment can be changed through enforcement of desired behaviour by managers (Quinlan et al. 2010).

Thirdly, in spite of the vast body of empirical studies on the subject of accident causation, the OHS literature has failed to produce a research approach which focuses on migrant worker emotions, perceptions and experiences relating to their working lives and therefore their health and safety. Recent literature suggests incorporating psychological, social and workplace interrelational factors, such as management culture and practice, in the analysis of how migrant workers perceive and respond to risks. This would imply that researchers should search for new paradigms within a multidisciplinary approach, including experts familiar with immigrant communities (Holmes et al. 1999; Quinlan and Mayhew 1999; Hahamovitch 2003; Quinlan and Bohle 2004; Abbe 2008; Sargeant and Tucker 2009; Schenker 2008; Quinlan et al. 2010.

As the working relationships of contingent migrant workers are hidden within the many layers of subcontractors and sub-subcontractors involved in the construction industry, who are generally at the lower end of the subcontracting chain, the burden of risk is shifted from employer to employee, increasing the risk of occupational illness. Migrant worker ability to exert influence on the decision-making process concerning health and safety standards is limited (Holmes et al. 1999; Dainty et al. 2001). In addition, these firms operate within a multilayered contracting system in which construction workers are recruited through main contractors, subcontractors and labour intermediaries. The development of a multidisciplinary framework as a platform for the research would serve to simplify and develop a new approach to the research of OHS of migrant workers (Abdul-Aziz 2001; Quinlan and Mayhew 2001; Dainty et al. 2001; Nosar et al. 2004; Baram 2009; Sargeant and Tucker 2009; Schenker 2008; Quinlan et al. 2010).

Vulnerable Migrant Construction Workers in Kuwait

Currently, the population in Kuwait is almost 3 million in which 34 percent are Kuwaitis and 66 percent are expatriate workers employed entirely in the private sector. The discovery of oil in Kuwait in 1934 has led to an exponential growth in the wealth of the country. This rapid growth in the strength of Kuwait's economy has led to a surge in construction activity and therefore the availability of employment in that sector. Migrant workers are attracted from all parts of the world, employed in a range of occupations from engineers to domestic workers and, in particular, in the construction industry. The segmentation of the labour market, however, is unofficially divided along the lines of ethnicity. Europeans tend to be employed in professional occupations, such as engineering, logistics, human resources and education. The less skilled and manual occupations, commonly referred to as 'dirty, dangerous and demeaning', typical of the construction industry, tend to be dominated by workers from the Middle East and Asian countries. Although limited, government work-related injury and fatality statistics show that migrant labourers in the Kuwait construction industry are over-represented. In 1999, 98 work-related injuries per month occurred in the construction industry and, as Table 12.1 depicts, most of the injured workers in Kuwait were migrants. Table 12.1 shows the distribution of labourers on construction sites and their nationalities in 2002.

Table 12.1   Kuwaiti injured workers by percentage and nationality (1999)

Nationality	%
Egyptians	58.4
Indians	10.4
Syrians	7.1
Pakistanis	5.2
Iranians	2.6
Bangladeshi	3.2

Source: Adapted from Tabtabai (2002).

The creation of the term 'Perfect Immigrant' by Hahamovitch (2003: 70) describes a disposable, cheap source of labour recruited through temporary labour schemes brokered by host countries, designed to maintain high levels of migration at a very low cost in order to placate internal anti-immigrant movements. Although Kuwait supports internationally accepted labour practices, there is an inward resentment of the dependency on migrant labour for increased profits in the face of rising unemployment levels for Kuwaiti citizens which led to the recent introduction of legislation to 'Kuwaitise' the Kuwaiti labour force (Loew 2000: 110). This results in the covert subjugation of migrant workers through a managerial culture dominated by autocratic tribal values and familial ties (International Labour Organisation 2001; Loew 2000). Moreover, although the notion of emotional vulnerability of construction workers has been identified by Kartam et al. (2000) as a possible cause of accidents in Kuwait, the concept of construction worker vulnerability is nevertheless still a victim blaming approach, referred to by Quinlan et al. (2010: 177) as 'a more subtle and apparently benevolent fashion of attributing, for example, migration strain, as a contributing factor to occupational illness'.

From a sociological, biological and demographical viewpoint, these workers are further made vulnerable to subjugation through common characteristics, identified by Abdul-Aziz (2001) as follows:

- *Age*: those seeking employment in the construction industry in Kuwait are young, able-bodied, and in the most productive years of their lives. They also stand the greatest chance of recouping the cost incurred through payments made to labour agents (Abdul-Aziz 2001; Schenker 2008).

- *Gender*: the construction industry in Kuwait is dominated by young men, in keeping with international trends. For example in 1997 foreign male workers in Malaysia comprised 80 percent of the construction industry labour force of 130,000, compared with 60 percent in 1987 (Abdul-Aziz 2001; Schenker 2008). The Kuwaiti construction industry is similarly dominated by young males, partly due to the heavy work involved and partly due to the fact that women are not permitted to work at night or in hazardous occupations under the Private Sector Labour law which covers construction workers (Kartam et al. 2000).

- *Reasons for seeking work through migration*: results of a study of Malaysian, Indonesian and Bangladeshis (Abdul-Aziz 2001) revealed that one of the main reasons for migration is that ethno-linguistic subgroups regard migration as a valuable intrinsic process in attaining manhood. Other reasons given are parental pressure, abundant job opportunities (75 percent); better work offers (20 percent) and higher wages (6 percent). These percentages, claims Abdul-Aziz, concur with a survey in 1996 by Kassim which revealed that foreign workers seeking employment valued greater employment opportunities over higher wages by a margin of 75 percent. This has led to the employment of large numbers of foreign workers in the construction industry, with higher risks of fatality. In addition, Abdul-Aziz's (2001) study found that subcontractors applied a rating scale to their workers in which the willingness to work long hours was rated top (86 percent), followed by obedience (74 percent) low wages (74 percent) and lack of fastidiousness (58 percent). A similar situation exists in the Kuwait construction industry (Kartam et al. 2000).

- *Ethnic and social origins*: most foreign construction workers come from rural backgrounds and have little experience interacting with different ethnic or social groups. According to Abdul-Aziz (2001) this is another contributing factor to the unofficial stratification of labour by contractors, with corresponding discrimination in wages between groups. Common criteria for contractors in determining wage segmentation are skills variation, docility, nationality and willingness to work in hazardous conditions. Several authors have rationalised the willingness of workers to accept lower wage rates based on nationality, claiming that wage structures reflect the willingness of nationalities to work for different wages (Dacanay 1982; Wells 1996). However, 57 percent of the workers surveyed by Abdul-Aziz (2001) thought that wage equality prevailed whilst 25 percent were uncertain. Thus it is of crucial importance to research salary structures, the influence of worker cultural and social origins in shaping work and social clusters as well as the impact on safety for workers within the employment relationship in Kuwait.

- *Previous work experience*: in Abdul-Aziz's (2001) study, 43 percent of Indonesians surveyed had previously been occupied in farming, whilst 12 percent had been employed in the construction industry.

In comparison, 46 percent of the Bangladeshis had previous experience in petty trading, factory work or had been previously unemployed. Thus it is important to determine the effect which previous experience in the construction industry has on worker health and safety for migrant labourers in Kuwait.

- *Educational and language*: a common finding in the literature is the low level of education, including literacy, among migrant construction workers, including Kuwait, which has a negative impact on worker ability to be trained or understand written OHS instructions (Kartam et al. 2000; Abdul-Aziz 2001; Schenker 2008). In addition, the lack of ability to interact with contractors because of language differences leads to miscommunication, loneliness and depression.

- *Alienation*: site operatives in Kuwait live in self-contained areas, many of which are located on the construction site itself. Alternatively, workers are transported to and from compounds where sanitary conditions are generally unhealthy. Often workers will be housed in apartment blocks away from construction sites and populated areas. In some cases up to 20 people will be forced to live in one apartment with shared toilet facilities with other apartments in the same block, leading to high stress levels caused by low pay, long hours, poor hygienic conditions, poor quality of food and water. This isolation leads to the spread of diseases due to low resistance levels exacerbated by heavy smoking and, in non-Muslim countries, heavy alcohol consumption (Kartam and Bouz 1998; Valcarel 2004; Xia et al. 2004; CARAM Asia 2007; Tinghög et al. 2007; Anya 2007; Lay et al. 2007; Passel 2007; Wong et al. 2008).

Because health and safety strategies, processes and procedures specifically aimed at protecting migrant workers are non-existent in Kuwait, a situation which is exacerbated by worker lack of access to regulatory protection, there is a need for robust analysis of the way in which employment relations is managed within the Kuwaiti regulatory framework, where smaller subcontracted and sub-subcontracted companies with poor management skills and lack of awareness, knowledge and commitment to applying OHS practices and regulations, are heavily involved in construction projects as a direct result of the practice in Kuwait of accepting the cheapest tender bid (Kartam and Bouz 1998; Kartam et al. 2000). The fact that many of the owner/managers of the subcontracted firms have limited business acumen increases the likelihood of non-compliance with OHS regulatory standards (McVittie, Banikin and Brocklebank 1997; Lamm, 2002).

Employment Relations and Occupational Health and Safety in Kuwait

The health and safety requirements in the oil sector are most stringent and great care is taken to ensure that project management consultants assume responsibility and accountability for ensuring that the workplace is safe for contractors. However, this system of ensuring the working environment is safe becomes defective when a breakdown in the chain of command and control occurs as a result of contractors subcontracting to subcontractors who in turn subcontract the work out. The relationship between these layers of subcontracting and the loss of control of OHS policies and practices is an emerging area of research (McVittie, Banikin and Brocklebank 1997; Sargeant and Tucker 2009), and is one of the key areas of investigation in this study.

Complex legal structures surround accident reporting and workmen's compensation and the way these are managed by Kuwaiti governmental bodies which are culturally suspicious of all expatriate activities. This discriminatory attitude, the social exclusion of migrant labour and the covert discouragement of union activity is entrenched through the unofficial stratification of expatriate labour by occupation and the housing of migrant labour in compounds or accommodation either on site or in the isolation of outlying regions of Kuwait. This prevention of the labour force interacting socially within Kuwaiti society, exacerbated by poor communication and language difficulties, has given rise to under-reporting of accidents, thus significantly hindering the process of evaluation and improvement of systems and processes aimed at improving health and safety conditions on construction sites (Kazemi and Ali 2001). Current literature does not explore or analyse the above factors from a worker perspective.

The government in Kuwait comprises essentially members of a few prominent families, many of whom control Kuwaiti businesses. The population is classified into Kuwait nationals versus expatiate, non-Kuwait nationals. This classification is institutionalised through migration legislation and decrees that support familial and tribal ties through the need for migrant labour to possess a business sponsor before residency status is granted. Loyalty takes primacy over managerial ability and the allocation of state resources and tenders are therefore familial and tribal based, which further strengthens these ties and reinforces conformity to traditional customs and values (Longva 1993; Loew 2000; Kazemi and Ali 2001; Metle 2002). The fear of invasion from its neighbouring countries and the tension associated with a dichotomous society in which Kuwaitis have become the minority ethnic group by three non-Kuwaiti nationals to one Kuwaiti national pervades the country (Loew 2000). These social and cultural schisms are reflected in Kuwaiti employment relations law.

Kuwaiti employment relations law is covered in three separate statutes: (1) the Kuwait Public Sector Law which applies only to Kuwaiti citizens; (2) the Oil Sector Law which applies to Kuwaiti citizens as well as government approved Gulf Nationals employed in the Oil Sector; and (3) the Law of Labour in the Private Sector. Migrant workers, who are covered by the Private Sector labour law, and particularly those employed in the construction industry, are largely ill-informed and ignorant of their rights due to language, communication and cultural barriers. This situation creates the possibility that abusive practices may occur in the Kuwait construction industry and that those workers who are involved may have no knowledge of, or recourse to, legislative protection (Kazemi and Ali 2001).

Residency visas are allocated according to contract duration and are negotiated directly between project owners, project and subcontracting firm managers and/or labour agencies in accordance with the duration of the contract. Thus, few individually signed contracts between contract owners and labourers are evident and workers are remunerated by sub and sub-subcontractors, minimising contract owner liability. Workers have no right to remain after project completion. Migrant workers are typically financially indebted and/or bonded to their labour/immigration agent and many of these workers do not see their families for at least two to three years (Kartam et al. 2000).

On 21 February 2010 a new Law of Labour in the Private Sector was gazetted designed to improve the working conditions for all expatriate labour except domestic workers and male workers employed as unofficial taxi drivers for Kuwait households. These workers are not officially employed by companies in the Private Sector, under private contract to households. A great deal of pressure is currently being brought to bear on the Kuwaiti Government to include these domestic workers into the same category as other expatriate labour, in order that they will come under the protection of the Private Sector Labour Law. At present the only way in which a domestic worker may lodge a complaint against their employer is either through the Department of Immigration who then refers the matter to the contract labour agents, or the domestic worker can lodge a complaint with the police if it concerns physical or sexual violence (Kaaki 2005). Although the new Private Sector Labour Law has generally been favourably received, there is growing concern by employer associations regarding the long-term effects the revised law will have on the supply of acquiescent labour. There is also concern over how the law will be implemented given the already complex system of administration, lack of communication between ministries and history of suspected collusion between contract labour agents and employers. This study will seek to explore the way in which changes in the law affect the experiences and perceptions of workers in relation to their employment relationship and their health and safety.

The Kuwaitis are well renowned for their strong nationalistic culture. This national pride became more evident after the Iraqi invasion of Kuwait in 1990. The cultural effects of having gained independence only because of American intervention has paradoxically strengthened the rift between espoused and practiced Kuwaiti values and ethics. Publicly and outwardly, Kuwait supported and still supports the United States government, however inwardly Kuwaitis resent being dependent on a Western culture for their independence, and seek to subjugate Westerners through a managerial culture dominated by autocratic tribal values (International Labour Organisation 2001; Metle 2002).

There is, additionally, a general and pervasive cultural and class tension between the large migrant population and the dominant Kuwaitis. These tensions have been exacerbated by external pressures applied by the ILO and other overseas human rights agencies endeavouring to introduce 'Western conceived' human rights, including non-discriminatory practices. Moreover, this uneasy cohabitation between the large multicultural migrant population and Kuwaitis is further complicated by Kuwaiti's three powerful neighbours, Iraq, Iran and Saudi Arabia, who have traditionally attempted to influence Kuwait's domestic policy (Shah et al. 1991). Thus, there is some fine juggling occurring within the Kuwaiti government and Kuwaiti businesses in which they endeavour to protect themselves from their intimidating neighbours by parlaying with powerful international interests whilst struggling to control a large migrant population of expatriate workers, which Kuwaitis have become reliant upon (Loew 2000).

OHS law and, in particular, its enforcement in Kuwait, is still in its infancy. Government agencies are at present keen to promoted better working conditions and foster a co-operative government and business alliance to address work-related health and safety issues of their Kuwaiti workers. The effectiveness of current OHS regulations and government enforcement, however, has yet to be tested. Regardless of the fact that migrant labour are generally considered to be at a lower social level than the Kuwaitis and are subject to covert discrimination, the expatriate project management consultants are expected to be responsible for satisfying international pressures by ILO and OHS agencies to ensure that employees adhere to health and safety standards. These responsibilities operate within the context of little or no autonomy, tight financial margins and pressure to reduce costs wherever possible, all of which may undermine the health and safety of the migrant workers (Kartam and Bouz 1998; Kazemi and Ali 2001; Xia et al. 2004). The effectiveness of OHS legislation enforcement directly affects worker health and safety and will form the contextual elements through which worker perceptions and experiences will be analysed.

Occupational Health and Safety Management Systems in Kuwait

The pressure to continually cut costs inherent in multilayered subcontractor arrangements affects the employment relationship in various ways. Informal and indirect employment via foremen or intermediaries is common practice in the construction industry, however it is particularly so in Kuwait. The fact that workers are itinerant and move from site to site significantly increases their vulnerability. This situation is exacerbated by language and literacy barriers, as outlined above. Migrant workers in Kuwait are mostly uneducated and functionally illiterate and few if any, understand Arabic or English (Kartam and Bouz 1998). The lack of a common language among the workers and employers and the transient nature of the work are often cited as root causes of many of the work-related injuries and fatalities that occur (Valcarel 2004; Xia et al. 2004).

In Kuwait the large construction projects are dominated by the oil and petrochemical industry. Kuwait law prescribes the terms and conditions under which contracts are managed. Large projects are sent out for bidding to an approved list of contractors appointed by the project owners. These major contracts are administered by the Kuwait Central Tendering Committee under their rules and contracts are always allocated to the cheapest bidder. The appointed contractors are legally required to subscribe to the safety protocols laid down by the oil and petrochemical companies which comply with internationally recognised Health, Safety and Environmental (HSE) standards. These principle subcontracting companies are generally free to appoint their own secondary subcontractors under approval by the oil and petrochemical companies as the approval process for sub-subcontractors is not overseen or directly controlled. The problems with OHS begin to emerge at this level as it is at this level where labour hire agents are widely used by subcontractors (Kartam et al. 2000). These smaller, secondary subcontractors are short of capital and under great pressure to cut costs at the expense of safety, and therefore do not invest money in health and safety training and equipment. In addition, they cannot afford, and more significantly, do not recognise the need for the services of safety specialists or instructors, resulting in lack of safety organisation culture either off or on site (Kartam et al. 2000).

According to Kartam et al. (2000), there is notably an absence of a unified set of safety regulations in Kuwait. In 2000, the Ministry of Public Works developed a safety chapter in its manual for construction practices. The oil sector has it own manual based on international oil standards, and no standard safety manual existed at the Kuwait Municipality. Moreover, Kartam claims, international standards do not necessarily apply to the Kuwait working environment, since methods of practice in advanced countries differ from Kuwaiti methods. For example, there is no rule against using wooden scaffolding, secured with twine or rope of unspecified quality, in any of the local standards (Kartam et al. 2000: 173).

It is the project management consultants on large projects in the oil sector who form the interface between project owners and contractors. They have the responsibility and, moreover, the accountability for ensuring that all contractors, both principle and secondary, abide by the health and safety standards prescribed by the oil and petrochemical and affiliated companies. The channels of communication between project owners and contractors inevitably break down as a result of lack of education, lack of communication, lack of managerial experience and safety culture, language barriers, worker inexperience and lack of training (Kartam and Bouz 1998; Kartam et al. 2000).

Thus cost cutting, subcontractor and sub-subcontractor qualifications, training and management, their willingness to enforce OHS safety and training, to provide safety equipment and the role of project management consultants, all affect the working lives and experiences of contingent migrant labour in the Kuwait construction industry and form the context within which these experiences will be analysed.

Conclusion

The Kuwaiti political, social, economic and legal milieu discussed in this chapter has had a significant impact on the currently developing occupational health and injury status of contingent, migrant labour. These factors have hitherto been given scant attention. As a consequence, such complex influences must be taken into consideration when examining the OHS of migrant workers in Kuwait.

In conclusion, owing to poor injury surveillance data available in Kuwait, in particular in sub-subcontracted scenarios, we do not know the true extent of the problem, namely how many migrant workers are being injured or killed as a result of work, what medical and rehabilitation attention have they received and what, if any, workers' compensation they receive. This study will examine the way in which projects are managed and the effects of the employment relationship on the lives, experiences, perceptions and health and safety of the migrant worker himself – the person who is invisible and does not have any voice because of all the factors contributing to this invisibility.

References

Abbe, O.O. (2008) Modeling the relationship among occupational stress, psychological/physical symptoms and injuries in the construction industry. MSc.Thesis. Louisana State University, USA.

Abdul-Aziz, A. (2001) Foreign workers and labour segmentation in Malaysia's construction industry. *Construction Management and Economics.* (19): 789–798.

Anya, I. (2007) Right to health care for vulnerable migrants. *The Lancet.* 370(8): 827.

Baram, M. (2009) Globalization and workplace hazards in developing nations. *Safety Science.* (47): 756–766.

CARAM Asia. (2007) *State of Health of Migrants 2007: Mandatory Testing,* CARAM Asia Berhad, Kuala Lumpur.

Dainty, R.J., Briscoe, G.H. and Millett, S.J. (2001) Subcontractor perspectives on supply chain alliances. *Construction Management and Economics.* (19): 841–848.

Hahamovitch, C. (2003) Creating perfect immigrants: guestworkers of the world. *Historical Perspective Labor History.* 44(1): 69–94.

Holmes, J., Lingard, H., Yesilyurt, Z. and De Munk, F. (1999) An exploratory study of meanings of risk control for long term and acute effect occupational health and safety risks in small business construction firms. *Journal of Safety Research.* 30(4): 251–261.

International Labour Organisation. (2001) *Overview of the Thirteenth Asian Regional Meeting*. Available from www.ilo.org/public/english/region/asro/bangkok/arm/kwt.htm, accessed 20 May 2010.

Kaaki, W. (2005) *All the Kuwaiti Laws you Need to Know in Plain English*. D and K Publishing and Distribution, Kuwait.

Kartam, N.A. and Bouz, R.G. (1998) Fatalities and injuries in the Kuwait construction industry. *Accident Analysis and Prevention*. 30(6): 805–814.

Kartam, N.A., Flood, I. and Koushki, P. (2000) Construction safety in Kuwait: issues, procedures, problems and recommendations. *Safety Science*. 36: 163–184.

Kazemi, A.A. and Ali, A.J. (2001) Managerial problems in Kuwait. *Journal of Management Development*. 21(5): 366–375.

Lamm, F. (2002) OHS in small businesses. In Lloyd, M. (ed.) *Occupational Health and Safety in New Zealand: Contemporary Social Research*. Wellington, Dunmore Press, 93–118.

Lay, B., Nordt, C. and Rossler, W. (2007) Mental hospital admission rates of immigrants in Switzerland. *Social Psychiatry and Psychiatric Epidemiology*. 42: 229–236.

Lewchuk, W., de Wolf, A., King, A and Polanyi, M. (2003) From job strain to employment strain: health effects of precarious employment. *Just Labour*. 3.

Loew, H. (2000) *Analysis of the Kuwati Culture*. Available from www.everyculture.com/Ja-Ma/Kuwait.html, accessed 15 July 2009.

Longva, A.N. (1993) Kuwaiti women at a crossroads: privileged development and the constraints of ethnic stratification. *International Journal of Middle East Studies*. 25(3): 443–456.

McVittie, D., Banikin, H. and Brocklebank, W. (1997) The effects of firm size on injury frequency in construction. *Safety Science*. 27(1): 19–23.

Metle, M.K. (2002) The influence of traditional culture on attitudes towards work among Kuwaiti women employees in the public sector. *Women in Management Review*. 17(6): 245–261.

Nosar, I., Johnstone, R. and Quinlan, M. (2004) Regulating supply chains to address the occupational health and safety problems associated with precarious employment: the case of home-based clothing workers in Australia. *Australian Journal of Labour Law*. 2: 1–24.

Passel, J. (2007) *Unauthorized Migrants in the United States: Estimates, Methods, and Characteristics*, Working Paper 7 OECD. Available from www.oecd.org/els/workingpapers, accessed 30 May 2010.

Quinlan, M. (1988) Psychological and sociological approaches to the study of occupational illness: a critical review. *Australian and New Zealand Journal of Safety*. 24(2): 189–207.

Quinlan, M. (2010) Vulnerable employment and health: lessons from history. Health and safety and vulnerable workers in a changing world of work. 8 June 2010, Middlesex University, London.

Quinlan, M. and Bohle, P. (2004) Contingent work and occupational safety. In Barling, J. and Frone, M.R. (eds) *The Psychology of Workplace Safety*. Washington, DC, American Psychological Association, 81–105.

Quinlan, M. and Mayhew, C. (1999) Precarious employment and workers compensation. *International Journal of Law and Psychiatry*. 22(5–6): 491–520.

Quinlan, M. and Mayhew, C. (2001) *Evidence Versus Ideology: Lifting the Blindfold on OHS in Precarious Employment*. The University of New South Wales. Department of Industrial Relations. Papers, 138.

Quinlan, M., Bohle, P. and Lamm, F. (2010) *Managing Occupational Health and Safety, A Multidisciplinary Approach*, 3rd edn. South Yarra, Australia. Palgrave Macmillan.

Quinlan, M., Mahyew, C. and Bohle, P. (2001) The global expansion of precarious employment, work disorganization, and consequences for occupational health: a review of recent research. *International Journal of Health Services*. 31(2): 335–214.

Sargeant, M. and Tucker, E. (2009) Layers of vulnerability in OHS for migrant workers: case studies from Canada and the UK. *Policy and Practice in Health and Safety*. 7(2): 51–73.

Schenker, M. (2008) Work related injuries among immigrants: a growing global health disparity. *Occupational and Environmental Medicine*. 65(11): 717–718.

Shah, M.N., Al Qudsi, S.S. and Shah, M. (1991) Asian women workers in Kuwait. *International Migration Review*. 25(3): 464–486.

Tabtabai, H.M. (2002) Analyzing construction site accidents in Kuwait. *Kuwait Journal of Science and Engineering*. 29(2).

Tinghög, P., Hemmingsson, T. and Lundberg, I. (2007) To what extent may the association between immigrant status and mental illness be explained by socioeconomic factors? *Social Psychiatry and Psychiatric Epidemiology*. 42: 990–996.

Toh, S. and Quinlan, M. (2009) Safeguarding the global contingent workforce? Guestworkers in Australia. *International Journal of Manpower*. 30(5): 453–471.

Valcarel, A.L. (2004) Safety and health in construction work. *Asian-Pacific Newsletter on Occupational Health and Safety*. 11: 4–7.

Wells, J. (1996) Labour migration and international construction. *Habitat International*. 20(2): 295–306.

Wong, D.K., Xuesong, H., Leung, G., Lau, Y. and Chang, W. (2008) Mental health of migrant workers in China: prevalence and correlates. *Social Psychiatry and Psychiatric Epidemiology*. 43: 483–489.

Xia, Z., Lu, G. and Liang, Y. (2004) Challenges and strategies of occupational health and safety in the construction industry in China. *Asian-Pacific Newsletter on Occupational Health and Safety.* 11: 8–9.

Yun, A. for the International Labour Office. (2007) Regulating multi-layer subcontracting to improve labour protection. Available from http://www.ilo.org/public/English/protection.

Index